SISTERLY LOVE

Sisterly Love

© Diana Hutton and HPEditions 2019
© cover design Diana Hutton and HPEditions 2019

**Categories: Literary Fiction, Social Issues,
Family Life, Ageing, Fictional Biography**
All rights reserved under all international and Pan-American Copyright Conventions. No part of this text may be reproduced, transmitted, downloaded, decompiled, reverse engineered or stored in any information storage or retrieval process in any form without the express permission of the publisher.
The moral rights of the author have been asserted

Digital edition by HPEditions, July 2019 available everywhere
Print edition by HPEditions also available from Amazon and most major retailers

ISBN 13: 978-0-6485686-0-5
ISBN 10: 0-6485686-0-1
ebook edition ISBN-13: 978-0-9875212-4-8
ebook edition ISBN-10: 0-9875212-4-1

Length: 98,000 words
Published by HPEditions

Dedications
For Eloísa and Jaime

Summer is gone with all its roses,
Its sun and perfumes and sweet flowers,
Its warm air and refreshing showers:
And even Autumn closes.

Christina Rossetti

Some words from the author

Am I telling a story in this book? It is certainly not a story with its conventional beginning, middle and end, although all that does happen in it. But I have wanted to depict eras and places through the lives of two sisters and these come and go at will, following the need that each of the sisters has to relate her memories or to comment on her present. So I suppose I could say that there is a story-line, but it is not conventionally told. Also, my use of capital letters in mid-sentence and unusual punctuation may seem strange to the reader. It is my way of emphasizing, or of introducing a thought or comment. I hope that you can appreciate these features.
D.H.
Madrid, 2019

TABLE OF CONTENTS

Dedications
Some words from the author
I   Peasoupers and Brass Bands   1
II   Octogenarian Scratchings   21
III   The Professional Lillian   48
IV   At Horace's   70
V   Elsie's Reminiscences   97
VI   Lillian's Men   127
VII   Waiting for Lillian's Train   153
VIII   Australia and a Wedding   181
IX   Almerian Rains   212
X   Horace's Decline   224
XI   Elsie and Horace   239
XII   Those Senescent Years   243
XIII   The Land of Opportunity …at Last   254
XIV   Incongruous Endings   260
Before You Go   269
About the Author   270
Other Books by Diana Hutton   270
A Grave above Ground   271

I

PEASOUPERS AND BRASS BANDS

Sisters, that blood relationship, is a complex mesh which intertwines in painful proximity sentiments of the greatest contrast. It is both a haven and a prison, a relief and a frustration. It is part of the condition into which we are born without our having asked for it to be so. It is part of the burden we carry with us to the grave. It is part of the joy we carry with us to the grave. It is a love we bear within us despite ourselves. It is an unchosen love.

I was born in London in a swirling peasouper, of the sort which made me wish I'd never been born. I was propelled out into the light on a mid-January morning back towards the beginning of the twentieth century. Yet there was no light. Or was Light that grimy haze, whose turbid yellow swirls pressed ghost-like against the pane of my mother's bedroom window? For I was born in her bed. On her bed in a whoosh of warm pink fluid flung forth onto a sea of rough-starched white sheets and in front of the inquisitive gaze of the detested aunt Emily.

The detested aunt Emily.

It was like that then, in those days when most cousins and sisters and aunts knew about delivering babies, admittedly many of us were lost or went astray, miscarried, during the complicated pregnancies of over-worked mothers, or were yanked harshly out into the world with a pair of forceps and half maimed for life. Nevertheless, it was a time when we were all less squeamish and not so put off by a bit of blood and guts, not so hygienic as we are today, towards the close of the century, the twentieth century, that is. Perhaps I should be thankful to have been born into the murky light of a peasouper, the dubious glimmer of those hazes over the world, over London which was our world and indeed the whole world at that time for us. Perhaps the glare of a bright summer sun would have been too great a contrast with the dim glow of my progenitor's womb. I might have been shocked for evermore were I to have squinted my way out into the brash light of a summer's day. As it was, being born into a peasouper meant that I was forced to struggle to see anything at all, struggle with my vision for long hours, peering into the mysterious yellow substance on the opposite side of the bedroom window, wondering, wondering .... if indeed a baby wonders. That struggle has made me a fighter ever since.

Peasoupers are virtually unheard of nowadays, now that the air has been supposedly cleansed to look like natural cloud, to make us believe we are breathing in fresh air. Though the way they talk about pollution in the present times, you would think it was worse than those peasoupers. Youngsters today can't imagine what they were like! I can remember trotting off to school on freezing cold mornings, my woolly balaclava clinging to my ears, my fingers tingling inside a pair of mittens, my unbecoming grey socks rucked around my ankles, limping because I had a large hole - potatoes our mother called them, or spuds rather - cutting into the skin around my big toe and a laborious piece of darning under my heel which rubbed me to red-raw discomfort. There wasn't the cash for more than two pairs of winter socks each and mother was an awful darner. I reckon that she spent more time and effort on poultices for the blisters caused by her awful darning, than she would have spent money on a new pair of socks for me. Occasionally she knitted our socks, but she left ridges around the toes and they were lumpy and bumpy and we complained bitterly, so she gave up and knitted us jumpers instead. Lillian used to cry in those jumpers. She thought she was pretty and that they made her ugly. As for the socks, we changed them only once a week, on Sundays when we had our weekly dousing in the bathtub. By the time Saturday night came they could stand to attention by themselves with all the dirt and sweat impregnated into them.

Apart from experiencing a peculiar affinity with the peasoupers, more than likely because I had been born into one, I was always glad when they appeared because then the other children couldn't laugh at my chafed blue knees which went purple in winter. They were invisible in the thick fog. I remember stretching my arm way out in front of me, slowly, and watching my hand gradually becoming invisible. That was exciting, a mystery to us, and my sister Lillian said it made her think of ghosts. No wonder the English are such a ghost-obsessed race, phantoms in the swirling mists, phantoms of the opera, haunted houses, witches on the moors way back even in Macbeth's time, unexplained clanking chains and dour dungeons, modern spooks, fairy tales of goblins, a never-ending list of literary protagonists such as Jack the Ripper all looming forth from one peasouper or another. No-one ever thinks about such things on bright sunny days and as England can't boast of having too many of those, our propensity for the shadier areas of existence is explicable. Horace, our younger brother, who used to trail along somewhere behind us kicking up loose gravel until the soles of his shoes became loose, said we were pathetic with all our talk of ghosts, You're *pathetic,* both of you, *pathetic,* he said. He was a bit of a boss really, has been all his life. Still is, I suppose.

My name is Elsie by the way. If a name matters. How *can* a name matter when it is nothing but a chosen label from an arbitrary list which one's mother has spent hours of pregnancy time pouring over, even pining over, as though it were an insoluble problem of the utmost importance? And in those days, the problem was doubly insoluble and the list doubly long because the sex of the baby to be remained undisclosed right up until the time of the baby's birth and so there had to be an equal variety of male and female names. But how can a name matter so much? I mean, would my knees have been any the less chafed if they'd called me Dot or Eugenia or Victoria, instead of Elsie? I wonder if Queen Victoria had chafed knees? Blue they might have been because of her blood. But chafed? I expect not. She wouldn't have had to walk to school through any peasouper fogs anyway. She would have had a tutor charged to instruct her within the precincts of her castle. That's why royalty's something to look up to, something to revere. A true monarch shouldn't mix with his subjects, besmirch himself against the riff-raff with chafed knees. I always think that monarchs should sit cushioned against satin folds, drip with ermine and bejewelled robes. I love that. It makes them different to the commoners. I mean, you can dream about that .... escape from reality, dreaming about the monarch on his throne, surrounded by all his servants and beefeaters, That's kindness too, caring that all those people have a good job looking after you. All those strange countries in the world without a king or a queen, *republics* they call them. How they manage I shall never know, being in the hands of ordinary people, riff-raff who've known what it was like to have chafed knees in peasoupers. No, we all loved the monarchy in our family. We were a true British family in that, faithful to our traditions. When the brass bands played the national anthem in the local park on Sundays, we used to stand up straight without moving an inch, like soldiers on parade, my father stiff and immovable under his bristling moustache, but mother could never remain in this posture until the end of the anthem because of the emotion she felt. Half way through, the tears would well up and she'd have to reach for her handkerchief. She always wept, every time, thinking of all that ermine, I expect. I mean, if you compare the ermine with the darns in our socks, it was worth spilling a tear over.

But back to the peasoupers. You can imagine how criminals like Jack the Ripper were bred in those fogs, real criminals who crept around in the half-light and seized women from out of the thick folds of the mists, like the days of Dickens with horrible little hunchbacks living by the dank misty bogs of the Thames. None of the open-air terrorists who shoot people dead in the bright light of day. Life was more sinister in those days, in the days of the unfurling peasoupers. I never dared to go out, for instance, not even down to the garden gate after dark. I was far too scared. And Lillian, who was decidedly more puny than me, was even too scared to go alone to her bedroom. If I remember rightly, that was Horace's fault because whenever those fogs came down, Horace always steered the conversation at tea-time around to spooky things, as though the thick mists spurred him on to show the sinister side of himself. Lillian would quake in her seat. She never spoke a word and she was the eldest of the three of us, sitting there trembling like a baby. Horace and I used to sneer at her. Then mother would make us go to bed together, up the stairs holding hands for mutual support. I must confess that I wasn't as brave as I might sound. I didn't like the long passageways and winding stairway in our old house. There were cupboards on the landing which had creaking doors and gaping black innards. Horace used to hide in them amongst all the clothes and jump out to frighten us and Lillian would scream then, but I would be livid and fight back with the bundles of clothes aiming at his ears hard with the folded bullets of our lumpy grey school socks, yelling war cries, I aimed at his ears because they were pointed and red and I hated them, Long ears, long life, mother used to say, my ears were short..... and Lillian there, like a ninny, pressed against the wall watching Horace and me deliver battle. In a way I felt sorry for her. In a way I remember thinking she was a coward, soppy, namby-pamby, the odd one out, always scared of everything, always clutching dolls. Still, I had to muster all the courage inside me to climb that hated stairway on foggy nights. During those journeys to bed in the peasoupers I must have laid the foundations for my metallic nature. Lillian and Horace always tell me even now that I am hard-hearted and outspoken. I simply know how to defend myself in a cruel world, that's all.

Then cringing fearfully between the ice-cold sheets, they were cold like sheets of frozen metal, although an hour or so earlier mother had placed hot-water bottles in our beds, the old stone bottles, not rubber bags in knitted or crocheted covers, which meant that there was one warm patch for your bottom in a sea of icy cold. We only possessed two of those bottles so that once we had fallen asleep she would withdraw them and re-fill them for her and father's bed. But as there were only two and we were three, she would swap them round our three beds every quarter of an hour and after her last swap Horace would race upstairs and put both bottles in his own bed, one for the patch under his bottom, the other for his feet, We must buy another bottle, my mother whose name was Nell, sighed each night to my father. She couldn't manage Horace, no mother could have managed Horace, he was unmanageable, except to father who caned him on his bare bottom with Lillian snivelling and me giggling, made to stand by both of us and witness as a forewarning what would befall us if we dared to cross him. I did, on more than one occasion and I knew what the tip of that cane felt like, so it should have been the other way around, me snivelling and Lillian giggling, Lillian who'd never felt the tip of father's cane because she always managed to divert the blame from herself, or was too scared to do anything which would provoke a caning in the first place.

In those ice-cold sheets I used to rub my heels vigorously up and down, except when they were blistered from Nell's, mother's that is, lumpy darning. I rubbed them so hard that I nearly took the skin off them and my chafed knees stung against the cold rough-starched sheet. Warmer, I used to lie there *listening* to the peasouper. When you listen to a peasouper, you have to strain your ears until they feel as though they are going to split. You strain and strain because all sounds are transformed, you no longer recognise them, they are muffled and distorted, weird and they conjure up vivid imaginary things. It isn't really the peasouper you're listening to, it's that you're trying desperately hard to identify the meaning of the sounds you hear caught up in its folds. Its folds swirl and move and creep against the window-pane and that is why you imagine you are *listening* to the peasouper itself and are actually *hearing* it. From the safety and relative warmth of my bed I found it both fearful and exciting, for a man's footstep sounded like a big unknown animal padding along the path, the bang of a neighbour's door like a superhuman cough, the far-off bark of a dog like a child's distant scream, the cracking of the twigs on the branch of the tree outside like a long witch's nail scratching on the window pane. All those sensations attract and yet terrify a child. And I can recall peering out into the black night, *watching* the peasouper through the latticed window pane and I remember *feeling* the thick texture of the fog, *feeling* it without touching it, *feeling* that it was pressing down hard against the window and walls of our house, so hard that it would secure us hermetically in its wreaths and that soon we would be unable to breath and then I started to perspire in bed, with fear not heat, my whole world became clammy and suffocating, filled with ugly goblins and their leering grimaces, with great big evil men wielding axes in their hands, with enormous ferocious dogs more like dragons than Smokey our harmless wire-haired terrier, all coming for me but not quite reaching me, dangling they were outside my bedroom window, hanging, treading water treading fog, in the peasouper swirls. Sometimes I prayed hard to God, but mostly to George V, to save me. I never quite knew if I was asleep or awake, if it was reality or nightmare, but after listening-to and watching the peasouper, I would smother my head with the blankets to eradicate the frightening visions, smother my head hard and then ....

It would be morning, time to get up and be hustled off to school, Horace still with remnants of sleep stuck in the corners of his eyes and on the tips of his lashes, Lillian snivelling because she'd forgotten to finish her homework and was petrified of the teacher, me with my socks rucked around my ankles and my chafed blue-turning-to-purple knees, all three of us out into the yellowing swirls of the peasouper to be separated in a jiffy from Nell by the invisible/visible curtain, there she was waving us goodbye from the front doorstep of our house, Take care children, Nell, mother rather, in her dressing-gown, that ugly brown garment she wore every morning to mix our porridge over the black iron cooker of the living-room, dirty it was because she used it to stoke the boiler too, which meant that the coke-dust ingrained itself into the dark fabric. Lillian would recover from her snivelling when we started to play at stretching our hands out in front of us, marvel at them disappearing like magic into the heavy yellow air, again and again all the way to school we played with the magic, shunning our hands, casting them away disparagingly, pleading with them to return, willing them and, *abracadabra*, here they are again. When we tired of that, or tired of Horace accusing us from his straggling behind of being *pathetic*, we focussed all our attention on our breathing. We were smoking then, like father, grown-up and important, blowing our puffs of imaginary cigarette smoke and watching them hit out against the peasouper and disintegrate into its thicker swirls. We puffed out our frozen red cheeks and let the breath-smoke out in short sharp spurts until we nearly burst in the attempt, burst from holding our breath, burst from stifling giggles. In retrospect, they were some of the better moments with Lillian. Playing together in the peasouper was a way of forgetting that we were so cold, cold in the freezing fog, cold with each other. It was as though the fog bound us together. When it lifted, our friendship lifted, waned and drifted away with the mysterious white swirls. It had something to do with needing one another, I suppose, building up a common front against the intruder, but when the intruder-enemy-fog dissipated, our common front dissipated too. So much for peasoupers and friendship. Both come and go.

I have said that we were doused once a week. On Sundays to be exact. It was an event. It happened on Sunday mornings. Not that we were spruced to go to church or anything like that, like many of our neighbours. In our family, it was only Nell who went to church. She used to attend the Catholic mass in the little stone church pre-Henry VIII two streets away. She wouldn't give up her religion even for father, she'd been with it until she was eight, so it was hers for life. Although father was a master-builder, like God was, he built only houses, not human beings. Perhaps he realised he was a master-builder of the inferior sort and that was why he never deigned to set foot inside a church. Professional jealousy. He liked to profess that he was an atheist, the closest he came to brotherly love and charity to neighbours and peers, was his freemasonry. But he tolerated his wife going, in fact he quite paled into insignificance with his atheism when the Irish priest told him that the Lord needed his wife and somehow, amidst struggles of which we were then unaware, he came to terms with sharing her with the Lord. The price Nell paid for her Sunday escapades to mass was unswerving obedience to the old man in every other area of her existence which did not fall immediately under the Lord's jurisdiction, that is, unswerving obedience in anything at all outside *her* Father's house, and inside *our* father's house. Some sort of fear he must have had, my father, for the Irish priest or I doubt that he would have tolerated this assault on his authority. From this I deduce that his atheism was half-baked only. I mean, it can't have been the priest he was scared of, that insignificant little man half his size with a jovial face and plump baby-shaven cheeks, Irish-whisky-swilling cheeks. So it must, on all counts, have been God he was afraid of. So much for atheism.

But I was on to bathtubs before I was wheedled away to mass. We were spruced for Sunday lunch, not for mass. And I was the only one of the three of us who hated the dousing. More often than not there were coke smuts in the bathtub because the coke cellar was a large door-less cavity right next to where the old enamel tub stood on its sturdy metal legs. They were dingy days those, coke-carrying days to and from the boiler. Lillian enjoyed her dousing,

Horace enjoyed his dousing, Nell said proudly They're water-babies, because they both learnt to swim. I hated the dousing and I never learnt to swim but Nell never called me an earth-baby, father just called me a coward. It was early days for me to be proud of not being a water-baby, leave that to others, to the Olympic medal winners-swimmers of the universe. The pride and self-confidence came later, both growing side by side with the metallic nature. But at the time I was mortified because I was not a water-baby. There is no doubt in my mind that I have never learnt to swim because of this childhood mortification. Never can I understand how people desire that bodily contact with the transparent hot or cold liquid which runs free from taps, or with the chlorinated water of swimming-pools, or with the murky sinister depths of rivers, or with the salt-hazed unquiet waters of the sea. Never can I understand .... Horace actually became a brilliant diver, a medal-winner for his school St. Olave's for Boys Only. Lillian and I used to go and watch him take off, like a swallow they said, from the highest tower. I suppose I felt a vague admiration - it was, after all, my brother way up there - as I poker-faced, watched him poker-faced, plunging headfirst downwards like a streamlined missile. Lillian bit off all her finger nails during those dives, she bit them right down to the quick, down, down as Horace climbed up, up to the highest springboard, by the time he launched himself off into mid-air the nails were well on their way down her digestive tract. She bit her nails alternately, one for Horace's dive, one for Horace's mate Mike who used to sit two benches away staring at her, staring and sniffing and smiling like a puppy slobbering. Even then she was a one for the boys, Our Lil she's a one for the boys, aunt Emily would spill the beans to Nell with a sort of hesitant admiration,

the admiring Emily,

relating that she had watched the plump slobbering Mike in his knee-length St. Olave's flannels follow Lillian all the way home from school one day. I was glad Mike didn't slobber over me. But neither did any other boys.

Sunday mornings then were chaotic. Why the dousing had to take place before Nell wanted to get away to mass, I shall never know. She never contemplated setting up the bathing procedure on a Saturday evening; perhaps she never contemplated stepping out of line with what the neighbours did and even though we never went to church, another of the prices Nell had to pay for going herself to mass was that we, her children, did not go, I'm not tolerating more than one bible-basher in the house, my father made it very clear. We nevertheless had to be spruced for Sunday lunch. So Sunday mornings were packed with feverish activity: the chaotic dousing, the escapade to mass, the preparation of the roast-something and Yorkshire pudding and gravy and roast potatoes and boiled unsalted vegetables, remember we are in England, let it never be thought that we transgressed venerable traditions, a sedate walk into the local park to listen to the brass-band, all this activity culminating in an afternoon nap, for the adults at least. I was at a loss to see why these important preparations didn't have a more scintillating ulterior motive. We were doused and dressed and spruced to sit through the interminable Sunday lunch in the company of Nell and father and aunt Emily whom we loathed,

the loathed Emily,

so that the adults could say, Let's have a snooze, or sometimes they didn't say it, sometimes they just did it, and if we wanted to go outside to play, You mustn't dirty your best clothes, and all the ribbons had to be discarded, the frilly Viyella best one-and-only dresses with embroidered collars undone, the black patent shoes and white socks pulled off and in their place the old corduroy skirts with darned rents, the woollen leggings worn at the knees, the jumpers-for-playing holed at the elbows and the faithful mud-caked wellies donned. I mean, all the dousing and the fuss over the dousing. For nothing.

And at bath time I always clamoured to go first, get it all over with quickly. The other two never minded, it was one thing we didn't fight over because if I went first then they could play longer in the water. In fact Horace practised becoming a gentleman on those occasions, Ladies first he always said, a true gentleman thinking of himself first. So the tub was filled to half-way mark, Nell carefully testing the water for temperature and when I'd removed my grimy week-old undies, things like my vest and my liberty-bodice and the dreaded darned grey socks, I was expected to take a gleeful plunge into the aqueous depths/shallows, like Horace into the pool with his swallow dives only in miniature, they'd forgotten I was a coward, an earth-baby. The contact with the slopping, lapping water caused my very soul to shiver. I would have quaked in my boots had I had them on. As it was, I shivered until my teeth chattered, Such a baby, look at you! Nell would exclaim, She's scared. She's scared, Lillian shrieked gloatingly from the side-lines and the Mortification would begin.

When I look back on the dreaded Sunday dousing, I think it was like a preface to hell, certainly a stolid training for it anyway. The dousing in that scummy coal-smutted bath tub, ablutions beside the coal-hole on the gelid Sunday mornings when the whole house seemed to be in the grip of frost-bite and the steam from the bath-water rising in pearly curls of damp vapour up towards the small square window cut high into the wall as though they'd forgotten to put in a window and had remembered afterwards, an after-thought of a window, a window which didn't serve to see in or out of, which failed to let in the light it should have let in and was too high to reach and which Nell could only open and shut with the aid of a broom handle, balancing herself precariously on the side of the bathtub and succeeding with nervous exasperated little jerks of her arm. An abortion of a window. And me under it in the tub feeling Mortified and far too wet for safety. Nell had an aluminium mug and mugful after mugful of the warm liquid she splashed over my bony shoulders, not forgetting to wash behind our ears now, nor in our ears, we must get rid of the potatoes, everything was potatoes to Nell, dirty wax in our ears, holes in our socks, the round white starchy things we ate mashed or boiled or roasted ..... Nell rubbing my neck vigorously, Goodness me, where do you collect all these spuds! She scrubbed my back with a boar's hair scrubbing brush, stiff harsh bristles, the stiffer and harsher the better, to make it shine she said, ineptly scratching red marks up and down my little girl's skin as I shied away, I'll splash you, I'll splash Lillian if you hurt me, I hurled. Rough towels and rough scrubbing brushes were synonymous in those days with stoicism as well as with precarious incomes. Then down to the *'portant place* in between my legs, there was some sort of mystery about that place that Horace was never allowed to see, at least when mother, Nell that is, was around. When I stood up in the bath shivering, now fully Mortified and just beginning to feel thankful that the ordeal was coming to an end, she whipped the rough towel around me with the speed of lightning to hide the *'portant place* from Horace's prying eyes, like a purifying action before she attended mass. But before I had stood up to shake the dripping drops from my skeletal frame, my head had to be thoroughly doused, mugs full of water poured at great speed, cascading one after another down through my long hair, soap lathered with the help of a little vinegar to attenuate the abrasive London water, gathered in my locks, fizzed in my ears, oozed down my forehead into my eyes, It's stinging, *stinging,* I yelled trying to wipe it away, the hateful sore stuff, *S-t-i-n-g-i-n-g,* with the soapy backs of my hands. Never once was Nell, darling Nell, the adorable Nelly to her friends, dear mother, capable of washing my hair without the soap finding its way to my eyes, two minutes' temporary blindness every Sunday morning for years of my childhood. Sad to remember, that. Then more cascading water, bubbles around the nose, dribbling of vengeful tears from the sore eyes, soap suds flowing away, water water everywhere and ne'er a drop to drink, and now *thoroughly* Mortified, I would rise from the scum, hair like rats' tails hanging in cold lank strands around my shoulders until Nell brought a smaller, rougher towel to the rescue, winding my strands into a turban, Just like one of those Indian princesses, whoever they were, she would say, rubbing me dry with the larger rough towel and There I was doing my act of stoicism, no more vengeful tears from the smarting eyes, being vigorously rubbed, trying to look like the Indian princess I could never hope to emulate, not that I was ever very sure what was expected of me if I were to emulate an Indian princess, I just knew that she must be someone very very nice. Nicer than me with my chafed knees and smarting piggy eyes.

More warm water was added to the scum I had left to posterity and Lillian could then splash to her heart's content in the lapping liquid beside her floating liberty-bodice which I had thrown from vengeance against her gloating into the grimy wavelets, whilst Nell turned with her customary bird-like energy to do battle with the knots in my hair, there was no such thing as softeners in those post-Victorian days, in those smutty coal-carrying days around our bath tub, when we would call on George V to save us from whatever and on God to save him in tune to the brass band in the park. Knots are the bane of people's lives. Knots torment. Knots pull. Knots frustrate. They defy combs and baffle brushes. They are alive and kicking, full of fight, retaliating with their nerve-racking persistent labyrinth of twisted strands. Knots were certainly the bane of my Sunday mornings and it was Nell, my beloved mother, at her most merciless, pulling the comb insensitively through the matted locks, *O-u-c-h,* as though she were raking the autumn leaves across the grass with a wire rake. I would clutch onto the roots of my hair with clenched fists and lips pursed tight, muster every ounce of the stoic in me, this was much worse than the rough towels and harsh scrubbing brush. The knot-eliminating session was an inescapable fact of life, you put up with it or your hair remained unwashed and that, Nell would never have permitted and worse it was because Horace got off scot free with his short crop. It was woman-suffering from the earliest of ages. Nell pulled, I screamed. Nell tormented, I shrieked. Nell raked, I protested. But never once did I cry. If the tears ever did reach my eyes, they were tears of rage and spite against the raked knots. They were war-waging tears.

The blubbing was Lillian's prerogative. Her hair was longer and thicker than mine. Elsie's is rarer, poorer hair, scoffed the detested aunt Emily whining through the sharp point of her long thin mean nose, her ferret's nose,

the whining Emily,

every Sunday at lunch when every Sunday at lunch Nell recounted the knot-liberating episode of the morning and I would seethe underneath my stoic countenance and Lillian would swing her thick glossy plaits proudly within inches of my portion of Yorkshire pudding and I would think how spiteful she was, just like Emily the ferret with her spiteful remarks, they were two of a kind, *birds of a feather* I whispered to myself through gritted teeth wishing that her shiny plaits would dip into my gravy and besmirch themselves.

How our mother could face the Irish priest after her battles with the knots, is beyond me. How she could even so much as approach the Lord on bended knees, the Lord who needed her, after waging war on our knots and, as a consequence, on us, I am at a loss to understand. Perhaps it was because He needed her. Maybe that is precisely why she went to pray, scurrying along the road, her worried little face poking anxiously out from beneath her felt beret, her thirty denier Sunday stockings wrinkling at the ankles, my problem with the grey school socks was hereditary by the way, clasping her handbag to her bosom, her voluminous handbag filled with a clean handkerchief in case the Lord brought tears to her eyes as George V was wont to do, and a penny for the oblation which she'd surreptitiously subtracted from the meagre allowance father gave her from his master-building. And nothing else. Hers was a handbag-for-*occasions*. She went to pray and to confess her sin of war-waging, to purify her knot-liberating fingers, to substitute my piercing shrieks and Lillian's sniffing and blubbing with songs of praise. Perhaps it was thus that she eradicated from her soul the onerous smudge of being a child-tormentor. Some sort of peace of mind she gleaned from the Lord, or from the congregation, or from the Irish priest with whisky-swilling cheeks, because she would leave the house of *our* father with a purposeful grimace and enter the house of *her* Father, late, during the chanting of the mass, the confessions and pardoning of erred souls, the partaking of the body-bread and blood-wine, the reprimanding sermon, And return to the house of *our* father cleansed and purified with a radiance which lasted almost all of Sunday, including her afternoon nap.

Sunday was a family day. Never, for that reason, could I understand why aunt Emily had to be there when she wasn't even a real aunt. She was an *ersatz* aunt, a hanger-on,

Emily, the hanger-on,

merely the friend of one of father's far-removed cousins, who lived her lone spinster life close by, too close for comfort. I think he felt sorry for her, or something of the sort. I think he even had his eye on her because years later, after several thousand Sunday lunches more, when Nell died prematurely, father asked Emily to become his second wife to appease his longing for apple pie, if there was one thing she was good at it was cooking, and she snaffled up the opportunity as though she'd been sniffing it out with her ferret's nose for years. Fortunately those nuptials occurred years after we'd all left home and gave us little cause for discomfort. The discomfort was her presence at our childhood Sunday luncheon table. She was a veritable dampener on the atmosphere. She was bespectacled on her sharp pointed nose, so thin and insubstantial that those flimsy metal-rimmed spectacles had a hard time finding a point to grip and they would slide down towards the tip and she would frown at them drawing her brows, also thin and insubstantial, together in a series of impertinent little dives which made her look like a frustrated owl. Sometimes she was the owl, sometimes the ferret. Never very wise, never very quick. Quick only to lash out at our misdemeanours with her poisonous tongue, more like a snake than a ferret I suppose.

Emily the snake.

She would turn up, hammering at the back door which I, spick and span and shining being the first to have finished the dousing, would have to open. I had difficulty turning the door knob as I reached up waveringly on the tips of my toes and the moment she saw from the outside that the knob moved slightly, she would cease her hammering and push with all the force of her wiry body and I would be flung backwards to land sorely on my bottom and Emily would enter the kitchen victorious and stand pointing at me, laughing her raucous laugh at my humiliation.

The detested Emily.

Flinging a greeting at Nell-washing-Lillian she would poke her ferret's nose into the oven, whip her snake's tongue across her lips, brush back the wisps of hair falling from her bun and advance into the living room where she would deposit her bag on the chair she took possession of on her visits, the chair I liked to sit in. Then she would go to the sideboard, authoritatively, like one who unswervingly fulfils commitment, and between mutterings and humming and callings-to-Nell, pick the pieces of cutlery from the drawer, rasping, Don't stand idle, child! Here are the knives and forks. You know what to do with them. Look at that chafing on your knees, worse than ever it is, Nell, N-e-l-l, it's more cod-liver oil Elsie needs you know! How I hated the weekly lining up for doses of cod-liver oil and milk of magnesia spooned by Nell, dear dutiful and caring mother, from a greasy brown bottle and a dark blue bottle with white sediment encrusted around its stocky neck. Nauseous life-giving liquids of the era taken by us in protesting obedience to supplement the lack of vitamins in those pre-first world war years, worse and more frequent than any cough mixtures, the evil brown potions administered by our local doctor. The child's knees look dreadful! I'll try and remember to bring some ointment next Sunday .... Ointment from Emily's first-aid kit, not on your life would it get anywhere near my knees! I'd never hear the end of it were I to be cured by anything she gave me, I told you so, I told you so. Just what would you do without your aunt Emily? Your mother doesn't know how to handle these things, and so on, resounding in my ears. Poor Nell, she really wasn't such a good friend of this bossy neighbour. Why couldn't she persuade father to stop the Sunday lunches in her company? Impossible, he was working up to his apple-pie retirement. Unawares, naturally, but working up all the same.

The table set and the lunch *under control,* dear Nell would unobtrusively, almost surreptitiously, depart for her rendezvous with the Lord, and as she fixed her felt beret on her greying curls she timidly instructed Emily to meet her in the park by the brass band with the three of us spruced and father bristling. See you as usual! Sunday after Sunday we whetted our appetites for the roast-to-come, listening to stentorian brass airs which hurtled forth into the cold bracing morning from trumpets, saxophone and cymbals. Analysed from across the years, it was execrable sound really. Execrably played too. Yet father liked it. It braced him the way the cold air braced him. Emily put up with it for the sake of currying favour. Mother was moved by it. But Horace and I used to nudge and kick at one another, for something to do. The whole outing bored us. Lillian told us that we were immature. You don't understand good music, she said. Listen to her! Emily grimaced at us with a threatening twist of her mean lips, father grew dour and twitched and bristled his moustache and Nell, still panting from her late arrival after mass, placed a delicate finger to her lips bidding us to be calm and controlled and well-educated. Always calm, always controlled, always well-educated. It was easy for her. She had just come from a session of spiritual replenishment. Her calm and control lasted only until the band began to play the National Anthem, then her tears would start to trickle and she would retrieve her handkerchief from the voluminous handbag-for-occasions and begin to dab, to dab, to sniff, to dab, to sniff again, without calm, without control, but always well-educated. Apart from Nell dabbing and sniffing and Horace and I nudging, Emily grimacing and father bristling, nobody moved a muscle during the Anthem.

Heads high, backs straight, heels clipped together, shoulders down firmly pinning feet to the ground, chests flung forward, arms stiffened backwards into straight-jacket poses, what *must* we have looked like! And not a hiccough! Still, it's with me to this day. I always stand to attention when they play the National Anthem even though it's our queen Elizabeth now, not George the fifth, even though I hear it on the television or radio and I'm alone in my little flat, I still stand to attention. When it was all over, they let us run on ahead across the park so that we could have a swing and a roundabout and a slide, just one of each, before trooping home together. Emily and father did the talking, Nell was way outside thinking about her mass, or the Irish cheeks of the whisky-swilling priest, no doubt. Father always said she was different on Sundays. Emily did most of the screeching too, to us, such a problem it was with the best clothes that were never to be dirtied. Once home we piled around the dining-table wishing it was any other day of the week than Sunday because then Emily wouldn't be there pushing her way in between us and father and mother.

The jealous Emily.

You wouldn't believe it possible for an adult to be jealous of a child, but I know for a fact they can be, Lillian used to feel jealous of our nieces when she was nearing sixty and they were in their early twenties, jealous because they had it all before them I suppose. Emily was jealous of us because she'd never had us, because no man would have her. The only good thing about Sundays was that we got a decent meal, not like the bubble-and-squeak and semolina of weekdays, and we were ravenous after the dousing and the brass band. The helpings of roast-something and Yorkshire pudding with steaming gravy, followed by chocolate steam pudding and runny brown velvet chocolate sauce put new fire into us. We stuffed ourselves to bursting, Horace and I racing through ours to see if we could steal a bit of Lillian's Yorkshire crust, Look at that bird outside Lil, Sunday after Sunday she fell for it and the adults fell for it while Horace's fork pronged the largest crust and mine the smallest leaving Lillian's plate as good as empty. She never even had it in her to protest. You've done well with your eating dear, Lillian was Emily's favourite, At least you're sensible, not hogging it down like the other two. Look how fat they're getting! Emily always defended Lillian. Something to do with the birds of a feather that I mentioned before.

Bear with me, reader, if I recall these fragments from my past. Less are they memories than an attempt to delve backwards into the pettiness responsible for the situation I am presently living, the situation of having this sister anchored to me in my dying days. Against her will. Against my will. Believe me when I tell you that this is not a book of memories. Of memories, no. It is a book about causes and effects.

II

OCTOGENARIAN SCRATCHINGS

I'm going to make a cuppa. Would you like one?
What sort of a cuppa?
Tea. What else do you think it'd be?
With you making it, it could be anything at all.
That's not very kind Elsie.
It's not meant to be kind.
I always love a cuppa now. Don't you remember when mother and father used to have one after their Sunday afternoon snooze, just like us? It helps to wake you up.
Speak for yourself. I don't need waking up.
Haven't you been asleep then?
No. I've been reading. What do you think, that we all sleep our lives away like you?
That's not true Elsie. I've seen you asleep often after lunch.
How could you see me if you're asleep yourself?
Oh, I only doze now and again, cat-nap with one eye open.
What was all the snoring about then?
I don't know. Was I snoring?
Enough to prevent me from sleeping!
Thought you said you were reading. Didn't want to sleep. Make up your mind! And make up your mind about whether you want any tea or not.
Well, you make it for yourself. I'll have a cup later. Don't feel like it now.
You normally have a cup. What's got into you?

Nothing.

Tetchy.

Just don't feel like it, that's all.

Elsie at her most contrary.

You have one.

I don't know if I will now. I don't know whether I feel like it either now.

Then why did you say you did? Why did you say you were going to make a cuppa?

Well, I've changed my mind, haven't I? I can do that, can't I?

Of course you can. But it seems silly to me. Just because I don't want a cup, you suddenly decide you don't want a cup either. You've never been able to make up your mind, have you? Not even over a cup of tea.

That's not very kind Elsie.

It may not be kind, but it's true!

Then I *will* go and make a cup and I won't so much as ask you if you want one or not!

Do you think I can't make my own or something? The way you go on, it's as though I needed you to wait on me hand and foot.

Well I was only asking Elsie. No harm in asking, is there?

Elsie muttered, dithering old cow!

Lillian fumbled her way to the kitchenette. She placed one cup, just one, on the dresser. She filled the electric kettle she had bought for her sister as an act of ingratiating intrusion into Elsie's tea-times. Small, beige, with a floral pattern circumnavigating the base and a pair of elements encrusted with lime from years of boiling up London water. It was hardly a salubrious kettle now, but Elsie never worried about that sort of hygiene. She had reached the threshold of her eighties having consumed litres of unfiltered tap water so the lime-encrusted elements were of scant consequence in her days. If anything, they added history to her kettle. Lillian waited. She pressed her fingers nervously into the thick woollen tea-stained cosy. She whimpered within as she waited for the water to boil. She felt her soul stained like the tea cosy, not with tea leaves, but with one insult after another, with one Mortification after another. She was paying now for the Mortifications Elsie had suffered as a child at her hand. Unbeknown, she was paying for the gloating over her sister in the bathtub, for having Emily as her accomplice.

Emily the accomplice.

She's always so cruel to me. I must go. Leave. Get away from her. Why should I have to stay with her like this every week? She's rude to me. Unkind too. What have I done to deserve the treatment she gives me? I'm always trying to be nice to her and all I get from her are her surly answers. I *will* go one day. Away somewhere where she won't find me. Then she'll realise. Then she'll remember all I've done for her. Like that dish I brought her from my last trip to Cyprus, such a pretty dish and she just went and stowed it away out of sight at the back of her clothes cupboard, hidden away it was behind her knickers. I saw it when I went to borrow a pair. Unkind, she is. It was as though she didn't want to remember the dish because it was me, I was the one who'd bought it for her. Jealous of my trips abroad, that's what it is. Well, that's her problem if she doesn't want to get away herself. Sitting here smoking and reading and drinking gin won't do her any good. She always says *I* drink too much. I only have the odd whisky at night, one or two at lunchtime occasionally. That doesn't hurt. I don't need it the way she does, the way Horace does. I suppose they got that habit from father and Emily.

Emily the tippler.

They used to drink a lot. Nell no. Nell was teetotal. She never touched a drop, the dear little thing. Except the odd glass of Guinness, that was. Guinness for her blood pressure. Guinness to keep her strength up. But I remember how father and Emily used to get sozzled at Sunday lunches and have to sleep it off afterwards. Nell slept too, just out of politeness, because it was the thing to do. I don't know what it would have looked like if father and Emily had slept it off by themselves. Nelly would have felt very left out. Father didn't drink as much during the week, only a bottle of ale. When he was working on the building site, Nell used to pack up his sandwiches in a small basket with the bottle of ale beside them and Smokey, our dog, used to carry it up to the building site. Such a clever dog he was with the basket swinging around his neck. Very proud of himself.

Do you remember old Smokey Elsie?

A cautious crackling call from kitchenette to lounge. Elsie was snoring lightly, twitching the tip of her splayed nostril. The few stout hairs which formed her greying moustache, yellowed from repetitive contact with tobacco smoke, were moving rhythmically with each light snore. No, of course, *you* never sleep, never dose off in the afternoon, do you? I'll get you a cuppa now and wake you up to drink it, you tyrant. Then try telling me you never sleep after lunch! Lillian reached up for another cup and saucer which she placed beside her own on the kitchen dresser. Steam shot forth in a disciplined spray from the spout of the kettle. She turned off the gas and purposefully removed the lid from the kettle, bubbling spitting water and vapour billowed up into her face and she burnt her fingers. All those years making tea and she'd never learnt to be careful of the steam. She let go of the lid with a short sharp squeal, Beast of a thing, and it dropped to the ground clashing noisily against the tiled floor.

What's going on out there? Is my tea coming yet, or not?

Thought you didn't want any! Lillian retorted.

Well, you said you were making it, didn't you? I may as well have one with you.

And she goes on about me not making up my mind, I ask you! You need to be armed with patience to put up with her. With resentful vehemence she spooned four piled teaspoons of tea leaves straight into the boiling kettle where they floated, misplaced and wan, forming brown saturated patches on the steamy bed of water, rather like damp toasted cress. The teapot remained empty.

Do you want sugar? she called to Elsie.

She always forgot whether her sister took sugar in her tea.

Won't you ever remember that I take two?

Perhaps you'd better put them in yourself then, hadn't you? I can't remember everything around here.

Trouble is, you don't remember anything, do you?

Lillian put *three* sugars into both cups and poured a little milk from the carton into each. The milk was on the turn and glutinous lumps of creamy sourness stuck to the sides of the cups. She added tea from the kettle, steaming pale brown water with leaves floating on top. Evil brew it was. With shaky hand she carried one cup and placed it on the small wooden table by Elsie's chair beside the ashtray filled with butts. The table was badly marked where smouldering cigarette ends had smoked their way into the wood leaving behind them dark smudges, miraculously salvaged before they could set serious fire going. The beige carpet beneath her feet was pock-marked too, holed by cigarette butts dropped into space between table and floor as Elsie's brain battled with life through a haze of gin. She tippled from the bottle on many a lonely night.

Wake up! Wake up! Drink your tea while it's hot.

Alright. You don't have to yell at me.

They were crusty with each other, perpetually on the defensive. When not on the offensive. Elsie was normally on the offensive, Lillian on the defensive. It was their particular method of communication, their way of life, a way of self-affirmation, being on the offensive or on the defensive. Time had to be passed. The offensive and defensive are opposite poles, a perfect sort of opposition for people living in each other's pockets. A meaningful solution, in a way, to the business of living.

So you did have a sleep, you see! Lillian could not resist the jibe.

So what if I did. Doesn't matter, does it?

Ooh, I thought it did matter. I thought it was a crime.

Who told you that, you silly thing?

I think it was you that told me that.

Go on with you! I wouldn't say a thing like that. You must have been dreaming.

Perhaps I was.

Lillian fell into a bout of surmise as to whether one should or should not feel penitent for dossing off in the afternoons. She concluded that if her own father and Emily had permitted themselves to partake of so luxurious an activity, then little fault could be found with it. Besides, that was a way of proving Elsie wrong, of hitting back, of standing up for herself, something she had never known how to do in her entire life, and a way of defending herself from the beastly comments, the whiplashing from Elsie's tongue. Their very own father's dozes were living proof that such a habit was permissible. I could tell her that outright, she conjectured. I could do, yes, she murmured audibly.

What are you on about?

Nothing. Nothing. Only thinking of old Smokey taking our Dad his lunch. Do you remember old Smokey?

The faintest, very faintest, smile of condescension wavered on the extremities of Elsie's lips.

Yes, of course I do, she said abruptly. He was a lovely old thing. We used to go with him when we were on holidays from school. He knew the way to the building site better than we did; don't you remember? They never let us on it though, did they? But old Smokey used to get through that hole in the wire with the basket swinging around his neck and find Dad amongst the workmen standing around the site or warming their hands in groups around small fires. They all knew him too. I remember Dad telling us that one silly old fool gave him beer to drink one day and Smokey flopped down in a pile on his wobbly legs and slept all the afternoon until the men had finished for the day. A hangover, he had. Elsie softened with reminiscence. The normally discontented corners of her lips livened as she continued. He guarded those sandwiches, too. Never once tried to eat them himself and, don't you remember, he growled at anyone who tried to get close to him. Amazing it is what dogs know.

Lillian softened too. I love dogs. There was moisture in her eyes. We've had a lot of them really, haven't we? Whisky and Joe and Rufus and Peter. All of them came after Smokey. Smokey used to be Nell's favourite.

But Elsie's memory was sharper.

He was the only one she knew, you silly thing. We had the others after we'd left home and married. After she'd died.

Oh, I do believe you're right.

I am right.

The tetchiness had returned. Lillian cringed at being told yet again that she was silly. Elsie was made of metal. Not of velvet or satin, nor even of the mellowing wholesomeness of wood, nor of the floating ease of water, nor the flighty ethereality of air. Hers was a metallic nature. They'd always told her that. Let them never forget it. Let it never be forgotten. Lillian never forgot it.

What *have* you put in this tea? God only knows what it tastes like! I wish you'd let me do it?

Lillian clicked her tongue in nervous guilt. By the taste of the tea she knew she had blundered somewhere, but couldn't remember where.

The milk's off. Look at it floating like scum. Why didn't you use the new bottle?

Mustering and rallying courage,

Well you shouldn't leave it in the fridge should you? After all, it is your fridge.

You use it enough, don't you?

There was bitter accusation in that phrase. Elsie fumbled for her glasses, fumbled for a cigarette. Only two left. I must have another packet somewhere. She picked up her book, the latest Barbara Taylor Bradford, and immersed herself in page one hundred and four for the fourth time with a determined pursing of her lips, a determination that silence reign, that she not be interrupted in her repetitive reading by any more of her older sister's idiotic remarks.

Lillian took the hint, grimaced, felt lonely and hunched her short thick neck into her thoughts. Her thoughts were rarely disturbed by reading, only by her ceaseless remarks and her roaming in and out of the transitory activities which had become part and parcel of her existence, which were in fact a prolongation of the multiple ephemerae with which she had crammed her days and the long years leading up to this eighty-third of her life. Her thoughts, when they were permitted to flow uninterrupted by trivial movement and conversation, were of a fragmentary superficial nature, smatterings, ends of thoughts, ends before they were ever beginnings, thoughts which were hesitant, shoddily formulated, thoughts pleading to be interrupted for fear of becoming entangled. For Lillian was at ease with the simpler things, with uncomplicated observations. She clicked her tongue. To herself. A nervous habit it was from way back, the tongue-clicking and the knee-rubbing. She would sit forward on the chair as if in a state of perpetual anxiety, hug her own knees in her own arms with a strange and pathetic longing, her back slightly humped, then she would relax the hug and rub both knees with a smooth circular movement, untiring, interspersed every seven or eight revolutions with a methodical little slap on each calf and a click of her tongue. A nervous habit it was. And then she was away, off into the tangled ends of her thoughts. Perhaps all this nervous activity helped her to stifle the solitude of living alone in a small bedsitter behind the London Law Courts, her days replete with nothing but her own unfulfilling meanderings and her weekends replete with Elsie's whiplashing. Rubbing her knees was comforting in the silence and she rubbed them now, on the defensive against Elsie's impertinent reading... as she reminisced. Why they'd ever sent Horace off to piano lessons, she couldn't make out. He'd hated those lessons, drumming out his unmelodious mistakes on Miss O'Riley's keyboard. He cursed every evening before the weekly class the way he'd heard father curse. He used to look pointedly at Nelly, who was responsible for forcing him to continue with the tormenting classes, and proclaim unabashedly that it was all God's fault and Nelly was aghast and promised to pray in mass the following Sunday for her blasphemous son. Of course it was a pipe dream sending Horace to piano classes. Horace's soul was not akin to music. He hates the rowdy rock of today and has never liked classical music. Neither did he appreciate opera the way I used to. He even *looked* silly playing the piano, Lillian mused, his footballer's legs swinging out of time, dangling from the piano stool. He was too rough and ready for music lessons. His legs were rough and ready, hanging in the air like that. His friend Mike used to peek in through Miss O'Riley's French doors beckoning Horace to hurry up, come to the swimming pool. Horace said Mike even poked his tongue out at Miss O'R. Once she saw him and she screamed, shrilly her voice was, like the top notes on the piano, You wicked children, I shall tell your mother, oh you horrid little boys, the tip of her nose turned white with rage and she twisted the end of her neck scarf in anguished frustration. How am I ever to teach you properly with interruptions from that mischievous little beast you play with? Horace slumped lower on the stool in reply, crushed by his lack of enthusiasm for his music career. He used to tell me and Elsie, whispered quietly in private that was, that he played the wrong notes on purpose so that Miss O'R would become exasperated and pack him off early before the end of the lesson. But I think he played the wrong notes because he was incapable of playing the right notes. Miss O'R was a bit of a tartar to poor Horace who was built to be a footballer, a swimmer, not a pianist. I remember the carry-on, him and Elsie poking and nudging at each other on Sunday mornings when the brass band played in the local park. I used to love watching the players and listening to the loud blasts they made in the Sunday morning air. Their music mingled with the church bells from Nellie's little church nearby. But Horace and Elsie spoilt it all for me. Insensitive to good music, they were, nudging and stifling giggles. At least Emily kept them in order.

Emily, the disciplinarian.

Music, good music that is, was wasted on Horace. The piano was wasted on Horace. But it took Nell, dear little mother, a good many years to realise that. He was only rescued from Miss O'R's clutches because old snoopy Morrison who snooped around behind classroom doors wiping his moustache on the hinges whilst spying on his pupils Horace told us, complained that he wasn't keeping apace in class. Not a question of being any less bright than the other lads, just a little rusty on the uptake, Morrison always said *rusty* when he meant *slow*, must dedicate more time at home to studies, relinquish superfluous activities. Horace saw his opportunity when father summoned him gravely to attention. He might have been rusty on the uptake with his schoolwork, but he was quick and cunning when he wanted his own way. What's it to be my boy? father had admonished. Diving or piano? There was no doubt about it, Horace was a medal-winning diver for his school and father's appreciation of music was limited to the brass band. The males won and Nell had to masticate failure. It was mostly the way. It was a relief to Miss O'Riley and an appropriate attenuation to the annals of music.

Lillian paused for a while on Horace's fate as a music student, her mind dangling a little out of tune like Horace's legs from the piano stool. She was small of stature, her bones were fine, her fingers slim, unlike her sister's thick-set knotted stumps. Her ankles were skinny. She was prone, they said, to osteoporosis and bronchitis, dealing with both in valiant solitude because she half believed in Christian Science and abhorred medical help. She was thick around the girth, solidly ensconced in a well-padded midriff. A large round hump was gradually deforming her spine, dwarfing what had once been a softly sensuous body into *old* old age, it was seeing the world from a slightly crouched position, only slightly, but that perpetual looking upwards was a dubious business, made even more dubious beside Elsie's sprightly perpendicularity. Lillian's was a sinking downwards, a premature moulding into the earth which would ultimately take her to its bosom.

She nodded imperceptibly and glared at her reading sister, if she'd been able to see better, she would have noticed that Elsie's book was still open at page one hundred and four. Elsie was reading page one hundred and four for the eighth time. Lillian felt lonely again, even the faintest bit jealous of her sister who had this facility for immersing herself, forgetting time, in books. For re-reading. The way Horace had immersed himself in water. Or something like that, she reflected. She reminisced fondly. How she'd admired his swallow dives. How I used to admire his swallow dives! Of course, they did make me nervous because I used to wonder if he'd have sufficient breath to come to the surface in time. He used to pop up in a frill of frothy bubbles, his black hair gleaming against the white and blue of the water and there was everybody clapping like mad, applauding my brother. The girls at the Brown School were jealous of me and Elsie because of Horace. They didn't have brothers who dived off the highest board like him. Once they pushed me and Elsie into a corner and threatened to tie us up if we didn't stop Horace beating one of their brothers at swimming. St. Trinian's wasn't a patch on those girls. I was scared of them, about six of them there were, and I cried. Elsie didn't though, she went for one of them, Elspeth I think her name was, and punched her hard in the stomach. That winded Elspeth and she fell down. We all bent over her thinking she was dead until Miss Harris, the history teacher, walked past leaning her arthritic body on her walking stick, that stick we were all so afraid of because she used to wield it at us, brandish it dangerously in front of our faces, threatening our backsides, snipping at our ankles, I think it was more her defence against the girls than a support for her arthritis. She pushed her way between us and poked Elspeth with her stick and demanded that we confess. Then those nasty girls split on Elsie and she was carted off to the headmistress and caned across her palms for being outrageous. She didn't even flinch an eyelid under the cane. She said, I just went very red in the face. I felt proud of her in a way. Lillian reflected on Elsie's courage in the dimming afternoon light of her bedsitting room seventy years later. Although of course I knew she shouldn't really have done it. Lillian reflected on the Brown School. Not that that was its name. Its real name was Lady Martha Bottomley's School for Young Ladies, but they called it the Brown School because the uniform was Brown serge, Brown stockings on lumpy adolescent legs, such a jaunty Brown beret with the school badge on the crease perched on my glossy plaits, she remembered, and pretty beige poplin blouses. Ooh, we did look smart in those uniforms! Chocolate Brown ties, she remembered fondly.

I wouldn't mind returning to those days. Happier days really, she mused without further analysis, as the dimming shadows crept into the room enshrouding the two human forms and the dregs in the teacups and the antique bits and pieces of furniture.

The twilight was a limbo, a hesitant waiting before the plunging into darkness, before the electric light was snapped on bringing its garish jolting into another consciousness. Life and objects were cruel or bizarre under neon streaking. In Elsie's bedsitter the neon flashes infiltrated with crude insistence into the modicum of life going on behind her windows. The cups and the objects in the china cabinet danced in sudden and rhythmic unison, or in stops and starts and spurts, to the bawdy neon signs of the Chinese and Italian restaurants opposite. Red, yellow, green. Announcing nightfall. Announcing to Elsie that it was pointless to start on page one hundred and five or she would completely ruin her already failing sight. Detaining Lillian from rising to take the empty cups through to the kitchenette. Detaining. Retaining life on a threshold, in one fragile moment of breathless indecision, a passing spirit, the guardian of day relinquishing its post to the guardian of night. Twilight is a magic moment of uncertainty, the uncertainty which accompanies transition.

Elsie's book, which Barbara Taylor Bradford had spent hours of her life creating, exhuming from the bits and pieces of her own imagination and experience, fell to the floor with a derogatory flapping of pages and a hard-backed thud onto the carpet holed by cigarette butts. Elsie preferred hard-backed books. She considered they had greater substance than paperbacks. She jumped out of the gloom as the hard-back thudded to the ground, emitting a sharp exclamation which set Lillian off into a bout of nervous clicking.

I'd better get these things washed up, she hastened, servilely grateful at being permitted to spend the weekend in her sister's flat, to drink her sister's tea.

I thought you said you were going to Horace's this weekend, Elsie retorted as if the sudden awareness of Lillian's presence in the twilight had come on her like an unpleasant surprise. Her going to Horace's would be a way of not having to put up with her, of not having her fumbling around.

Was it *Elspeth* that girl's name? Lillian ventured, her hand poised on the tea-stained saucer.

Which girl's name? Elsie's voice rasped through the cigarette smoke and out of the stupor of having read page one hundred and four, four more times.

The one you hit below the belt and winded. She giggled nervously.

What *are* you talking about now? I don't remember any Elspeth!

Yes you do. The one who threatened to tie us up at school that time because of Horace.

You do talk a load of rubbish.

Your memory's not as good as you say it is any more, is it?

I don't know. Maybe it isn't. Elsie was resigned. Then decided, characteristically enough, to defend herself.

I may not remember trivial little things from way back, but I do remember the important things.

Like forgetting to take your pills, spat Lillian.

Oh *that's* not important. Then in begrudging acknowledgement of Lillian's feat of memory,

Anyway, I *do* remember that Elspeth, now you come to mention it. And I remember the caning they gave me for it, too. Nasty old woman, that headmistress.

But you did nearly knock the girl out. You could have killed her, you know. Lillian welcomed the chance to admonish.

Oh well. It's a thing of the past. Elsie brushed her own misdemeanours away with disparaging disrespect for the present. Because your past makes your present. Lillian seemed to have more respect for her past, at least if respect was nostalgic longing and fantasising over what could have been and what hadn't been. She stared at Elsie's book idle on the floor. She wished she could read like that. Everywhere she went she picked up other people's books wishing, always wishing, that she could bring herself to read, force herself out of her dithering thoughts to concentrate just long enough to read a novel. She admired the readers of the world. But every time she'd tried to read seriously, she found herself wishing that the glossy pictures of a women's fashion magazine supplant the endless lines of small print. To be honest, it bored her, that detailed concentration on the written word. It bored her but she longed for it all the same, like hankering after tangible contact with the members of the royal family whom you could never touch or see in the flesh but whom you could dream about. And then Horace had a daughter who knew foreign languages and Lillian spent many a moment on the occasions when they coincided in Horace's house fondling the foreign books the young woman left on the breakfast table, caressing them between her long fingers, clicking her tongue over them, trying with all her might to decipher the strange words. It was then that she felt a sense of exclusion as though she were being cruelly barred from important and mysterious areas of existence. *Après*, yes she knew that, it meant *after*. She'd learnt that at Lady Martha Bottomley's for Young Ladies. She'd tried hard with her French. She had almost won a prize which would have taken her across the Channel for a weekend, but they'd given it to another girl who managed her irregular verbs better than Lillian.

Her fingers still poised as if to pick up the saucer, she riveted her gaze onto Elsie's book and there was an unmistakeable flint of jealousy in her eyes now. Elsie passed many an hour reading. Admittedly books took her four times as long as anyone else to read because she read each page at least four times. But at least her reading, her re-reading, occupied her, occupied and interested her mind as little else did. She did have a few droppers-in, *my friends* she called them, from the neighbouring bedsitters. Lillian knew the white-haired Kathleen who was still a youngster, only seventy-five. She'd known more exotic, quite dramatic days really. She had danced away several years of her youth in a ballet chorus, modern stuff actually not too highbrow, plenty of leg-kicking for the benefit of the men in the audience. The *boards* were her life, she would say with a dramatic gasp, but she forgot them quickly enough when she caught a man who'd left his wife and he whisked her off to Bangkok. He in turn left Kathleen, in favour of a particularly sweet and obliging little prostitute who passed him the venereal disease she was incubating. Neither lasted long and Kathleen was left alone in that *devastating* city to find her fragmented way back to London. Never again did she entrust her life to a man. No longer did she dance on the *boards*. Her bosom had overgrown and prospective producers of ballet *shows* informed her with an appropriate sigh of sensitive remorse that she was *not quite dainty enough* for their requirements. Kathleen still had an ample bosom from which she breathed deeply and heavily, her voice blowing forth in whispering gasps. She wore, at seventy-five, kittenish clothes, flimsy white cottons with frills and sleeveless they were too, to reveal the sagging skin of her aged arms. She still walked quickly, with light balletic step, head held high, back straight, pausing on thresholds with her feet in second position, and she made everyone else's business her own, *took over* if she could. That was what Lillian didn't like, the competition with this Kathleen who was invariably on Elsie's doorstep when she arrived there on Friday evenings, organising one portion or another of Elsie's life. She was on the Neighbours' Committee and knew all the gossip in the flats, that old Mr Wadham across the way ate a trout every night for supper because they'd told him as a youngster that fish gave you brains and he still believed it and he fed his tabby exclusively on trout heads and tails, that young Mrs Barnley's mother was dying of drink, that Mr Robinson had struck his wife, cocksure fellow he was, and the wife had run out on him. That was the gossip. But being on the *NC* as she called it, Kathleen also told Elsie in advance when the rates were going to be increased, when the refurbishing of the south wing was to be concluded. Vital titbits of information they were, emanating in gushing waves from her balletic bosom. She knew more than Lillian. Lillian consoled herself by saying that it wasn't her block of flats anyway.

There were times when she would attack Elsie for reading so much. I don't know why you're always reading, ruining your sight like that, with all the other interesting things there are to do.

Like what? Elsie was bleak, metallic.

It was years since she'd ceased to find any real stimulation from outside events. She was swathed in a certain crust of boredom as far as exterior stimuli were concerned. Her metallic soul was sufficient unto itself. Occasionally, she would pull herself away from Barbara Taylor Bradford and take her small sprightly body, like a little bird really, off to see the tulips in the park. She had a passion for tulips, their harsh lines, their sentinel quality, the unmistakeable clarity of their colour, their unimaginative severity suited her character. Tulips brightened Elsie's day, but of course they didn't flower for long, just as her brightness didn't flower for long. Lillian, on the other hand, preferred the daintier, less jarring contours of lily-of-the-valley, the softness of the small pink rose, not the vibrant patriotic rose, but the tender petals of the wishy-washy rambler, rambling and unoffending like herself. She liked pretty, inoffensive things, minute detail, fussy china objects where years of dust lodged in the inaccessible nooks and folds. Where Elsie was impatient, Lillian had all the time in the world which meant that punctuality was a dictate to be obeyed by others only. She dithered to and fro as her bird mind hopped rapidly, with superficial touch, from one subject to another, from one object to another. But now she remembered the teacups.

Leave the teacups. I'll do them. You made the tea, so I'll wash the cups, said Elsie with efficient logicality. Then bossy,

You turn on the lights and switch on the tele. We may as well see what's on.

She saw *what was on* every night of her life and would never have turned the tele off had the programme not been to her taste. Television was her unfailing evening companion. Both sisters were hooked on television, hooked indiscriminatingly. Lillian snapped on a wall switch. No light came on. Blast, she muttered in low tone, hoping that Elsie would not hear and discover the mistake she thought she must have made.

What's the matter? Elsie called suspiciously from the sink behind the dividing partition which separated the kitchenette from her lounge. She never misses a thing!

What's wrong now?

Nothing, nothing.

Silence reigned as Lillian thought desperately hard why the light had not come on with the switch. A fumbling silence it was, tinged with embarrassment, a silence laden with Elsie's spying, with her waiting to pounce and point the finger of judgement.

Nothing! Nothing's the matter, she repeated. She looked around her, clicking nervously, as if expecting the four or five bulbs in the room to miraculously respond with a sudden shower of light. But they didn't.

I don't know Elsie, she ventured apologetically. There doesn't seem to be any light at all this evening.

Well, have you pressed the right switch? asked the cantankerous sister, distrusting.

I think so. I've done it before. I ought to know where it is, oughtn't I?

Yes, you ought to. What are you doing over in that corner? She peered around her prefabricated partition, her red stumpy fingers dripping with fairy liquid bubbles. Already she was accusing, standing there dripping soap off her fingers onto the beige carpet in frothy damp splodges.

Well I'm turning on this switch, aren't I?

That's not the one for the lights! Can't you see you've turned on the little foot heater!

Ooh! So I have! Do you know, I thought it was feeling warm around my ankles! Lillian giggled her nervous giggle, admitting, Aren't I silly!

Silly cow! muttered Elsie into her stout grey whiskers, snapping on the light by the partition and splattering fairy liquid onto the wall. Lillian didn't hear the insult, she intuited the insult. She must get her own back.

Look at you, dripping soap suds all over the wall and floor. You'd best be getting back to your washing up. I'll turn on the light.

Well I've already done it, haven't I? And they're not *suds*, she retaliated, they're *fairy liquid*.

Lillian turned away, defeated on every count. Well, there was always the tele, she reflected. That was some consolation. And she'd go to Horace's soon, get away for a bit. Under careful analysis, Lillian was a *hanger-on*. She had been a hanger-on all her life. Her life had been a constant participating in other people's intimacies. It wasn't that she had meant to clutch on like that, she wasn't intelligent enough to have ulterior motives, at least not far-reaching ones. But she did need to escape from the annihilating silence of her own company, she feared solitude to the point of phobia, she preferred to feel an intruder in the intimate patchwork of her relatives' lives than to face up to the bare facts of her childless widowhood. During those times when she was unavoidably alone, she took refuge in the warm glow of her whisky glass, it helped a little, it brought on crocodile tears, the consoling cape of maudlin self-sympathy, things became warmer, pleasantly befuddled. Her mind ebbed then in the muted gold liquid back and forth as the gentle lapping of a full, still sea against a lone rock. Her own body was the lone rock, the liquid the undulations of her mind. She'd hung on, clung on, for decades now. There'd been Australia on two occasions, prolonged occasions when on each count she'd gone, *just until I get a place of my own* she'd written on the card announcing her arrival in Sydney. Both times the *occasion* had lasted three and a half years, it had been a long series of occasions really, stretching out over seven years when the *place of my own* had been but a particle of her dream world in the down-to-earth reality of Horace's household. Before, in between and after Australia, there had been London where she had clung like a leech to her sister, working outside, true, but sharing the evenings, their evenings, butting her way into Elsie's married life, not that that was bliss in itself, but Elsie's husband, Roland, did become embittered, *fed up*, with the extra female around the place. Horace's wife Mavis, in Sydney, had a nervous breakdown over Lillian's presence. Because wherever Lillian went, went and stayed, she scrutinised the lives of her hosts with a critical eye and saw to it that her presence was felt by subtle or not so subtle comments of disapproval, by passing moods of Christian scientific devotion which pushed their way under others' skins, by disapprobatory stares and clicking, the stronger her disapprobation, the louder her clicking, the more frenzied her knee-rubbing and calf-slapping. Horace and Mavis had three children who used to laugh at her and loathe her by turn, imitating her knee-rubbing amidst shrieks of hilarity and sometimes putting up with her. Their tolerance was dependent upon their transitory humours, upon the stretching and shrinking of their growing days. Lillian's moments of condemnation of her brother's and sister-in-law's and her sister's and brother-in-law's ways of life stemmed from the feeling of guilt which she could never shake off at being a *hanger-on*. She convinced herself as the days and weeks went by that she was as necessary to them as they were to her. In reality, she was doing them a favour by staying. I mean, when Mavis had that breakdown because Horace used to tipple, over-tipple and take too much notice of other women, I used to spend my well-earned weekends cleaning up the house for her, dusting and hoovering on Saturday mornings after I'd been at the office all week. I was such a help to the poor woman. But Mavis always complained that Lillian dusted and hoovered with a cigarette hanging from her lips and dropped long flakes of ash over the recently dusted furniture and recently hoovered carpets and that she did the dusting and hoovering on Saturdays because she had nothing better to do. There are always two sides to everything. In her later years Lillian did hire a place of her own. A bedsitter like her sister's, only smaller. Roland saw to that. He ousted her for outstaying her welcome and for telling Elsie how to run his, Roland's life, not that he was difficult or incompetent, a gem of a man actually, too weak in fact for Elsie's metal edge, but he saw to it anyway that Lillian be removed from his days, if only around the corner, at least *not anymore* under the same roof. So she packed another seven years of her life into a suitcase and retired to her new lodgings behind the London Law Courts, a room with a kitchen stove and surface tucked away behind a concertina door. After Roland died, after Mavis died, many were the nights she spent with Elsie or Horace respectively, still repeating *I must go really, I must go back to my place.*

I really must go down to see Horace. Poor fellow, all alone he is down there.

I shouldn't think he'll be any the happier with you there, you know what he's like. Elsie bit disparagingly through her yellow teeth; she attacked, spitting the words from under her moustache.

What are you watching there?

I don't know. Something. A historian was speaking with the reflective precision and moderated tone, the natural product of his intellectual baggage, bringing snippets of Lenin's life into Elsie's living room.

Since when have you turned communist? she barked.

Communist? I'm no communist! They're dreadful people, they are.

Well, what are you looking at this programme for then?

I don't know. It just came on. What is it, anyway? Who's that fool yelling his head off at the crowds? Fancy believing anyone like that!

Can't you see you've switched it to BBC2? It's One we want. Or ITV.

Sometimes they have good things on Two.

Since when have *you* become highbrow?

The shrieking laughter of a studio audience crashed into the room startling Lillian, raucous bursts which matched the psychedelic shafts of neon streaking which shot from the street across the screen. Elsie had switched to One. Irritable, she pulled the curtains on the night outside. That's better. Then peremptorily. Now, I'm going to have a gin.

What about you? Whisky?

I don't mind if I do.

Lillian never said no, though she'd disapproved for years. She was too weak. It was too much to expect of her to say no, to openly disagree. She only disapproved behind furtive glances, black-browed peering, tut-tutting and clicking. None of her disapproval ever really came out into the open. Clearing the air was not her way. Besides, the taste of whisky wasn't altogether unpleasant. Elsie crossed to her cocktail cabinet squinting against the smoke which rose in twirls irritating her eyes from the cigarette stuck between her lips. A long worm of ash flaked to the ground. She trod it into the carpet. Good for the moths, she spluttered on the final note of a rasping cough which left her watery-eyed and puce in the face.

You really ought to keep off the cigarettes you know, Elsie. They're no good for you.

Listen to who's giving advice! You've smoked and coughed your way through your whole life up until a couple of years ago. Besides, the day you give up whisky, I'll give up smoking.

I can do that easily, though I don't see why I should have to give up everything when others give up nothing. But I could give it up without any trouble at all.

Don't talk rubbish. You'll never give it up.

I would if I went about coughing like you.

You may not cough now, but you dither instead. And you've forgotten how you always used to cough when you had bronchitis.

Yes, well I gave up smoking, didn't I? That's the sensible thing to do.

Elsie's cocktail cabinet was small. Its carved wooden top lay open for the world to see its contents, such as they were. A depleted assortment of bottles, two full of dry martini and one empty dry martini bottle, two and a half containing gin, Gordon's gin. A mixture of gin and dry martini was Elsie's preferred indulgence, whereas Lillian had succoured her body over the last fifty years on Scotch. There was half a bottle of Scotch only in the cabinet. There were a variety of corkscrews dating back across the years: the plain metal corkscrew with a wooden handle from way back, the more elaborate French corkscrew which Elsie's niece had brought her from Paris on one of her flying visits, a sudden vibrant invasion into Elsie's days, not altogether disagreeable, chatter overflowing, bear hugs, effusive expressions of affection, I've brought you this, the pressing of a small gift *for my favourite aunt* into the old woman's hand. With that corkscrew the bottle-opening revolution had hit the market, from then on bottles could be opened with disarming ease. And the latest corkscrew, Elsie couldn't remember who had given her that one, Italian this time, not made of metal, but of white plastic. You twisted effortlessly as the screw penetrated the cork and kept twisting as the cork gently levered itself up and out, in no time. Ingenious, thought Elsie. There were also two small collections of coloured cocktail sticks, a plastic bunch and a metal bunch. And three liquid measures with ludicrous faces. All three were thickly coated with dust. Disused. Forgotten remnants of a gayer past. Stuffed untidily to the back of the cabinet was a set of coasters, a cheap souvenir of London with Tower Bridge sliced in half on one of them where the picture had peeled off leaving a jagged white strip of rough paper, on another Westminster Abbey reduced to creases where the paper had dampened under wet glasses, and the Guards of the Changing beheaded by disfiguring smudges of spilt liquor. Elsie's drink cabinet smelt abominably of stale alcohol, dropped ash working its way day after day into the wooden carving, stains from the gin of overturned glasses soaked and dried and defaced the wood pattern. It was a cocktail cabinet with a history, with character, with a grottiness that attuned to the grey smuts of London City's streets. It was a cocktail cabinet fitting snugly on its squat legs into Elsie's life. To her, it was an object of endearment.

Elsie poured the drinks now. Strong, well-laced for herself. Weaker, cheeseparing for her sister.

I must go you know, Elsie. I really must go soon.

Go where you like, Where do you want to go to anyway? Her voice was abrupt and tinged with impatient inquisitiveness.

Well, it's a long time since I've been down to Horace's. Poor fellow. All alone he is down there in the country with no-one to talk to since Mavis died.

That's what he prefers, isn't it? To be all alone.

Oh no! I get on alright with him. He likes having me there. He enjoys the company.

Only so he can push you around.

What rubbish! He doesn't push me around. Nobody pushes me around.

Lillian took an enthusiastic swig from her glass, smacked her lips and clicked her tongue.

I think I'll add a bit more whisky to that, if you don't mind. It doesn't taste very strong.

Add what you like, said Elsie, indifferent.

I think I bought you a bottle last week, didn't I? apologetic of her need for a stronger drink.

Maybe, I don't know.

I must get another bottle to take down to Horace.

Lillian added whisky to her glass, then parted the curtains and stood staring out into the darkened street. She clicked her tongue quietly to herself. Late office workers scurried along in the wind, coats blowing around their knees; some clutched plastic bags full of items shopped in one-hour lunches, others grasped briefcases with determined fist making their way purposefully towards the black hole a few yards down on the opposite side of the road which was the entrance to the underground. Others stood more or less patiently in queues waiting for the red double-deckers to come hurtling and lurching along Faringdon Road. Others hailed cabs with impatience. The City was emptying its streets. Each bus, each train, each cab relieved the pavements of a few more scuttling bodies. Lights in office buildings snapped off as the occupants hurried home to supper and tele chewing the day over in their minds, contented at last to recover the four walls of their own intimacy. Those more reticent to return to homes and children and wives, lingered on over the papers of an office desk, or lounged against the counter of a pub. Their presence meant that the City was slow to settle to the deserted rhythm of its night-time streets.

A newspaper vendor with red raw bulldog cheeks stood in the cold by his stand of tabloid litter blowing on his fingertips which were peeking through the frayed woollen edges of his soiled gloves. He stared dejectedly at the rapidly thinning mass of passers-by, stared with a hunger in his eyes as if willing that he become part of their lives - it was cold and bitter and lonely on the streets early on in the night. A dog lifted its leg against his paper stand. Get aat yer dirty git! he yelled, raising a threatening arm. Lillian flinched for the animal. The dog cowered and trotted to take cover in the entrance of the building behind the newspaper man. It sat shivering with fright on its haunches, watching the movements of the street. Watching and waiting for the meanest morsel to come its way, its brown eyes liquid with wanting. Was it lost? wondered Lillian. Its pointed muzzle probed the air nervously, jerking this way and that. It was black and mangy white, poor white, off-white with dirt. Unkempt. And looking for someone, its owner or any owner. It was a stray with a set of protruding ribs and a mournful whine. The newspaper vendor unwrapped a cold sausage roll from a piece of crumpled brown paper. His supper, doubtless. He bit into the pastry with voracious unselfconsciousness and the dog was there, in a flash, before him, wagging its skimpy tail, ingratiating, pleading, whining. Ere y'ar then! The poor share more easily than the rich. When you've been without on many a night, you know what the pains feel like, the knots in your stomach, the nagging hollow and, after all, a dog was as good a friend as any man. The animal wolfed down the manna as if from heaven fallen, almost half the old fellow's supper. It gulped in grateful satisfaction and sat on expectantly.

Evenin' George. Looks as though you've got yerself a friend there!

The caretaker from Elsie's block of flats passed by on his way to The Peddlar's Arms.

Looks as though I 'av, dun it? And to the dog, Eer y'ar, yer rascal then. Cum awn!

The dog approached gingerly in answer to the man's coarse cajoling. It sniffed warily at the grubby elongated arm.

Cum awn chum! he insisted, friendly now.

The animal licked his dirty fingers and evidently relishing the taste, whined in grateful satisfaction. It curved its skinny body around his calves with pleasure, nosing the faint pong of urine on the baggy trousers which flapped in the wind. He patted its head and caressed the fur on its back. Eyes of dog and man misted over with the haze of long-desired affection.

Oh I say! Look at that, Elsie! That dog with the old paper bloke. He's been sharing his supper with it. Look! They're friends now. Dear old dog. Look at it wagging its tail. Dear thing, it is.

Lillian had always had a predilection for dogs. She was overcome in a moment with soppiness. The incident had diverted her attention from the nostalgia she felt for the hurrying homeward-bound office workers. She had been filled with sentimental memories of her own office days as she'd watched the life on Faringdon Road gradually diminish, as she'd observed the night beckoning them to their homes, as she'd felt pangs of envy for her long-flown youth. People working. It was an honourable thing to do. Lillian sniffed and clicked her tongue yet again, a metallic little sound it was like drops from a tap falling quickly and distinctly into an aluminium basin. She clicked as she thought and wished she could again form part of this beehive of laborious souls, glorified and magnified in the thousand insignificant activities of vast companies, labyrinths which consumed their souls, stripped them naked of their sense of independent will. In those places, people allowed their foibles, the personal push and stimulus of their lives, to merge into the harsh sound of tapping machines, to be annihilated by senseless directives, to be squashed beneath the weight of unanswered memoranda. They rushed hither and thither in flurry and flummox obeying orders, answering telephones, barging thoughtlessly through the day. Stones perpetually rolling and gathering little, if any, moss at all. Yet Lillian remembered her working days with reverence and gratitude. And she missed them now, confined as she mostly was to the silence of her own bedsitter, or to sharing the embittered remnants of Elsie's and Horace's lives. She compared her reverent gratitude to the diminished activity of her present days, sobbing inwardly for the bright company of office companions. She missed the laughing and the joking. Lillian had always been full of fun, she'd had sex appeal, they said, and had doted on the men's attentions. Moreover, she missed the responsibility and sense of achievement which her job had given her. Time dragged for her now in comparison.

I must go to see Horace, she said aloud.

For the umpteenth time. A trip to the country would fill the blank in her days and she associated it in her mind with an obligation, of the sort which the sight of the day's workers produced in her.

Goodness knows how many times you've told me that today.

You ought to come too, you know.

She didn't mean a word of that. She never wanted Elsie with her on those trips. Her journeys down to see Horace were an artifice to escape from her sister. But she invited her, nevertheless. Lillian rarely meant what she said, nor said what she meant.

No. I don't want to go now. You can have him to yourself. He can't stand me, anyway.

Well, you always rub his back up the wrong way.

You always kowtow to his whims!

You do say a lot of silly things you know, Elsie.

I know. I was born silly. She sounded resigned. But not as silly as some, she grated poignantly.

This is intolerable, Lillian thought to herself, feeling accused. Really, she had no option but to get away for a spell. Elsie's cruel manner more than justified her going. I shall be leaving in the morning, which sounded like the first irrevocable decision she had made in her prevaricating life. Elsie simply shrugged.

III

THE PROFESSIONAL LILLIAN

Of course in those days, it was upper-crust, a department store with style, selling only the best, on a par with Harrods, Liberty's, with sophisticated clients. No riff-raff there. It was a shop which sold exclusive things too, articles of clothing and food items from abroad. Lillian was fortunate to be accepted there, I mean, *we* weren't upper-crust at all. Nicely spoken though. They'd taken care of that at Lady Martha Bottomley's. And neat. Lillian dressed well and she was pretty. Emily had drummed that fact well into her, and into me, when we were small. Lillian will be the glamorous one of the two, she'd asserted with conviction. No-one ever questioned Emily's claims to knowledge

Emily the intellectual,

least of all father who, unbeknown to us then, had his eye on her and who professed to know little of good looks. He obviously didn't because Emily was decidedly ugly with her ferret face. Father's was not an aesthetic nature. Whatever Emily said, Nell would never have dreamt of disagreeing with her, through politeness and because Nell was submissive and Emily was domineering.

The domineering Emily.

Though Horace never took any notice of Emily.

The unnoticed Emily.

To him she might simply have been another piece of furniture which, more often than not, stood in his way barring his vision to more interesting things; and I could hardly, at so tender an age, be expected to defend my snub nose against Lillian's supposed glamour.

So it was Lillian's good looks that acquired her a position at Selfridge's. Perhaps they did play a part in it. Her very first job! She was engaged as a typist destined for the offices. Long were the hours she had studied at her typing machine, tapping away mechanically, copying reams of pages from textbooks, beating herself against the clock, faster and faster, more and more accurate. And her hieroglyphs on small lined pads, Pitman's she called it, all good businesswomen needed Pitman's, shorthand for recording the spoken word at great speed. I thought then that she had chosen the right career and that I would automatically follow her golden example. Selfridges, then, engaged Lillian as a typist destined for their offices, but sent her down to sell underwear at a counter on the ground floor where she stayed for six months working in a draught near the main entrance. It was an arbitrary, unexplained decision. She stuck it out that selling, always dreaming of the promised typist position, dreaming daily, weeping nightly in her humiliation, but not daring to complain to the powers-that-be. People in those days had respect for their employers, or they feigned to have respect. At business college they taught us that respect for the boss was all-important, no matter if your respect was hypocritical. Whatever his attitude towards you, you respected him, and it was normally *him*, very rarely *her*, he was a busy man with a burden of crucial responsibility on his shoulders. You were there to help him. Above all to respect his decisions, at all costs. Even if his decisions took the shape of unfulfilled promises about your work post, even if there was less in your pay-packet at the end of the week than you'd been promised when he'd offered you the job, less because the company was going through hard times and *we all have to make a sacrifice*. We were, above all, grateful for a job, grateful to our employer. Lillian and I sincerely believed that, even though Lillian used to weep at night because they'd done the dirty on her. She said that some of the girls incited her to protest, that she had *workers' rights*, like the Russian women, they said. They said she was weak to accept such a slap around the chops without standing up for *her rights*. But in Lillian's mind, she was not a *worker*. Workers worked down mines, built roads, swept streets. Menial tasks were theirs. Typing wasn't menial. It required training, dedication, a knowledge of good spelling. *Workers* didn't have those qualities. Lillian was convinced of her qualities and esteemed that her training had hoisted her into a sphere which could in no way be compared to that of the *workers*. She had been taught to admire her elders, her bosses, to hang on their every word and, above all, to obey their commands and to feel privileged obeying them. There was nothing subservient in that. She couldn't understand what those Russian women were on about. A fuss about nothing, probably. Continentals were like that, they over-dramatized, Nell used to say they were *histrionic*. I never knew where she had found such a word. Nell seemed too small to use words like that. So Lillian went on dreaming and weeping, yet respecting and not daring. Be submissive, advised Nell cringing from a corner of our lounge one evening. Just you go on working hard and being submissive and you'll see how they'll take notice of you one day. But why did they take me on as a typist? wailed Lillian, by then at the end of her tether and almost hysterical. They have their reasons, Nell comforted. Just be patient.

Nell chaperoned Lillian to her job on the underwear counter each day. She didn't actually dare to enter the store for Lillian preferred not to be seen with her mother, not that she was ashamed of her, but most of the other girls found their own way to work. However, Nell didn't trust people. She considered it one of the duties of maternity to deposit her daughter safely at her place of work, conveniently chaperoned and therefore unmolested by any young men curious about her daughter's developing charms. Because Lillian did have charms. Her dark brown hair was abundant, falling in light waves about her shoulders, glistening in the sunlight and in the light of Mr Selfridge's chandeliers. Her nose was long and straight and fine, unlike my wide snub. She had a beautiful skin too, like an English rose, Emily always pointed out. She wasn't very tall, but tall girls were gawky, she was slim with a blooming bust, her bust was too large really for her hips and thin legs. I used to think she sometimes looked like a bird with her breast perched heavily on spindly legs. I was jealous though of her bosom because mine was under-developed and I had no waist which made me look like a sack of potatoes tied in the middle. Emily said that, anyway.

The spiteful Emily.

But Lillian's big bust meant that her waist looked small and she was getting to an age where she used to pull her belts in very tightly to make her hips more noticeable. She knew how to move her hips too. They swayed now, as she walked on her newly acquired high heels, in a way they'd never done at school. I used to notice that boys would stare at her when we walked down the street together and she would flick her hair back in a haughty manner and her cheeks would flush pink. Sometimes she even stared back at them, even smiled at them sometimes. Then if they said anything, she would giggle her nervous giggle, clasp my hand and pull me away rapidly. Sometimes she'd look back again, longingly, and slow down to a linger, just out-of-reach of them. Acting the temptress.

Nell mostly went to pick her up too when she'd finished her day on the underwear counter. But when I left school the following year, also bound for business college, mother relaxed her chaperoning. Lillian had been her first child and it was logical that she display concern. It was *done* that she display protective concern. Emily too would delight in recounting sinister stories of young beauties enticed into dimming alleys by gentlemen dressed in suits who turned out to be devourers of maidens

Emily, the story-teller

and that convinced Nell to maintain a motherly grip on her eldest daughter.

I remember one Saturday morning, Lillian worked by the way at her underwear on alternate Saturdays, mother and I went along to Selfridge's to wait for her, *just outside the store on the right of the main entrance.* I stared up, intimidated, at the impressive doors and experienced a certain pride that my sister was working behind them. Even if it was only underwear she was selling. She learnt very quickly to call it *lingerie* and took pleasure in describing in minute detail the colour and texture and cut of panties and brassieres and petticoats. She did her describing at night when we both went to bed and it left a funny feeling in my stomach. She had to sell to some very elegant ladies, she told me, perfumed and powdered, who fingered the *lingerie* with slender white fingers which had never seen a wash tub and nails they had painted in a leisurely fashion. Some even went to buy their underwear accompanied by their husbands, most of whom conveniently averted their gaze when they saw Lillian's cherry red lips poised above the panties they were to purchase for their wives. Lillian told me of their looks. In secret, too. Very much in secret, because it wasn't so long ago that I had been at school, at Lady Martha Bottomley's for Young Ladies. She dropped me subtle hints about those looks from her sheets at night in the bed across the room. So subtle that I barely understood. She meant it that way. I was strangely flustered by her air of superior knowledge, her bird-droppings of information which incited my curiosity but never satisfied it. I remember thinking that she was doing it on purpose, making me feel small and inadequately young so that she could act important. Sisterly love, they call it. I never really thought that Lillian would do anything, well, *naughty,* with a man. Not that I was very sure at that stage what I meant by *naughty*. I just knew that some of the girls at Lady M B's used to go behind bushes with boys and show them their bottoms for a farthing, or a sweet, or for a kiss, a peck on the cheek. But there was something deeper and darker about Lillian *being naughty.* For a while, it haunted me and more particularly after that Saturday morning.

It was cold that Saturday morning. A crude wind whipped papers down Oxford Street, past Selfridge's, towards Marble Arch and gritty specks blew into our eyes. Nell's hair was lifted by the wind and by the time we arrived at our destination she looked like a parrot with its crest ruffled. All the world seemed to be in a hurry with the wind. London has some of the windiest streets in the world. Glacial winds they are, whipping as they do around corners, biting into people's faces, howling past their ears. I hate the wind. It still, to this day, makes me feel uneasy. A trolley bus trundled past us as we approached Selfridge's and people stumbled off it at the stop looking bewildered as people do when they alight from transport in a place they don't know. But rapidly they dispersed towards the various department stores. People pushed past us on the street. Nothing like they do today of course. They were more educated then, more full of *sorrys* and *pardons.* People today are a barging mass, a hazard for the old and infirm on the streets. But it wasn't quite as bad then, or was it that we were younger and better able to defend ourselves from the surging and shoving. We waited for a while outside the big doors of Lillian's store and a woman on the other side, *just outside on the left of the main entrance,* another chaperoning mother maybe, kept on staring at Nell. She had a bulbous nose which fascinated me because it was so ugly and she was gross under her shapeless winter coat. I stared at her, but she kept on staring at Nell and at Nell's ruffled parrot crest. I put my hand up and tried to smooth it down and with an impatient little gesture she smacked my hand away. I realised then that she was embarrassed under the woman's gaze. Had I been older I would have understood that the woman was staring out of ignorance and because we were the only others waiting as she was at the entrance to Selfridge's. She was staring at Nell almost unseeingly as you might stare at television in a bar because it draws your gaze hypnotically, not because it interests you. But Nell felt scrutinized and embarrassed. Her embarrassment pushed her to do something she would never in normal circumstances have dreamt of doing.

She suggested we actually take shelter *just inside* the entrance, *unobtrusively,* we could go out again when we saw Lillian coming and nobody would know that we belonged to her. She wouldn't have to be shamed by us. So without more ado and shunning the woman with the bulbous nose by not so much as casting a glance in her direction, we pushed our way through the great swing doors.

It was like passing from a troubled and ugly world through a passage of time into a world of miraculous beauty, a dream world. Outside the tempest was goading human beings. Inside there reigned a calm splendour. An odour of exotic perfumes filled my nostrils, it was as though the luxurious face and body creams on sale at the counter directly in front of us delicately moistened the air to a perfect texture, expensive costumes, leathers and wood, glamorous silks and satins draped on all sides. I gasped and held my breath slightly, aghast as I gazed upwards at the glinting chandeliers. Nell and I were small and insignificant amidst all this finery. It was the first time I had ever been inside a big department store and I felt uneasy, admiring, true, but out of my depth. I came to after the initial impact and began to look around for Lillian amongst the lustre and lights. Can't see her anywhere, can you? exclaimed Nell, too self-conscious to look very carefully.

I peered around me watching all the people intently, the milling customers who walked with slow and measured step, speaking softly to each other, hesitating here to look at jewellery, there at cosmetics. My attention was caught by a small group of ladies exquisitely dressed in wide-brimmed velvet hats; their features mysteriously concealed behind the fine gauze netting which descended from their hats over their faces. Young and inexperienced as I was, I could appreciate the fine cut of their clothing, the sheer sheen of their stockings encasing long slim legs. They were four in all, two middle-aged women of exceptional elegance both in feature and in gesture and two younger women, both of whom were dressed strikingly to match the dramatic lift of their countenances, the smooth olive texture of their skins. They were studying some pieces of jewellery displayed in an illuminated case and exchanging comments as they did so and laughs now and again which exuded a vitality which was not common then to England. They appeared relaxed and warm, not tensed and cramped with cold as we were. The youngest of them, older than I was and probably older than Lillian too, stretched out a perfectly manicured hand. She waved it in front of the others as if to admire her finger bedecked by one of the rings in the case. Was it her mother or her aunt helping her to choose an engagement ring? I'd rather have an aunt like that one I thought, than Emily, who was only a fictitious aunt anyway and a disgrace to any family!

Emily, the disgrace.

I couldn't keep my eyes off those four attractive people. I told mother to look at them and she sucked in her cheeks as if incredulous that people could look so beautiful. She looked small and innocent to me in comparison. We had never seen anything like them on the streets where we lived. There people were shoddily dressed with ugly purple hands from cold and overwork, with thick woollen stockings or, at the best, a strong-meshed thirty denier. Neither did they smell of all this pungent sweetness which was expensive perfume, they smelt of bars of household soap if they were lucky or if they weren't so lucky, of unwashed clothes and sweat in the summer months. The men had dandruff on their jacket collars too and some of the women went around with darns on the elbows of their cardigans. Of the youngsters, the less said, the better. The four ladies walked towards us, poised in every one of their movements. I saw Nell visibly shrink into her heavy lace-ups and feel backwards to the wall for support. That girl wasn't much older than Lillian, I thought, smugly pleased that for once Lillian could be unfavourably compared to someone. I was normally the one who was unfavourably compared to her. As they passed by us, we paled appropriately into insignificance and I heard them say words to each other which were foreign to me. Foreigners! I gasped to Nell. It was the first time I'd set eyes on anyone who wasn't full-blooded true blue British. Foreigners! And the word conjured up all sorts of enticing visions in my mind. Real foreigners all the way from the *Continent.* How have they come here? With plenty of money! retorted mother curtly as though wishing to dismiss the episode as quickly as possible. Of course, Nell thought those people were histrionic and unnecessarily flaunting. But I looked down at my ugly stockings and heavy shoes and thought that they weren't.

Where was the undies counter with all this? I looked around and saw it diagonally to one side behind us. I was just about to point it out to Nell when I stopped, stupefied in my intent. A glimpse, nothing more than a glimpse, had I caught of Lillian. Half an arm of Lillian, for she was shielded from my sight by a broad-backed man who seemed to be speaking in earnest to her, both of them behind the undies counter. I glued my eyes to them without a word to Nell. Lillian so close like that to a man. Then I noticed that his shoulders began to shake, with laughter evidently, and I saw him pick up a brassiere and wave it in front of her. She doubled up with mirth and, horror of horrors, he touched her around the middle, that hand so near her bosom. Who was he to be doing that? And what was worse, Lillian appeared to be enjoying every minute of it. He deposited the brassiere again on the counter and then playfully taking her hand in his, gave a mock bow and raised her fingers to his lips, playing the gentleman and, as he bent lower, I could see Lillian's breasts, the tops of them that was, the *cleavage*, peeping out of the top button of her Selfridge's blouse, the white uniform blouse I'd never seen her dressed in at home. The man withdrew with a wink and jocular salute and she posed her lips as if to blow him a kiss. All lips and big fleshy breasts, my sister was. And he was gone. Lillian stared challengingly at some approaching customers. Brazen, she was. What was it father used to call dancing girls, *brazen hussies?* I felt the life force drain out of me and I looked at Nell bashfully to see if she'd noticed anything untoward. She hadn't. She still hadn't even seen Lillian. After the affront from the *Continentals* and her general discomfort at having to wait *just inside* the shop entrance, she seemed unable to muster up sufficient concentration to distinguish any detail in particular. Her face was flushed, red patches on her neck I noticed, and her scarf was askew. She looked generally flustered and as if her only desire be that the interminable wait come to an end. For my part, I swallowed my secret about Lillian behind a long sore gulp, so loud it sounded in my throat, my shame for her. I was afire with embarrassment, yet as I looked about me, life continued to ebb and flow as usual. It was evident to me in one burning glance that I was the only one who had noticed Lillian's imprudent behaviour. I longed to look her way again, brazenly too, accusingly, yet I couldn't. I was out of my depth with that sort of thing. I couldn't even look at her when she eventually joined us ten minutes later. I couldn't look at her during the whole of the journey home on the trolleybus. I couldn't even *speak* to her for a long time after that.

Not until she had tired of Selfridges because they never offered her the promised opportunity to type and she was losing her skills selling underwear, *lingerie*, over a counter and letting men play with her brassieres, certainly losing the skills she'd been trained for at business college, anyway. Until she gave them her week's notice in favour of an author. By that time, I was doing my business training. This business training for girls really was the fashion then, the height of female emancipation. It was Emily who'd pounced on the advertisement for Lillian. Imagine it, an *author* who wanted a secretary to type out his books. An interview was arranged at the Savoy Hotel. And Emily had to be in on it with her ferret's nose. That was only fair, she said. After all, if it wasn't for her, Lillian would never have known about the job and perhaps Nell wouldn't quite know how to deal with the prospective employer, authors could be such difficult people.

Emily, the boss.

And it was important to give Lillian that *moral support* she would need at such an important interview. Emily and Nell would both accompany her to the Savoy. She seemed fast to be developing a predilection for glamorous places. The three women went along to the Savoy while I remained at my typewriter practising to Mozart at thirty words per minute. I would have liked to have gone along too, but that was out of the question Emily said, looking distastefully at my hair. That awful fringe, it makes the girl so plain, she complained to Nell, not even directly to me and I was sufficiently grown up now to be spoken to, growing up I was and growing into an outcast.

Emily. Who *did* she think she was!

The truth was I hated her with all my heart and when they'd gone, I plastered my fringe even more determinedly down on my forehead. Horrid woman. Who was she to criticize plainness in anyone else? Had she never taken a look at herself in the mirror?

Lillian was offered the job with the author, Emily said because she had supported her, chipping in at the interview. But with one inconvenience, Nell said, one very big inconvenience. Lillian would have to go and *live* with the author in his house in Swansea. In a second my mind was in a turmoil when they told me the news, in an upheaval of Lillian's fleshy breasts mingled with the author's books and papers, an author looking down her *cleavage* while he was dictating to her. I suppose it's alright, Nell said, because there is *one* saving grace. The author was a reverend and had promised in a very kindly manner to *watch over* Lillian. He had a housekeeper, a good woman, who would also *watch over* her and she would be well fed and not overworked. Emily, knowing the church, had asked how much money Lillian would earn. Nell kicked her under the coffee table for bringing up such an indelicate question, though secretly she was relieved that Emily could be counted on to do the outspoken parts. And the reverend had looked at Emily condescendingly as if she were a very slight smell under his nose. She will be paid an adequate sum for her task and age, he directed straight at Nell. Don't forget that she will be having free board and lodgings and gaining much experience. Nell, wary at first, decided that the man could be trusted. Being a man of the church was a point in his favour as far as she was concerned, whatever Emily thought.

That night in bed Lillian confided in me that she was excited at the prospect of leaving home. I was silent. I was jealous of her opportunities. I was proud in a sense that she'd been chosen for a difficult job like that. She was my sister, after all. But I was uneasy, uneasy had I been ever since the day in Selfridge's when I'd caught her flirting. I was humiliated too because I'd never had the courage to accuse her about that. I was convinced, furthermore, that her escapade to the reverend's house had to do with that flirting, but I didn't dare say so. Why couldn't I talk about those sorts of things? I never had trouble speaking my mind about anything else. You don't sound very pleased for me, she said tantalizingly into the darkness. In fact, you haven't spoken to me for ages. I still didn't answer. Of course, I know what it is, you're jealous of me, aren't you? Jealous, that's what it is, she flared. Whether that moment was the root of all our differences or just a logical continuation of her goading in the bathtub, an affirming that I was to be well and truly Mortified by her, Mortified for evermore, for as long as I were to live on this Earth, I don't know. It certainly didn't help relations between us. I pursed my lips together. I hugged my silence hard in the darkness. The strains of life were emphasised in their tiniest detail in the shadows of our bedroom, sensitive to the touch like the strings of a violin, emotions pinpricking against the conscience. Grappling with emotion was terribly painful to me. I was not in the habit of displaying emotion, not the tenderer emotions anyway. I bottled things up, bit and fought my path through the days, skirmished with people. There was a bullying side to my nature, I have to admit, a need within me to demonstrate openly that I was tough, unflinching. Emotion I associated with tears and weakness. I didn't want to attach myself to anybody, much less to this namby-pamby sister who was turning out to be so successful and sought after. I identified better with Horace. He was somehow solid in his masculinity and that calmed me, he fought back at my outbursts, he didn't cave in under them as Lillian always used to. Not that she did anymore. The change in her confused me and I was perpetually edgy with her, nervous of her highly-strung temperament. She put me on my guard against her because I could never calculate how she was going to react. Our relationship worsened as I grew in consciousness. In consciousness of life and in consciousness of a certain rivalry between us. The rivalry sprang from our unequal natures and the disparity in our looks. Where she was soft and attractive, I was angular and felt myself repellent to people. Where she laughed easily, I grimaced. Where she wept, at times hysterically, I clammed my pain deep inside. Where she chattered, I was silent. Emily had always taken it upon herself, with what authority I shall never know, to point out the differences between us. You could at least say you're pleased for me, she insisted across the eons of night which lay between us. But I didn't. After another lengthy silence, she tempted me, It isn't that you'll miss me, is it Elsie? That hurt. Yet I was incapable of showing her the slightest tenderness, of stretching forth the tiniest tendrils of emotional warmth to this sister who was going away to Swansea. What would she be doing with her reverend author, I couldn't help asking myself? And she was egotistical, I thought ferociously. Selfish, talking ceaselessly about herself, about her own activities, with never a thought for me. Never once had she asked me how I was enjoying my business course, what I intended doing with my life. She was too involved with the admirers of her lingerie. Well the lingerie was coming to an end now. Serve her right! How her selfishness hit me hard that night. I pulled the blankets up around my ears and wished she'd already gone to her reverend/author. Let her go quickly, pull sharply away from the home fires, leave me alone to care for Nell who was often poorly these days, to keep an eye on Horace who was still irresponsible and father who was working long hours and drinking more than was good for him. Let her go and leave us to it. You couldn't rely on Lillian, whatever

Emily said in her favour. Silence and thoughts hung heavy in the darkness.

Oh well, when she was gone, I could bury myself in books which is what I most liked.

It was a shock to me though, her leaving. One of those very fundamental shocks which life springs upon us from time to time. I had until then been infantile enough to conceive of our family as an unbreakable nucleus, laudable in its solidity. It was unusual in those times for children to flee the nest at a young age and particularly for a girl to do so. Mine was therefore a natural sentiment. The way, I mean, that I believed in our family as a *whole* unit but with a sort of a growth on one side, which was aunt Emily.

Emily, the tumour.

It had been a comfortable sensation, that identifying with a whole, that unquestioning acceptance that this was your place on earth. I was even positive, in my subconscious at least, that it was a perfect sort of existence, this continuing the five, or the five and a half, of us together until death us do part. And it was wrong that it break up before time. Mine was an indubitable belief in the rightness of family life. To me, the only acceptable way out of the parental haven was by forming your own family and this, it was quite evident, was precisely what Lillian did not intend doing. Lillian was leaving to earn money, money for herself, for her own low-cut blouses and make-up and tight skirts, not money to help us out. Her departure I considered unnecessary. She could have found work in London, work which would have permitted her to return home each evening. Perhaps it was that I was incapable of accepting that she was *ripe* and I wasn't; ripe, that was, to fall from the paternal branch, out of the maternal lap, into goodness only knew what types of predicament. Perhaps it was that I too wanted to be *ripe,* but knew that I wasn't. Ripeness doesn't come upon us all at the same time. But that knowledge was a burden for me to have to shoulder because although I was the younger of the two of us, mid-way between Lillian and Horace who was the baby, I had always been accustomed to taking the initiative, to rampaging my way headfirst through situations and letting Lillian follow on as best she could. Time and the law would have it, however, that she was to mature before me, to come of age sooner than I was. To *branch out*, as it were. I had already caught a glimpse of her branching out that Saturday morning in Selfridges, laughing at a brassiere waved by a man. And in the black of our bedroom, I remember wondering where it would all lead. The brassiere, the author and the reverend.

It led to Jesus Christ. It was about that time, a little afterwards, two months afterwards to be precise, that I discovered that He used to travel on the train between Swansea and London. Not that I discovered this personally. It was Lillian who'd seen Him. It wasn't that I had any deeply religious convictions in that first year at business college, either. Indeed, mother was the only one in our family who claimed any knowledge of the Lord and His doings and misdoings. Despite my ignorance in such matters I was still incredulous that He would reveal Himself to someone of such precarious taste as my sister Lillian. I mean, the Lord was supposed to be Superior and Exemplary in His ways and although we were told that He was forgiving even to the most sinful of sinners, I found it hard to understand why He would manifest Himself to Lillian and much less on a commonplace vehicle like a train journeying between Swansea and London. But the fact of the matter was that He did. According to Lillian, anyway. When she related the encounter, Horace stared with enormous round eyes as I'd never before seen him stare, that was before he started disbelieving Lillian's stories, mother looked proudly intrigued and Emily, who happened to have dropped in mid-week

Emily, the dropper-in

sat on the side-lines with an expression of demure admiration, a faintly *I told you so* expression as if it was only to her favourite Lillian that such things could occur. Certainly not to me, anyway. Father was absent at his building site. We were all interested and excited to one degree or another to know Lillian's news. She had been away for two months with her reverend author. There had been the due interchange of letters between her and Nell, Lillian writing about the pads and pads of Pitman's which she had to transcribe each week. I'd seen her shorthand and knew her outlines were enormous and I thought to myself that if she'd done it as neatly as I did then there would have been fewer pads to transcribe. She said in her letters that there was a lot that the Reverend, she addressed him with a capital R for the respect she felt for him, dictated to her which she didn't really understand, but she could at least spell the words correctly and for this she felt gratitude to Lady Martha Bottomley's, correct grammar was a boon in life, and Nell replied to her that indeed it was, that potatoes had increased in price and that she was thinking of substituting them with rice although she was concerned that maybe your father won't like it and that she was glad that Lillian liked the meals which the Reverend's, she copied the capital R from Lillian's letters, housekeeper prepared, that Elsie was doing well too with her Pitman's.

I remember that Lillian looked glowing on the day she arrived. Her cheeks seemed ablaze with happiness and she was glamorous in her high heels and her belt pulled in tightly making her bosom of bountiful size. All I could see as she stood by the window, her profile softened by the hazy light of the autumn afternoon, Doesn't our girl look pretty murmured Emily, was the reverend author staring down her cleavage. I wasn't sure what he looked like but I'd conjured up a pale-faced lean man with a soft brushing moustache, not like the broad-backed fellow, the brassiere accountant, behind the undies counter in Selfridges. And in my imagination I saw him pining for Lillian's cleavage as he dictated his book and I secretly wondered, because you couldn't help wondering those things, if he wanted to brush her cleavage with the extremities of his soft moustache. Otherwise, why was she still wearing her belts so tight? She sucked in her cheeks, pouted her painted lips, assuring herself that her audience was receptive, even Horace was receptive that afternoon to his newly-arrived elder sister and had not gone *up*

Mike's as he normally did after school. Lillian was taller and confident, no longer the whining namby-pamby of our school days. Two months with the reverend author had given her grace. And by the sound of what was to come, the grace of God.

She'd been immersed, little after the train pulled out of Swansea, in her reading, in her conscientious pruning for errors in the latest notes she'd typed for the reverend author. Most of his work, she proclaimed authoritatively, was theological stuff, whatever that was I thought surreptitiously to myself, contemplations on God's divinity and man's imperfection, she continued intellectually, pausing to watch the effect her words had on us. Nell shifted uncomfortably from her left to her right foot, embarrassed that her heathen daughter's knowledge of things ecclesiastical seemed fast to be outshining her own, What had she understood, if anything, after a lifetime of churchgoing? Emily looked as intelligent as was possible yet the best she could manage with her ferret's nose was a series of sudden jerks from her emaciated face, jerks acknowledging Lillian's profound remarks. Let no-one ask her what was her opinion of them, for scant was the opinion behind the jerks. Lillian had noticed that her eyes were irritating her; every so often she'd had to look up and rub them taking care not to smudge her eyeliner in the process. She was alone in the carriage. Nobody else beside her. Nobody else in front of her. She began to feel ill as the train swayed onwards. Harsh pains in her stomach. Perhaps the reverend author's housekeeper wasn't such a good cook after all, Nell thought to herself after ascertaining that Lillian had eaten steak and kidney pie with boiled-dry potatoes and hard-yellow-peas for lunch that day. She sniffed remorsefully, as though imagining her ill-nourished daughter, destitute and infirm on a long train journey. She need not have worried, however, because Lillian was salvaged from her discomforts. The Lord had appeared to her, she said, in a shining halo, His entire body outlined in a bright light, she said. She said He said she was suffering, without even asking her. Imagine that, He *knew* without asking what she was feeling.

Horace's eyes bulged in tune to her tale. I wanted to rub my ears to see if I was hearing right. Emily said, what did He look like. He was floating, Lillian said, in a long white robe, His hair was long, shoulder length. He didn't 'ave a fringe I hope, she interrogated looking distastefully at my forehead. Oh no! There was no fringe. A high, pale brow, said Lillian dreamily. Yes, but how did you *know* it was Him? blurted Horace at last. Because He was there, simply there without entering through the compartment door. I told you. There was *nobody* else in the compartment with me. And suddenly, between stations when the train hadn't even so much as stopped, there He was. I will accompany you, He said. I said I was only going as far as London. He said that didn't matter, He would accompany me always. Where is He now? asked Horace, almost garrulous. Nell looked around as if expecting Him to walk through the door. By this time she was virtually green with envy. Emily jerked and fidgeted nervously. I stared hard at Lillian. I was beginning to think she was telling a story to impress us. I would extract the truth from her that night in bed. Well, you can't see Him like other men, said Lillian disparagingly. You have to be in a certain receptive state of mind, she said aloof now, perhaps even a *suffering* state of mind. All I know is that He cured my stomach pains and sore eyes and now I know I shan't ever have to go to a doctor again. He said He'll be with me always. Why *you?* I shot jealously at her. Don't ask me that. Ask Him! He chooses His people, you know; she remarked with a superior air. I was livid and marched out of the room, Mortified, yet again, by her supercilious answer. Horace came after me laughing up his sleeve. I think she's going mad, he confided, before going *up Mike's* There was no room for doubt in Horace's mind. In a way, I agreed with him, yet I was annoyed with myself for doubting at all. Emily and Nell hung around Lillian's tight skirt like a pair of pigeons waiting for more crumbs.

So Lillian had returned home after her first long absence, convinced of her rendezvous with Jesus Christ and with the first foundations for her Christian Science firmly entrenched in her soul. It took me a few years to realise that she used her beliefs as and when she felt, that they were beliefs of convenience, like a bag of tricks to be pulled out and discarded at will. But then in my youth and inexperience and business college, I felt hopelessly inadequate. I felt that there were in fact vast wastelands between us, of knowledge or of nothingness. Whatever it was, the separation was enormous. Under the weight of my discomfort, I lay in bed that night listening to her breathing before we slept. It had only been two months, her absence, but her presence once again in our bedroom was like an intrusion. I had become accustomed to falling asleep all by myself, without being lulled by the pulsations of another somnolent body close by and I noticed that she had put me on my guard once more. I imagined that a dog whose hackles had been roused must feel the same way as I did on that first night of Lillian's return. Well, I could bark at her then, like the angry dog I felt. I had to discover what sort of a turn her life was taking. I was feverishly curious about the brassiere, the cleavage, the reverend, the author and now Jesus Christ. They jumbled around my head like the clothes inside the drum of a washing machine in motion. Not that we had washing machines then but we have today and when I look back on that time, this is the best analogy I can draw. So I barked out into the night, into the tremulous shadows lying in wait around the objects on our dressing table, through the fugitive glimmer which appeared and disappeared mysteriously in the night-time mirror, between the minuscule creaks of the old oak wardrobe door which swung invisibly as Nell or father or Smokey the dog moved about downstairs, I barked gauchely incompetent, insensitively inquisitive, I barked, and my voice grated,

So what does your reverend author do to you then? I sensed Lillian stiffen at the blatant crudeness of the way I had phrased my question.

What do you mean, what does he *do* to me?

I asked first, I retaliated, sharpening my spurs for battle, I asked first, so you answer me first. Then I'll answer you.

The night was thick between us. She didn't answer. I persisted, spurs well sharpened,

Do you let him touch you like that brassiere man did?

I was willing her to tell me, I wanted to extract every detail from her, invisible and protected in my bed as I was, my expression of hurt and febrile curiosity concealed by the darkness. I was crazed with impatience to know what men did to women and apart from that I wanted to be able to accuse Lillian, make her aware that I disapproved of her carryings on. In short, in the smothering darkness, I wanted to *feel* the reverend author's moustache brushing against her cleavage.

Well, he dictates to me all morning in the dining room.

How does he dictate? I insisted.

Dictating! How do you think? Word after word. Sometimes quickly, sometimes slowly. Sometimes he takes long pauses and that gives me a rest from writing. It's quite easy really, she said airily, brimming over with confidence and inspired by the interest I was showing.

And what do you wear? I asked knowing full well she'd taken the Selfridge's blouse with her because I'd searched for it amongst the things she'd left and it hadn't been there.

Clothes of course. You don't think I sit there with nothing on, do you?

I refrained from suggesting that I considered her capable of doing just that. Dresses, jumpers, skirts, blouses.

That blouse! That white low-cut blouse you wore in Selfridges, I blurted out untidily. That day I saw you there, I was waiting with mother and you were letting a man, that man with the brassiere, touch you and you blew him a kiss and I could see everything you had tucked inside that blouse coming out of it!

There! I'd said it. Four months later it had burst out of me, four months marinating in my acid bile. I hated myself for saying it, but the force of my need to know was more pressing than my capacity to restrain myself.

Just what do you think you're talking about? she retorted, clearly edgy and on the defensive. I insisted,

And what did you get up to with that man on the train? You alone in the carriage with a long-haired chap with a light all around him? What are you trying to make poor mum believe? Saying he was Jesus Christ! They call that blasphemy. Something awful could happen to you for saying that. Christ'll get his own back on you.

I *did* see Him. It was true.

Where did He put his hands to heal you then? You'd better be careful Lillian, letting all these strange men touch you.

Just what do you mean by that?

Nothing! I replied, grumpily returning to my shell after having waged warfare. Nothing! You know what you've been doing. We don't.

I included the whole family here, smugly, as though Lillian's imagined behaviour was an affront to our whole perfect nucleus, an assault on our integrity as a family, in short, a disgrace to us. You're the only one who knows what you've been doing with the man on the undies counter in that posh shop where you worked, behind the boxes in the store rooms there, you know what you've been doing with your visions on trains, with your reverend author's moustache!

He doesn't have a moustache. I don't know what you mean!

Well, whatever he does have then. Whatever he does look like.

He's round and tubby with a red shiny face, no beard, almost bald, with a row of fluffy white curls surrounding the top of his head which makes his shiny forehead look enormous. His eyes are small, gleaming like two beads behind thick glasses and as he dictates, he puts his hands together, just so, as though he were praying all the time. He's very kind and nice to me, but when he's finished dictating I go away and spend all the afternoon typing my notes in my room. At night I eat my supper with the housekeeper and I don't see him until the next morning. She stopped to draw breath. Then slyly,

He doesn't come and visit me in my room if that's what you're thinking! She was sarcastic now, coming out in defence of herself.

With you, it's hard to know what you'd do with anyone, I said indifferently, tired of the battle now that I'd driven my spur in. Disinterested even, because it looked as though I had been proven wrong. The reverend author didn't have a moustache, he was hairless; and neither was he pale-faced, he was red and shiny. I grimaced, imagining his cheeks like the pink skin of a new-born piglet. And Lillian hadn't been touched by him. But she still hadn't answered my insinuation about the brassiere man. That I tucked away so as to have a trump up my sleeve and because I felt too tired to pursue the interrogation and because I sensed a certain discomfort emanating from Lillian's bed. I'd done enough damage for one night. There would be other times for more.

There never were other times though for more of that, because I completely forgot about the man on the undies counter, until now. Until I came to write all these things down about my life, these things which I insist are not memories, but causes. I forgot that at the time, or perhaps I should say that I only remembered it up until the day Lillian arrived home with her Indian prince.

IV

AT HORACE'S

You've come by yourself again.

Oh yes. Elsie couldn't make it this time. She has an appointment with the eye doctor later on in the week.

It doesn't matter. Probably better anyway. She always manages to annoy me, taking over, running the house the way she does.

She did send you her love, you know Horace.

Well, that's alright. I send her mine too.

You could go and see her in London sometimes. Now that Mavis isn't here any longer, you've a lot of spare time on your hands.

I'm not going to London. Can't stand the place, you know that. So don't keep on about it.

Would you like a cuppa? asked Lillian, wishing she'd never mentioned the excursion to London. Lillian always resorted to offering people *cuppas* when she felt that she had upset them in some way or another. She managed to get around them that way. Horace was an inflexible person. He never wanted to go anywhere. It was always her, or Elsie, or her and Elsie who had to do the moving. Not that she minded coming down to the country from time to time, but life would be pleasanter if Horace were a little more tolerant. Then Elsie would come down more often too, keep her company on the journey. She seemed to have forgotten that she'd come to the country to escape from Elsie's bitter tongue. Unlike her sister, Lillian enjoyed being in Horace's country cottage with its pretty garden. There was always plenty to occupy her there.

Kept her young, it did, that garden. She peered out of the window as she waited for the kettle to boil. The kitchen window had a view out onto a spacious back garden which gave in turn onto a field where horses and sheep grazed. Horace had always kept his garden immaculate in the past. Like a showpiece it used to be, she thought. Although that was in the past. Now he paid a man with a lawn mower to come in and cut the grass from time to time, having lost interest in it himself and the weeds grew at inexorable speed throttling space for any other timid plant life, except in the small beds of daffodils and hyacinths which she remembered planting herself a couple of years ago. Now the daffs were coming out, baring their yellow trumpets to the March winds. The snowdrops had died off. Lillian remembered their clusters of dainty white petals which she had picked in late January and placed in a small crystal vase as a centre piece on the dining table. She remembered too that Horace hadn't even noticed it, after the trouble she'd gone to, getting her feet damp on the dewy grass and bending over the tiny flowers. She'd wanted the house to look pretty, but he hadn't even noticed. Men were insensitive to those sorts of things. Elsie always told her she was silly to go on trying to make Horace's life more liveable with actions like that, Elsie said they were useless actions, imperceptible to a man like Horace. Anyway, what did Lillian want from him, she'd asked. Elsie was incapable of doing anything for anyone unless she had an ulterior motive, incapable of doing anything just for the *niceness of it.* And Horace did like her flowers, she was sure of it. He just didn't comment on them, that was all. Mavis had liked flowers, but she'd preferred pot-plants like African violets and had never taken the slightest bit of interest in the garden when she was alive, Lillian reflected. It was a waste on her really, this lovely garden. Fancy having a garden and not taking any interest in it. Mavis would have known all about it if she'd had to live in a bedsitter with nothing but a window-box to look out on. She'd never known what it was like to live like that. She'd been lucky all her life, always living well with big gardens. But towards the end of her days she didn't even bother to pick roses for the house. Those roses, they were the pride of the street, blooming in Horace's front garden the way they did, everyone admired them.

She opened the side window of the kitchen and peeped down cautiously, because Lillian was a cautious person, onto the bed of bluebells. It was here that Horace and Mavis had poured the tea leaves daily from the remains in the teapot. The bluebells thrived on tea, shooting up each springtime in greater abundance and with renewed enthusiasm. Lillian let out a short gasp of admiration and called to Horace, Ooh they're pretty these bluebells Horace. Very pretty this year! She had told Horace that every spring for the last fifteen years. Needless to say, he didn't answer her from his post in the lounge chair. Horace directed life in his house from the lounge chair. It was a sturdy armchair, stocky like himself, almost made to measure and covered in mushroom pink velvet, worn and grubby on both arms. He had wallowed and hollowed into that chair for years now and its cushion had become appropriately moulded to suit his bulky shape. The visitors sat around him. That chair was rapidly becoming his sole anchor on earth. Since Mavis had died, it was where he felt safest and even more comfortable than in his bed. He invariably sat up in bed too, propped against three pillows where he managed to balance his heavy frame during the whole night and sleep from time to time without falling out of the bed. A miracle because by the time he got to bed each night his body was beleaguered and his mind befuddled with his daily intake of alcohol. If he lay down at sheet level, he complained of claustrophobia, that he couldn't breathe. He had to be in an upright position from where he could control the nocturnal rhythms of his home. And upright too he was in his chair from where he controlled the diurnal rhythms of his home. Lillian tried often enough to encourage him to take a turn around his garden or to walk slowly up the narrow little road to the village shop. Such activity, although hardly dynamic, would have provided him with a slight variation of routine, but Horace had no desire to make any variation to his routine. Instead, he stretched his intolerance to an extreme by stating categorically each time she tried to persuade him, that he didn't want to go out because he might be waylaid by a neighbour. He feared the neighbours in the village with the fanaticism of an agoraphobic, he wished for no-one in his life who might criticise his way, upset his routine, make him do anything that he didn't wish to do. It was years since Horace had sorted out his thoughts in relation to the world and its inhabitants and true to the dictates of convention, custom and tradition, deep, deep roots, nobody or nothing would make him alter his ways. What's more, I'm right! he would declare without the slightest hint of modesty. He was not one to be crossed. It was years since Horace had constructed his own self-made cage where he lived in a state of listless indifference to the trials and tribulations of the world. The News was his only interest in external activities, but Let none of it touch him, not so much in the form of a greeting from a neighbour. And so he denied himself the pleasure of others' company, apart from those who were thrust upon him by blood relationship and whom he tolerated because convention had moulded him thus. Silly fool you are! Elsie used to say to him when he protested bitterly about meeting people. Oh, he isn't Elsie! Lillian would respond, sticking up for Horace. But when she was alone with Horace, she would insinuate quietly, You are silly, you know Horace, never going out anywhere. Lillian prevaricated, she was blown from one remark to another, like a blade of grass in a medley of breezes.

She looked out of the kitchen window now, she had poured the tea and was waiting for it to draw. The grass, she noticed, was longer than usual, thick and well-nourished after the winter damp and glistening green in the afternoon sunlight. And Lillian felt protected. Further away in the field at the back, she could see the three horses grazing. Lovely old things they are, she thought, except for the flies they bring in the summer. Fill the house with flies they do when it's hot. But one couldn't complain to the neighbours who owned them, such nice people too, even though

Horace didn't want anything to do with them either. The horses were a snippet of life in the quiet. Elsie said that. Elsie said that the horses were at least *some* sort of substitute for the London hubbub. I mean, if it weren't for those horses to look out on each morning, nothing moved at all in days down here in the country. Elsie was right. Lillian always wanted to come to Horace's, but almost as soon as she'd arrived, the deadly quiet, the stillness of the countryside, hit her and that was what Elsie couldn't bear, the quiet. Yes, Elsie was right. If you saw two people walk past the cottage each day, it was an event. She remembered ridiculing Mavis for jumping to her feet every time someone passed to see who it was. It was normally the same people at the same time each day, the old retired General with his black Labrador just on one in the afternoon and then Miss Fawkes the riding teacher on horse-back sitting astride her beast under the riding hat perched askew over her great hook of a nose. Mavis had been starved of company in her idyllic retirement cottage and the General and Miss Fawkes had provided her with food for comment to Horace. Yes, Lillian had laughed at her then, recently arrived down from her busy London life, but now that life in London was less busy and she was *down* more often, she too would jump to her feet and comment to Horace on the General and his Labrador and Miss Fawkes astride her horse. In fact, not a day had passed in fifteen years when Horace hadn't heard mention of them. He almost felt he knew them although he had never, even when out in his garden, so much as passed the time of day with them. Sometimes he would answer Lillian, as he had sometimes answered Mavis, That old fool, so it is!

Lillian poured two cups of tea and took them through to the lounge. As she placed one of the cups on the little table beside Horace's chair, the little table overflowing with bottles of pills to be taken twice daily, with the latest letter from distant relatives, with Horace's favourite photograph of one of his devoted daughters, with a glass in readiness for his next whisky, with his biro poised for the crossword puzzle, with the page from the newspaper of television programmes which he never looked at except for the News, Lillian caught sight of Miss Fawkes astride her horse under her riding hat askew over her great hooked nose.

Look! There goes old Miss Fawkes, she uttered as if for the very first time and nearly spilling the tea in her enthusiasm over the event.

That old fool of a woman, so it is! Miss Fawkes was duly despatched by Horace. What does she want to go riding around on horseback at her time in life!

Well, she's been doing it all her life, so I expect she likes it, doesn't she?

I don't know. Maybe you're right. But I can't think why.

Well, we can't all be the same you know Horace. It'd be a dull world if we all had the same tastes, she said. And thought, Particularly the same tastes as you.

What is it then, half past four? Must be. She always goes by at half past four. Like clockwork. You'd think she could vary her routine.

Well, everybody has to have a routine, Lillian was tolerant of everybody to the point of tolerating anything at all. After all, you have *your* routine, don't you? Horace hadn't altered his routine for fifteen years, since his retirement from the insurance company where he had bequeathed the entire range of his effort and intellect, squeezing himself dry for what was left of his days with irreproachable dedication to the insurance company cause. Lillian studied his dissatisfied expression and thought from behind her teacup that he was critical, too critical of other people. Intolerant, that was the word for him. One should be more tolerant.

Nearly time for the five o'clock news, he said. If you wouldn't mind turning the television on.

Horace directed life in his house from the lounge chair. With courtesy, it is true, but he *directed* all the same. Lillian had a painful back, weathered and slightly bowed under the creeping onslaught of osteoporosis, but she was light of spirit and believed in *keeping herself going.* Her Christian Science principles, if somewhat faded over the years, prevented her from complaining. Horace had nothing wrong with him at all, except that one of his feet shuffled and he played on his shuffling foot, using it as an excuse to be waited upon when others were around. Lillian, bent and stiff after sitting, rose as best she could and went across to the television which she managed to switch on although with perplexity for the knobs weren't the same as the knobs on Elsie's set or as those on her own. Horace then adjusted the required channel from his chair by means of his remote control. Horace had come late in his days to zapping, but had adapted to it with surprising agility considering his scorn for things modern. If he'd drunk more whisky than was good for him, he found it difficult to press the correct button on his remote control which meant that he *zapped* unnecessarily and cursed in no uncertain terms if the picture were to disappear altogether when he confused the sound volume with the off switch. He suffered incipient signs of deafness which he feigned to be worse than it was so that he could overhear much that was not destined for his ears when the relatives were around. It was another way of controlling from his chair, overhearing when others didn't realise. To sustain his image of a deaf person, he was obliged to be coherent and put the television up very loudly; he would press his *zapper* with vehemence and Lillian would jump out of her skin at the sudden burst of noise. When it was too loud, even for his own deceitful motives, he would point his *zapper* in not quite the right direction and begin pressing all sorts of buttons exasperatedly to no effect until, well under the influence of whisky - a *skinful* Elsie used to say - he would miraculously point it in the right direction and substitute ITV with BBC Two, make the sound disappear completely and the colour increase to the most lurid reds and blues, or cause the screen to flicker in vibrant irritating lines. Then he would curse vituperatively and Lillian, diminished and fearful of his obstreperous behaviour, would be called upon to rectify his viewing and have to try to *zap* back to ITV and turn the sound a little lower, an onerous task for her because she was not well versed in technological devices. Mind you, none of this clowning occurred when Horace was alone. It was contrived for the benefit of Lillian and Elsie. Horace was wily in his quest for attention.

Lillian and Horace complemented each other, each giving to the other what the other lacked. Horace gave Lillian direction in her life, so that she would not be blown about too much. Lillian gave Horace the adulation and attention he required, she nourished his ego and pandered to his whims. He gave her a nice cottage and a pretty garden which, for all her love and loyalty to London, she had to admit to preferring to the window-box of her one room behind the Law Courts. She in turn helped him to bed on the evenings when the whisky had seeped down to his feet, which was every evening, and his feet wouldn't respond to the hazy commands from his brain. Then Lillian offered Horace her old bowed shoulders as support and, comfort the one to the other, they somehow manoeuvred themselves along the passageway and found their respective bedrooms. But most of all Horace gave Lillian relief from Elsie, because although Elsie and Lillian also complemented each other, the arrangement didn't work so well: Elsie and Lillian were both women. And sisters into the bargain which meant that what Elsie gave Lillian, Lillian did not necessarily want, and the little Lillian had to give to Elsie, Elsie spurned.

What Lillian most loved about the country cottage was having a *whole* house to live in. Sad it is that she had had to wait until she was eighty to know what it was to live in a *whole* house, except that is for her Australian interludes, instead of a bedsitter or the small flats she had known during her unfortunate marriages, in a house with four bedrooms, a lounge *and* a dining room, a kitchen *and* a laundry, a hall *and* a porch. It was a luxury to live in and to be, now that Mavis' gentle life had withered to its end, the mistress as it were of a *whole* house and garden. It wasn't that she had to be mistress to a lot of people, for Horace was the only inhabitant of that house, but it did mean that she could organise the *female area* of the house at her ease, bring in snowdrops from the garden even if he didn't notice them, arrange the crockery on the kitchen shelves to her own convenience, wash the clothes in a proper laundry instead of in a bathtub, as she was obliged to do for lack of space in her own bedsitter. Horace even allowed her to decide on the menu although he did insist on having a cold lunch every day, so as not to alter the fifteen-year routine into which he had fallen and which he had no intention of giving up. Imagine, fifteen years of cold lunches when a little mid-day soup warmed the cockles of the heart, and ten years of prefabricated suppers, hot admittedly, but prefabricated. A boon for the aged, they say, those prefabricated meals, or perhaps an impediment to the imagination, a way of *giving in* quickly, of *growing old* before time. Most women who live to a venerable age make cakes until they are well into their nineties. They live on because they refuse to simply accept what is meted out to them prefabricated in plastic bindings. But Horace had adopted the prefab dinners as part of his routine and woe betide anyone who criticised them and Lillian, grateful to be permitted to stay on as *mistress* of his house, complied unfailingly with the ground rules. Cold lunches was one of them. She didn't want to rub Horace up the wrong way, not in serious things like that, anyway. Besides, she welcomed Horace's direction in her life, he was something of a guiding light to her really.

As Horace renounced his gardening habits and slowly but surely his enthusiasm waned for things green, Lillian also began to find herself *mistress* of his garden beds. His garden became her own private domain as, with ever more frequency, he would answer her requests to plant this seed or that bulb with an I don't care, plant what you like! And Lillian would catch the bus into the town the very next day and fill her bag with packets of seedlings and bulbs. If it happened to rain directly after she had brought them home, which was not infrequent, she would hobble out between the drops and place them on the workbench in the shed in Horace's back-garden and forget about them until her next visit three months later when it was invariably too late to plant them. Oh well! They'll be alright for next year, she would mutter to herself holding the packets affectionately between her fingers and peering with a certain nostalgia at the pictures of the bright blooms and caressing the bulbs as if putting them to bed for a year. And she would substitute her bulb-planting with her edge-clipping. Horace had an old pair of clippers with a long handle which meant that Lillian could cut the edges around the beds without having to bend over and a pair of rusty blades so that to make any substantial inroads into the overgrown grasses she had to clip at least four times around the same edge in the way that Elsie read the same page of her book four times. Sometimes when Lillian was feeling particularly energetic and attuned to her gardening, she would don a pair of old brown *crimplene* trousers from *way back*, a woolly jacket with beige and brown squares and frayed cuffs, that was when Elsie used to call her *a treat*, You do look a treat in that get-up, and Lillian, hurt, would take refuge in her battle with the weeds. She would sit her old humped frame on the grass and grapple with the weeds at her arm's length, tugging with the might which was left in her octogenarian body at the tenacious evil grasses, *les mauvaises herbes*, the French were right she thought to call them that, they entrenched themselves and their wicked roots far more deeply into the soil than any ordinary plant, as she pushed her wisps of perm off her forehead with the back of her hand decorating her skin with streaks of brown earth as she did so. It was hot work but she was mistress of the garden beds and in her element. She'd show Horace what she was capable of. She'd show him she was worthy of her keep, worthy of the whisky she drank. And she plunged her bare fingers down into the heavy earth, clogging her long fingernails as she did so, Lillian's fingernails added at least half an inch in length to her fingers and so there was plenty of space for the earth to clog there. She insisted on leaving her fingernails excessively long despite the fact that age played havoc with them. They were yellowing and split, one or two broken off, the others jagged, lethal weapons to her stockings. From time to time she still remembered to varnish them, usually vermillion. Elsie used to comment that she looked as though she still wanted to *dig her claws in*, but she would forget to remove the varnish when it started to crack and so most of the time her nails were unkempt, reminiscent of a past spent glory, nightclubs fast-disappearing into the mists of youth, dinner parties whose guests were but a fading spectrum of phantom visages. Lillian should look after her fingernails, Horace commented to Elsie in one of the moments when he felt ashamed to have her for a sister. But with all the gardening, what could you expect. For she found it easier to dig with her fingers than to use a spade. Eighty years were a lot of years for one to be expected to wield a spade.

Occasionally she would take the hoe which was lighter in weight and better suited to her needs and she would hoe around and about her seedlings, in and out of the dreaded nettles. She never waged war on the nettles, Those B.....s! as she called them to Horace when recounting her morning's work. She complained bitterly about the nettles, as indeed does any garden lover, but she was aghast when the man with the lawnmower came and cast a particularly strong brand of weed-killer onto the nettles and succeeded in killing off all the seedlings which she had painstakingly planted nearby. That'll teach you to plant anything next to the nettles, remarked Horace unsympathetically. True, the garden was a battle, but it was her domain. It kept her young in mind and healthy in body, as healthy as the creeping osteoporosis would permit. In the garden she could lord it over Elsie because Elsie detested the garden. Elsie was an indoor person who shielded her body from excessive light and hot and cold currents and whose lungs reacted in no uncertain terms against any onslaught of fresh air. She preferred the smoky confines of a closed room and boasted that after sixty years of *smoking like a chimney* the doctor had told her that her lungs were as pink as a baby's bottom, When they should have been black like tar, Lillian thought grimly.

And having her own room, too, a bedroom which was separate from the remainder of the rooms in the house, now that was really nice. Far better than her one-roomed-sitter where bedroom was lounge and lounge dining room and dining room kitchen and where the bathroom served equally for washing her body and her clothes. A bit of a squash that, really. She felt attached to the small room decorated with primrose paint which Horace had allotted her. Elsie had always preferred the bigger guest room with the old high bed and the polished wood furniture which had belonged to Mavis' mother who had lived many of her last years in Horace's home, like Lillian *hanging on*, or rather hers was more a case of *clutching on*. It was an old-fashioned room that one. Elsie felt happier, more secure, amongst quality relics from the past. Lillian, on the other hand, moved or floated or was simply blown with the times and adapted happily to her primrose paint, to her inbuilt wardrobe and to the three pieces of white-lacquered modern furniture which constituted bed, dresser and bedside table. It was neat and uncomplicated. Ideal for her because she did the complicating. She settled in amidst a medley of objects which had interwoven their mutual dependence the one upon the other over the years, she nestled in with her life-long habit of untidiness which was fast becoming an acute problem because she left her life behind and about her in the most inappropriate places, handbags full of the money she had just drawn from the bank on the benches of railway stations, the keys of her bedsitter in Elsie's drawer, and a long list of etceteras. The surface of her dressing table in the primrose room which Horace had bequeathed her in spite of himself was virtually invisible beneath the numerous fine hairnets woven around her nail files and caught onto hair pins, beneath the corn pads extracted from their empty boxes useless and littering, strewn beside a variety of powder compacts and empty lipstick tubes, letters and gift cards from the Christmas before last, expired gift vouchers for W H Smith's sent for her birthday last sixth of April eleven months ago, bows from gift wrappings, Lillian loved their pretty colours, sitting sadly crumpled under untidy piles of copper coins which she found too heavy to carry around with her in her bag when she hadn't mislaid it, pills of varying shapes and sizes and colours, pills obtained from the doctor when she had forgotten that Christian Science was supposed to do her healing, her travelling alarm which had stopped at five o'clock several journeys ago, nail varnish, her vermillion varnish, spilt onto the outside page of her cheque book. Any further unoccupied patches of the dresser which might have been visible were hidden under scissors and combs and shoehorns, a second or third toothbrush and accompanying paste, a spectacles case without the spectacles which she had left at Elsie's, unpaid bills from the Water Board and British Telecom. Lillian's dresser was a whole lifetime of accumulated objects, This travelling to and fro is a complicated business, having two homes like this, she would say, I need my lotions here and I need them in London too.

The truth of the matter was that Lillian had completely lost control down to the corn pads on her toes and the bills she received and didn't pay. It is hard to conceive of her ever having been the supposedly efficient secretary she had been when she dithered endlessly over where to put the most insignificant item of her personal belongings. Lend me a pair of knickers she would say to Elsie, when she stayed at her *third* home, I must have left mine down at Horace's. You never know where you leave anything anymore, Elsie would bite. You really ought to tidy your room you know, it's like a rubbish tip, barked Horace.

So Lillian lived in a muddle of borrowed knickers, talcum powders, an assortment of perfumes and large boxes of tissues. She had a mania for boxes of tissues, a veritable obsession for boxes of tissues, the 'specially large ones, the *men-size* tissues. Every time she went out shopping either to town or to the village store, she would intend to buy a box of tissues and sometimes she actually bought one. Do you need any tissues? she would ask Horace. Any tissues today, luv? Hannah the shop girl would ask her with a knowing grin. Lillian put her tissues up the cuffs of her sleeves, she left them half-used, poised on top of the thousand other objects on her dresser, she forgot them on the kitchen table where they mingled in with Horace's handkerchiefs and the tea towels waiting to be ironed, she dropped them down the side of her armchair in the lounge, That's funny, I thought I had a tissue with me. Just a minute Horace, I'll be with you, I must go and find a tissue. Lillian went to bed with tissues peeping out from under her pillow, with tissues beside the half empty whisky glass on her bedside table, with tissues tucked into the elastic of her knickers in case she needed them in the middle of the night. Hers was a genuine mania for tissues which far transcended any fixation she may once have had for pretty handkerchiefs.

There was a hazy nostalgia hovering over all Lillian's wisps of possessions. True, she'd been a hoarder throughout her life, but now there was a clinging quality, a sad neurosis around it all as though she were attempting to halt the passing of life, or at least to slow it down, to wrap it inexorably inside bits of Christmas gift paper, to trap its consuming power inside numerous hairnets, to grip small parts of it with hair and safety pins, to blow the chagrin of life into a thousand tissues which she then did not have the heart to cast away. It was as though it had become essential to her to impede the pace of those dying days by prolonging the payment of bills, they had to be paid so life in turn must prolong itself and give her the time to pay them. The same applied to Elsie's borrowed knickers, she'd promised to give them back *some time*, there was a life-prolonging element in postponing obligation. She had reached that point when it could be said that her muddle tied her down, fastening her with a physical force to life, more difficult it would be for Death to reach her with its gripping claw, semi-concealed as she was amidst her belongings, amidst the transient odds and ends which had no apparent sentimental value, or maybe that one was the hairnet she'd worn on a certain day when ..... Was it possible to remember the good times because of a hairnet?

Perhaps hers was not so much a hazy nostalgia as a purposeful intent to establish her identity inside that primrose room, dropping things around her the way a dog urinates in short sharp spurts to demarcate his territory. A desire to continue making her mark on the world, her own personal seal like the blob of vermillion nail varnish on her cheque book, her disarray was a way of forcing others to take notice of her, Horace had told her to tidy her room, hadn't he? He wouldn't have spoken to her at all if it had been tidy. And like the garden beds, that primrose room had become her own domain and there she could behave with unrestrained vent for her own wind-blown existence mingling all her bits and pieces together in an inextricable web, an orgiastic craze to recapture the ends of her life strings, a frenzied obsession to collect, to hoard the moments in laddered stockings, borrowed knickers and tortoiseshell shoehorns. The bows from the gift wrappings, the gift cards from the Christmas before last, the crimson lipstick consumed down to the rim, perhaps, after all, did have their meaning; they put the haphazard memories of her days into some strange perspective inaccessible to the objective observer who happened to be Horace with his unsentimental meticulousness. And lastly, her untidiness, her forgetfulness, was one of the luxuries of age. Growing old had to have some benefits and she enjoyed moulding herself into an unhurried relaxation, a life no longer parcelled between hours and obligations.

Proof that Lillian considered the primrose room as her own and proof that she was not entirely unaware of her foibles was that she didn't, apart from the tissues, litter the rest of Horace's house like that. She was conscious that her littering was a source of irritation to Horace and, above all, she valued peace and quiet, the absence of warfare, that is. She normally *came off worse* in arguments with her sister and brother and she had no intention of adding wood to the fire. She made a big effort to keep her untidiness to herself, within the confines of the primrose room. She knew that Horace hated untidiness, hated it with a fanaticism to the point where he was obsessed with the most insignificant of alterations in the position of his mantelpiece ornaments, rather like a sickness it was with him, in a man of his age, in a man of any age, thought Lillian, but she had no intention of ruffling him even more than life itself had already ruffled him. Not that Lillian herself considered that Horace had had a ruffled life. On the contrary, she esteemed that he'd been exceptionally lucky. Here he was finishing his days in a nice house and garden. He'd been happily married until his good wife had deceased, he'd travelled a lot and seen the world, he had three children who cared for him yet left him to his own devices which was as he wished. He'd never even had to go to the dentist in his life, his health was excellent except for that shuffling foot, he'd had a *good* job with his insurance company and didn't want for a penny or two now with his savings and part of his wife's inheritance. Exceptionally lucky, really, she mused. Yet all this moaning that goes on. He never stops, when he ought to be thankful that life hadn't dealt him any severe blows. Like it has to me, she went on musing, with my husband dying years ago and not leaving me two-pence to rub together. I've worked like a slave all my days. Then we never had any children. Nobody to care about me now I'm old. And a tear escaped from beneath her eyelid, splashing into the dishwater. Lillian was over the sink washing up the afternoon tea cups. She spent hours of her life washing up the dishes at Horace's house. Her dedication to the kitchen sink was part of the silent compromise she had, an unspoken unwritten contract, You can have the primrose room and drink my whisky if you wash up my dishes. She liked to consider it her duty anyway. Whether such a contract had ever actually crossed Horace's mind she didn't know, but the un-uttered agreement became part of Lillian's code of conduct, it was in this way that she justified to herself her long presences in Horace's life. The washing up filled her days in the cottage too. When Horace *did* for himself, he never allowed a piece of dirty crockery or cutlery to remain on the draining board, he was a stickler about dirty dishes on the draining board. Let no-one in his house leave them there either! Neither should a drop of water glisten in the aluminium sink nor moisten the tap after the job had been completed. Immaculate, spotless, it all had to be left. Even if the only dirty things were a knife and fork, a glass and plate, which was normally all there was when Horace was alone, he could not tolerate them being left to accumulate. He would drag his foot out to the kitchen walking with the help of his metal frame, lean against the sink, roll up his shirt sleeves and set to work. He would fill the sink to the brim with very hot water and with generous squirts of detergent, liquid frothing in excess, fruit of a life oblivious to want, fruit of a life of surfeit. He would plunge his eating utensils and his arms up to the elbows into the liquid and rub energetically. Horace actually seemed to *enjoy* washing up and it must be admitted that he did it very well indeed, even if he was too fussy. Did it well, except that he never rinsed the detergent away with fresh water. The detergent he wiped away with tea towels which he hung expressly for that purpose over the radiator to dry between meals. He put the kitchen radiator on in the height of the summer so as to dry his tea towels. Washing up gave tangible form to Horace's punctiliousness. The washing and the drying and the wiping down of his kitchen surfaces was a logical consequence of his meticulous nature. He had in fact done the washing up for quite some years. He had trained himself up to dexterity in the matter on many an evening when Mavis had complained she was too exhausted to confront the dishes smeared with left-overs.

However, when Lillian came to stay she took it upon herself to accomplish the task and did so, uncomplainingly, four times a day: the two breakfast cups and plates lightly bespattered with crumbs from the toast, again after lunch when two whisky glasses replaced the breakfast cups and a glass bowl sullied only by two or three drops of water where lettuce leaves and washed tomatoes had lain (Horace wasn't a one for cut salads and, even less, for salads with a dousing of oil and vinegar. That was for Continentals and Americans, No idea how to eat he used to say, they cut up all their food then eat it with a fork, highly uneducated and out of tune with British custom). The next washing up session came after afternoon tea when the cups could never be left to join forces with the plates from the evening meal. So between one session and another, Lillian spent at least half of the time granted her each day, she was slow and painstaking in the process and sometimes, forgetful, would wash things twice around. A whole half of her time over the kitchen sink washing up utensils which were hardly dirty.... Her hands were constantly in and out of soapy water and the three tea towels had to be used in rotation or they would never have had time to dry. When alone in her bedsitter, or with Elsie, she would also wash up every time she ate something but in London she was more slapdash, leaving the dirty water in between sessions, leaving the lather to disintegrate into grey slops, leaving the film of scum to appear, leaving the hot water to turn cold. A depressing sight that was and one which Horace would never have permitted in his kitchen. Lillian knew that and respected his desires, as always, servilely grateful, rubbing away the excess soap and drops of water from the draining board, making sure that the surface gleamed, unmarred by the tiniest spot. From the kitchen sink Lillian could look up from time to time from her task and see the horses out in the field, catch sight of that bit of life of which Elsie had spoken. That way she knew that all was not completely still in the village, that life maintained its vigilance in the horses munching and grazing. Sometimes they even rolled on their backs and chased each other about the field. Now that was *really* something to see, to comment on. If you could just see them, the dear things! she called to Horace. He took scant notice of her. He considered her *as soppy as a wagonload, Soft in the head, she is,* he would comment to Elsie.

Perhaps Lillian was rather *soft in the head*, but she was sensible enough not to litter Horace's house outside her own room, as we know. She would potter around with a duster drooping from her fingers filling up the hours she didn't spend over the kitchen sink or drinking whisky with Horace in the lounge. She would pick up the numerous little ornaments on the shelves all around the house, ornaments which were gradually beginning to weave their titbits of history into her own life, rub them ineffectually with the duster and replace them, muttering to herself in indistinct tones, the wheezy whisper of the aged. But she took great care never to move them from their position on the mantelpiece for Horace would have noticed. They had been in their *positions* like sentinels for the last fifteen years and never should they be altered. She feared breaking the ornaments. Years back, she remembered, in Australia that had been, she'd broken one of Mavis' favourite wedding presents, a small crystal lamp. Mavis had treasured that lamp and in her own quiet way had cursed Lillian for meddling in her life. Lillian had no wish to repeat such a fatality with Horace. He too was attached to his ornaments, seemingly more so than he was to the people around him. So she dusted in and out and around them with the greatest care, poking the edges of the duster timidly into curves and crannies and concealed spots where nobody ever looked. And she made a special effort to restrict her own belongings to the primrose bedroom, collecting up her magazines or photos or the cardigan which took on her bulbous shape, the nail file or the handbag crammed, jammed with the snippets and oddments of old years, whatever in fact she had happened to have beside her lounge chair, she would gather up and take to her room each day. She wanted her presence in Horace's house to be minimally intrusive. She did not want to be ousted.

It was an attractive house, airy with light, light with air, unlike the stuffy confines of her own bedsitter. You could breathe in Horace's place the way people were born to breath, swelling your lungs with wholesome country whiffs of fresh horse manure and cows' cud. The kitchen was large, a shower of brightness, with its double-facing windows and easy for a woman to manage, pleasant too to have your morning tea and toast sitting looking out at the green and the daffs and the horses. Just to drink in the quiet after the hustle of London, whatever Elsie mumbled about it being like death during life. In the dining room, Lillian particularly liked the old maple dresser decorated with pieces of silver and crystal, more wedding gifts, she'd never had anything like that when *she'd* married. Of course, there hadn't been the money that Mavis' family had, Horace had married money, *a good catch,* they'd said. And then they hadn't approved of her choice of husband so you couldn't expect them to shower her with lavish gifts. Her life had been difficult, she sighed, after all one couldn't order these things. Yet they'd all seemed to blame her for not having known how to choose a man. It wasn't fair. But Horace's dining dresser represented a lifestyle which titillated Lillian's imagination, it whispered messages from an elegant past that dresser and the antique table and dainty chairs. The lounge didn't have the same elegance, the wooden mantelpiece with its stone fireplace gave the room a rustic air, the beige carpet was worn thin from Horace's traipsing and foot-dragging from the entrance over to his chair, *his* area of the room was lived in, in contrast to the rest of it which seemed to be especially contrived for admiration from afar. Two newly upholstered armchairs had barely been used and were unwelcoming in their pristine state. And those ornaments on the window sill behind them belonged as if to another place, another time, like miniature statues from an occult past. That part of the room had without a doubt another personality, aloof from the grottiness which was fast surrounding Horace's chair. It was a cold area. Where Horace had his chair, it was warm. Lillian hated that chair of his. She resented its dominating presence on that side of the room. With begrudging disgust she would flick the crumbs dropped down the sides of its cushion during his lunchtime cheese and biscuits, for Horace no longer moved to the dining table for his meals. Lillian would set up place mats hopefully on the dining table each day, convincing herself fruitlessly that she would persuade him to leave his chair *just while you have your bit of nourishment.* But he was not to be budged and with a gesture of impatience he would bang his hands on the arms of his chair, I'm not moving, not going *anywhere*. This was his answer to any invitation at all, whether it be to go for a walk or to visit or to go to his own dining table for a meal. Nowhere at all, he would state in his dictatorial manner. Silly old bore, Elsie would jibe courageously behind his back. Lillian just tut-tutted and thought he was a silly old bore without saying so. She would never have agreed unconditionally with her sister. You really ought to come to the dining-room for your meal, she would coax. He didn't heed her coaxing. And with each refusal her resentment grew, grew to dimensions which caused the chair to become a problem in her life. She would dream about it some nights during her wispy old sleep, tossed and turned in Horace's chair she did. And there it was in the morning as she made her way, clicking, fumbling, tut-tutting, sleep still hanging to her old wiry hair, clinging to the lashes of her large faintly bulging eyes which watered in the early morning light. Behind her weakened tear ducts she could see the chair looming up at the end of the passageway, there, through the open lounge door, in front of her, but empty for Horace was behind her sitting up in bed, propped precariously against three cushions like a great barrel with a human form, snoring lightly in the early hours, sleeping away the turbulence of his thoughts, his mouth drooped open. He looks like a very old baby, thought Lillian. But the chair, there it was still, even more horrific when empty than occupied by its sole owner.

In the pale grey light of dawn it appeared to her

as a sort of a monster waiting to be tamed, possessed. She would conquer her revulsion for it and approach it with her inexact gait, staring obsessively at the worn pink velvet upholstery on its wide arms, eyeing with distaste the grubby edges of its staunch cushions, ugh! it seemed almost warm still from Horace's body of the day before. Icily warm in the cold grey light. Spots of dried spilt whisky stained its side. Indeed, it smelt of alcohol, a faint dawn waft which heralded the insipid routine of the day to come. Lillian sighed, the chair had an anchoring quality, it was anchoring her too, anchoring her to stilted routine, something she had managed to avoid, even if at other people's expense, nearly all her life up to now, up to these her dying days. From the monstrous chair Horace would zap in and out of his news programmes and control the television viewing in the room. Which meant. That Lillian, like Mavis when she had been alive, was never permitted to watch anything else but the News, four times a day admittedly, but only the News and the same news at that. Horace was too self-centred to allow attention to be focussed for long on anything which subtracted attention from himself and his own comments about his past life in the insurance company. As he was poor of hearing although not, as we know already, as poor as he liked to make out, he never seemed to catch on to what was being said in any other programmes and so he resented the fact that Lillian could participate, in her small way *become absorbed,* in the content of anything else that was on. Now that's a nice thing to watch, she would suggest with hope in her heart, seeing a ballet programme or a nature programme advertised in the newspaper. Sometimes she liked the highbrow stuff on Two. Now he's a very funny fellow! Haven't you ever seen that comedy? She really preferred the light entertainment on One, it was easier, you didn't have to think so much. In her London bedsitter she spent hours of her time glued to the box. You don't want to watch that rubbish! Horace scorned. What do you want to watch that for? Then, playing the martyr, Don't mind me, you can watch what you like! But if Lillian dared to take him at his word, he would sit in a state of perpetual irritation, of selfish petulance, interjecting her viewing with impatient remarks: I don't know what they're talking about, Don't think much of this, Can't stand this awful row. And there was Lillian immersed in her snatched moments of mirth, giggling behind pursed and dribbling lips, red in the face, spluttering from surreptitious laughter, laughing, pretending not to laugh, wanting to burst with all the pent-up silence of Horace's imprisoning routine surging just below surface in a mass of bubbles, exalted at her own daring for having twisted his arm, yet afraid of the consequences. And he would fidget. Pour himself another whisky on the sly as if to emphasise that if no-one wanted his company, he would drink himself silly. In short, he would *force* Lillian, finally intimidated by his infantile display of egoism, to tell him to zap the programme off and away. It wasn't much fun watching TV at Horace's. In fact, it was *impossible* to watch TV at Horace's.

The house had a roomy passageway and an entrance hall which was larger than Lillian's entire bed-sitting-room. Unfair it was that the lives of some were so wide, of others, so narrow. The ample hall space ran into a passage which wound through the house from bedrooms to kitchen uniting all the rooms. It was not a grandiose corridor by any manner of means, but it did have the advantage of being both cosy and spacious at the same time. It was a warm and uncomplicated passageway, a passageway with curves yet without obstacles. It was a passageway which beckoned you from one room to another, propelled you with ease on your journey. It was comfortable and comforting. Not like those long never-ending passageways in hotels which carried you past room after identical room, hotel passageways controlled by numbers and arrows pointing up and down, converging on lifts and emergency exits. In such passageways you could walk for minutes on end, strangely conspicuous in the silence, occasionally meeting a chamber maid on her cleaning rounds with her trolley of utensils, more often than not, hearing nothing but the sound of your own footsteps, the sound of your own breathing. Lillian knew that because she had worked in hotels. No, Horace's passageway wasn't like that. She loved the way it opened out into the hall space, like a meeting place with the little monk seat which her brother had purchased *for a fiver* many years ago, a half-moon mahogany table under a large circular mirror which gave the sensation of there being more people in the hall than there actually were. Even if she only looked at herself in the mirror, that made two instead of one. That part of the passageway ran off into the primrose room, *her room*. Horace's room, apple-green, was next door, and next door to that the lilac room with the *quality* furniture which Elsie liked to use. The salmon pink toilet and bathroom were on the opposite side of the hall. The bathroom had undergone recent renovation, the man from the renovating company referred to it as *the refurbishing*. Horace had obstinately refused to install a shower cubicle whilst Mavis was alive. He could manage, he said, hoisting his poor invalid wife onto a board self-rigged across the bath and sponging her down with lukewarm water and not enough soap, nothing like as thorough as his own childhood dousing, or as thorough as his washing up. I can manage ..... It would all have been that much easier with a shower, but Horace wouldn't be told. It would have been an insult to his nursing prowess. It was only when the paint on the bathroom walls began to peel off in shamefully tatty shreds that he could be persuaded to undergo the major upheaval of having the shower installed. Alas, it came too late to alleviate the inconvenience which Mavis had suffered during her ablutions. Destined never to see it, she died a week before it was installed. One of Horace's daughters who lived *on the Continent,* in Spain, wanted him to include a *bidet* in the refurbishing package too, but he wouldn't hear of it. Archaic things for *Continentals* who don't wash themselves properly, was his comment, An unnecessary waste of cash. Bidet or no, the shower cubicle improved Horace's bathroom, although Lillian was too frightened to shut herself in, Behind that spring door with all that water pouring down on my head, not on your life! Claustrophobic horrid little cubicle it was. The bath was for her. Baths were quiet and civilised, predictable and controllable, I mean you don't get into them until you've turned the water off, whereas with a shower you don't get into it until you've turned the water on, she commented with Aristotelian logic. Dangerous things they were, showers! The clambering in and out of a bath, the fear of slipping over, seemed to perturb her less than the idea of locking herself inside the miniature recess of the shower. Lillian had been reared in the *old way*, doused in the *old way*, and it was in the *old way* that she intended to remain. The way in which she still insisted on washing the clothes by hand despite the fact that Horace had allowed himself to be pushed, actually hassled, into buying a washing machine. For years he'd been convinced that he had no need of anything so ludicrously modern as a washing machine. He had a pair of hands, These are my washing machine, he would retort in headstrong pride to anyone who attempted to dissuade him from continuing along his obstinate path. He thought he could wash, but the truth of the matter was, he wasn't washing the clothes thoroughly. As he never rinsed the detergent off his dishes, so he didn't rinse the soap suds from his clothes. When his underpants and vests dried, small patches of stiffened soap clung in puckered blobs to the material and on any coloured garments, white flecks would have to be brushed away, tell-tale of Horace's deficient performance at the laundry sink. But Lillian was petrified of the washing machine. From the day they delivered it, it made an appalling noise, the drum beating hard against a metal bar which the deliveryman had omitted to remove. Not only was the noise horrific, but the whole machine, under duress after its careless installation, would move about the floor with a series of small jerks and Lillian, horrified, would stare at it as though it were bewitched. She really didn't think much of it at all. Even after it had been repaired she still glanced at it suspiciously each time it moved from one of its activities to another. Like anybody else, she wasn't happy when she felt disconcerted. She was suspicious of innovation. During her working days, she had always been contented to bash out her letters on an old-fashioned typewriter. Electronics were not for her. Let the youngsters battle with computers, she would continue in her own way, in the *old way* which had, for her, proven more than adequate. Anyhow, these youngsters today don't know what it is to work, she would mutter.

For Lillian muttered. She was prone to muttering most of all at night when nestling into the primrose room for sleep. Her mutterings consisted of veritable conversations, of an explosion to an imaginary interlocutor of her innermost thoughts and repressions. Lillian emptied her soul each evening into the phantasmal breast of her invisible companion. She muttered in loud whisperings which grated against the primrose paint. At times her tone was vituperative, her words blasphemous, a vengeful warning of the stale morsels of pain she repressed within, behind her smiling flexibility, the rusty lumps of hurt she contained behind her soft cajolements, her light-hearted innocence. Bitter mutterings. A soul full of vengeance against the world, against those who, if not kind to her, at least, like Horace, tolerated her. Fortunately for Horace, his hearing was sufficiently dulled for him not to be able to distinguish the details of Lillian's accusations, his imagination sufficiently stunted for him not to suspect that her mutterings might be directed at him because he had scolded her for being untidy, because he had not allowed her to watch television, as if she were a child, because he was perpetually grumpy and irritable and frankly impossible to live with. The blood in her old wizened body, thinned now by whisky, flowed on its haphazard course through her veins and arteries as she lurched back and forth against her bed and dressing table trying to remove her clothes, back and forth against the sea of recriminations which she had piled up in her mind during the day about the way Horace ill-treated her. It was at night when she thought about Elsie, all alone there in London. Lillian transmuted her own pain by attaching it to another. Her mind fled back to the good times they spent together, laughing, going for walks around the busy shops, watching television. They *did* things together. Of course, Elsie *was* a bit harsh at times, But I suppose I *am* rather silly and forgetful on occasions, she thought with apologetic nostalgia for her younger sister. Elsie knew that Horace could be a beast. She would commiserate with her. Strangely enough, Lillian felt protected when Elsie was around. She could sit meekly behind her sister's sharp lashing tongue when Elsie dealt out pieces of her mind to Horace, sit there in her protected innocence as though nothing of what was being discussed with such violence pertained to her at all. Elsie's a good scout really, she muttered. Horace humiliates me. I must go back to London. I must go soon. The night stilled her mutterings.

V

ELSIE'S REMINISCENCES

She accuses me all the time of being cruel, Too pragmatic you are, she says, Too outspoken. Yet she can't stick up for herself at all! Already, after only a week with Horace, she's on the phone again grousing about the way he treats her. She sounded near to tears today. She wants to come back to London. As if she has to ask my permission. Anyone would think we don't let her do what she wants with her life. If she'd have let us have more say in it earlier on, things might have been different for her now. Kathleen sat posed and poised on the edge of one of Elsie's lounge chairs, listening attentively, her head slightly tilted like a bird. She never looked as though she stayed for long anywhere. She stared forlornly at her friend, her large eyes those of a ruminating cow.

I wouldn't tolerate her moaning, I really wouldn't, Elsie. You're too good you know, my dear, putting her up the way you do.

She can stay if she likes, as long as she doesn't make a nuisance of herself. Elsie sounded grimly resigned to her fate.

But she does, doesn't she? Make a nuisance of herself I mean. You always say so to me, anyway.

I suppose so. But she is my sister, after all.

Kathleen rolled her cow's eyes with a certain sagacity and let out a long dramatic sigh.

I must be away, my dear.

She rose from the chair, pushing her balletic body up out of her feet in fifth position. She waved her arms with breathless exuberance. And slyly,

I must leave you to prepare Lillian's bed.

She can do that for herself, Elsie responded curtly with a sour grin. She saw Kathleen to the door.

My dear! I shall be seeing you ...

And Elsie's *friend* breezed away down the corridor, propelled along by her own dramatic respiration and enthusiasm for the gossip of life.

*   *   *

A watery morning sun caressed the beige print of Elsie's chair. It showed up the darker rims on the material where the city soot had crept in through the crevices between window frames and wall. Soot falls in fine and silent layers, so fine and silent as to be invisible on a grey day. Only in the brightness of the sunlight is its trespassing revealed, only then can one trace its intrusive powdering on the surfaces of tables and the rungs of chairs and its slow corrosive action upon the satin lining of cushions, the worn patches on carpets, even on the cracked tiles of the bathroom wall. There it was even more evident than in the sitting room because of the streaks left from the steam after Elsie had bathed herself. Elsie didn't notice the city grime coating her furniture and upholsteries. She was impervious to such observations. In reality, she knew nothing else, having always lived in the city of London. To her it was life-blood, warm with its thin film of silt covering everything and she detested the cold cleanliness of the countryside, that fresh and freezing crust on Horace's early morning windows congealed her soul. London, like a great dissected monolith with its crumbling derelict buildings and proud spires pushing up towards a sky mottled with clouds, with its rolling brown river parting the ways between north and south, with its royal palaces and stately homes and contingents of busby-ed guards, its polyglot restaurants, evidence of the immigrants' sweating brow and their culinary nostalgia for distant homelands. The monolith-city where rigid civility walks side by side with eccentricity up green-verged side-paths, through higgledy-piggledy back lanes, across wide belts of parkland, behind the Law Courts, past the Silver Vaults in Chancery Lane, glimpsing the dome of St Paul's from Bow Lane and Fleet Street. These landmarks were Elsie's stamping ground.

Occasionally she went further afield window-shopping in the West End, browsing around Dickens & Jones or John Lewis' or Debenham's, sometimes even as far as Selfridges in Knightsbridge, and that was when she'd remember Lillian's first job on the undies counter. Bond Street she loved too. She loved the whiff of exclusivity, the aura of a lifestyle which wasn't within her reach, but which she admired. Fur coats and expensive jewels appealed to Elsie. They were to her proof of success, they were the extent of her limited aspirations, they sang to her of a life liberated from the day-to-day grind which had been hers. She put the Bond Street boutiques on a pedestal in her mind although she complained bitterly to Lillian of late that they weren't any longer what they used to be. Then there were the pubs of London, those beer-swilling gin-tippling hours in the company of rosy-cheeked faces and jackets smelling of pipe tobacco. Elsie's husband Roland had been a publican, at least not when she had met him. Then he had been an accountant. But he *became* a publican, he *managed* a pub for one of the big London breweries, swapping the office desk for the counter of a saloon bar for fear of becoming *bogged down* in statistics. By dint of Roland's choice, Elsie had spent the best part of her days *pulling pints.* Not as a barmaid, mind you, but as manageress. The memories would clamour as she strolled around her London, past pub doors where noise and laughter and bubbling beer frothed outwards to meet her in the street. From time to time a lump constricted her throat and Roland would be there before her, tall and handsome with his sleek black hair, joking with the customers. And she would hurry on her way, fighting with the lump in the wind. Sometimes her outings would take her down the Haymarket where she would peer at the photos on the hoardings outside the theatre. Elsie had enjoyed the theatre in her day, not the small impoverished experimental groups who acted all that abstract stuff you couldn't understand, but the important companies who put on lavish shows or raucously funny comedies. But it was a long time since she had been to the theatre. It was expensive and Roland had gambled away a huge slice of the savings which should have fallen to Elsie when he died and had left heavy debts behind him which meant that she had to adapt herself to frugality in her widowhood. She simply couldn't afford the theatre and had to content herself with staring at the pictures on the boarding outside. In contrast to what might have been, what Elsie would have liked her life to be, she had spent many a morning in the past not browsing around exclusive shops, but hurrying to her butcher in Smithfield market for her meat supply, battling her way amidst the hanging carcasses, blood still fresh, their entrails oozing with offal.

There was a beat, a throb about London which connected with the innermost viscera of Elsie's being. She underwent a pathological suffering when she was separated from her beloved city, the pain and frustration of an unrequited love, the hankering after the indifferent object of her desire, she was assailed by a sense of being spurned, forgotten by London and the Londoners when she went away to another place. London was to her incomparable to anywhere else in the world. Born and bred in the Plumstead peasoupers, her heart marched in time with the pageantry of the British monarchy, ceremonious occasions like royal weddings and coronations made the blood thump around her veins with a patriotic pride which the most patriot of patriots of any other nation on earth would find it hard to measure up to. Elsie venerated the British royal family which she had hoisted to the uppermost reaches of her mind to the point where she was besotted by the fashionable style of every new hat worn by the Queen Mother, by the perfection of every pair of shoes on Princess Ann's feet, by the indefatigable array of handbags, most probably all empty like Nell's bag-for-occasions, carried by the Queen herself in her royal hands. Elsie defended the monarchy from the marrow of her bones to the tips of her toes and fingers. In fact, royalty was the one subject which she and Horace and Lillian agreed on in absolute harmony, the one thing common to them which they all actually agreed to have in common. And although there were *other* castles, like Balmoral or Sandringham, even Windsor, it was Buckingham Palace and the springtime tulips in the surrounding gardens, which moved Elsie's heart. Royalty held a gospel-like spell over her. Whenever she walked past Buckingham Palace, she felt a reverence for the loftiness of royalty, that distant family perched way above the commoners, and she consciously diminished herself to the status of a grovelling yet grateful subject, appreciative of having been born in Britain, of actually *having* something worthwhile to admire. It is no wonder, she thought to herself often, that all those people from India and Jamaica want to come and live here. Obviously they want to serve the Queen, be close to her, heap their allegiance on her. She never imagined that they had come for money, to escape from lives of misery in their lands. And all those grateful Canadians and Australians who come flocking to London too, just to catch a glimpse, if not of the Queen herself or a member of her family, then at least of one of her famous guards, the ones who never bat an eyelid even when provoked by staring onlookers, Wonderful men they are, A credit to the country standing to attention the way they do, Obedient through and through, Put the rest of us to shame. And then the Americans and Japanese, even the *Continentals* who come yearly to steep themselves in British pageantry, starved as many of them are of such glory. Poorly lives, thought Elsie, bereft of kings and queens. Patriotism was a solid rock to Elsie, an anchor in the world and she considered it inconceivable that anyone live without that perpetual aura of regal glory to revere. To her, other nations were lacking without the paraphernalia of royal coaches and processions which clung tightly to tradition. In her patriotic adulations, Elsie cut as innocent a figure as Nell had in the church. Elsie loved England and its royalty above all else, she loved them with a vehemence which was unhealthy because it excluded any other ways of running a country. Elsie was a defender of her nation far beyond any saner contemplation she might have had about the dubious morality which lies behind the protection of one race against all others. Of course, she was unaware that she harboured xenophobic thoughts within her breast and would have been aghast were anyone to have insinuated such a thing to her. But the truth was that she was frankly contemptuous of anything which occurred or was produced or could be seen or done outside England. Even Scotland, Ireland and Wales could not compete in Elsie's soul beside England. England was the pivot around which everything revolved and London was the summit of that pivot. And the pride would well in her breast as she walked past her favourite landmarks.

She closed the door after Kathleen's brief visit, Kathleen's visits were always brief and breezy for she teetered on the surface of life never allowing herself to plunge into its depths, to corrode her balletic bosom with scabs of disgust. She moved in the realms of the light and airy. Elsie was altogether heavier in nature and suffered Kathleen's levity because she was a helpful neighbour and Elsie was getting to a stage where she appreciated a little help with the more onerous responsibilities in the community of flats. She appreciated Kathleen's untiring supply of information about what the Town Council did or did not expect of tenants, she found their circulars confusing and didn't always understand what was expected of her. Kathleen always knew. Elsie went to her kitchenette to make herself a pot of tea. As she waited for the kettle to boil, she took her pen from a china mug full of pens and pencils which stood on the wooden dresser beside her telephone. She reached under her mattress for her pages of writing. She kept them there in hiding as she didn't want Lillian to lay her hands on them. Lillian tended to snoop into things which were none of her business. Her snooping was not so much a malicious snooping but was because she had a nervous fear of being excluded from things and didn't always have a very clear-cut picture of what was her business and what was other people's business. Elsie took her writing over to the dining table. She placed her pot of tea on a small raffia mat beside her, in a spot of watery sunlight, and took up her pen. Now that it seemed as though Lillian would soon be returning, she wouldn't have as much time to dedicate to her writing. Lillian consumed her hours when she stayed with her, pottering around the bedsitter all day doing nothing. Privacy was impossible with two women piled together in a small room.

Elsie's mind leapt back to the family house she'd lived in during her young years, as the words flowed from her pen.

* * *

It was surprising how quickly I became accustomed to Lillian's absence. It actually made me controller of the activities in our household. I was the only daughter left and I took pleasure in running errands for little Nell who was often poorly at that time. I worked hard at my secretarial studies and I felt strangely free not having to be constantly measured against my elder sister and her good looks. I was learning how sweet it was, that freedom from unjust comparisons, the freedom of only having myself to measure up against, because Horace didn't count. In those days, boys and girls were as separate and as unexpected to compete as dogs and cats. He was launched on the masculine path, I on the feminine. It was Lillian who had been the spoke in my wheel, not Horace. And so the *jolt* of her departure, the jolt which I most felt would have a negative effect on my future, had precisely the opposite effect. That was one of life's miracles, giving you what you hadn't wanted yet it turning out to be precisely what you did want. And what was good for you, what's more. For when Emily tried to chide me,

The chiding Emily,

I defended myself honourably instead of running off to mope in a corner or turning my sulky lips on her. Little by little she didn't chide so much and I could perceive that she was favourably impressed with the progress I was making. Of course, she would never have admitted that, never have admitted that she'd preferred Lillian because she was the more submissive of the two and the more glamorous, that she *looked up* to Lillian for the wrong reasons. But I could see that in Lillian's absence she felt something for me, almost akin to, if not affection, then compatibility. No, perhaps that's the wrong word, it was Lillian Emily had been most compatible with, but perhaps she felt the faintest glimmer of acceptance that I did have a *positive* side to my nature. She begrudgingly accepted that I was growing in the family circle and that I was capable and a force to be reckoned with. This sentiment deepened, not that I held any vested interest in Emily's sentiments for me, as long as she restrained her belligerence, but it seemed to take root at the time when Lillian started doing stupid things, undependable things like turning up on Nell's doorstep in the company of an Indian prince. I mean, we simply weren't of the category, were we, and I don't know where Lillian borrowed such ideas. We were agog. At that stage we were unaware that princes were two-a-penny in India.

Nell was ruffled that day, I remember it well. That very same morning she had had altercations with the neighbours. The neighbour, Maud – *aunty* Maud to us, like *aunty* Emily, *aunties* who fell somewhere between true blood ties and the formality of *Mrs*, or *Miss*, in Emily's case – was infuriated because our dog Smokey had taken to tormenting her cat. Just as her mangy mottled old tabby had finished its morning preening and had settled like a sphynx on the grimy window sill of her lounge, Smokey, who had been awaiting his moment, had hurtled through a hole in the fence which divided the two gardens, barking his head off and snarling ferociously at the tabby without the slightest intention of harming it. I think it just tickled the dog's sense of humour to watch the cat flee with a piercing yowl. It added drama to Smokey's day. The tabby would find refuge in Maud's muscular arms, but when she came over to protest, Nell diplomatically suggested that it was unwise to become involved in animal wars. So much for yer friendship! Maud blustered. Never do I want anythink, Nell occasionally cringed at Maud's *k's*, from the likes o' you again. She withdrew into the cavernous depths of her large old house, still nursing the offended tabby. Until ten minutes later, Nell was drawn away from the kitchen sink by a hysterical shrieking and the sound of objects clashing and thudding against the gravel on the garden path. She ventured out into the garden and ducked just in time to avoid a china coffee pot flying through the air. There were bits of smashed crockery all over the ground. Take yer weddin', Nell also cringed at Maud's missing *g's*, presents back! hurled Maud. Take that one fer yer wretched dog! and a saucer hit the retreating culprit on his hindquarters. It was the coffee set that our parents had given Maud and her newly-wed Cyril on their *happy day.* So much for life-long friendship. Though I think that people make a lot of unnecessary fuss over friendships, particularly between neighbours. Those are friendships which are based on favours and circumstance, hardly ever on mutual interest or attraction. But Nell was a sensitive little person and was saddened that the smashed coffee set had put paid to an episode in her life, to the normally peaceful cohabitation with Maud. Father, with his tone of deprecation for women commented that Maud was probably just going through *one of those funny periods* which women of her age went through. But Nell was ruffled.

Ruffled, as she stood on the doorstep squinting up at Lillian and her Indian prince. She had never before been so close to a turban. She stared quaintly at its intricate twisting and folds. She was small and the Indian was tall, so she had a good way to look upwards to the object of her scrutiny. She wondered ingenuously what was underneath the turban. Hair, obviously. But how much of it? Someone had once told her that *those people* never cut their hair. Did he take the turban off at night, or did he sleep in it? Did he have to do those pleats every day himself or were they sewn into one piece? Was it the only one he had, this donkey brown one, or did he have a whole selection of them? All these questions darted fleetingly through Nell's little brain before she had even had time to register surprise at seeing this dark handsome impeccable young gentleman standing beside her daughter. She had been perturbed by a turban before she had gathered herself sufficiently to ask herself the one all-important question of what exactly was Lillian doing midway between brazen and coy in the company of this exotic man. Ay Lillian! From the man on the brassiere counter, to an Indian prince, via a reverend-author. Where *would* it all finish? When Nell recovered from the turban, she came over all hot and confused, as was proper at her time in life. This is my friend, announced Lillian with a nineteen-year-old giggle and a tweak at the Indian hand beside her. Close beside her. And Nell felt immediately diminished. What was happening in her life? This sudden incursion of suspicious foreign blood. Now she felt anxious, as well as ruffled, anxious and ill-equipped to confront yet another mishap in her life which, if not as crude as Maud's casting of coffee cups over the fence, was deep and disturbing in a way that she could never have explained even to herself, let alone to anyone else. The Indian companion smiled with a dark and disarming flash of magnificent white teeth and Nell let out a little gasp for she had never seen such a perfect set of teeth in her entire life. The teeth she'd seen around the neighbourhood were yellow, or protruding, or plagued with gaps. This strange man, from another planet as it were, standing calmly, neatly, smilingly, on her doorstep, was perplexing to her. She couldn't get it all into perspective and her mind was a haphazard haze of smiles she didn't intend and words she didn't mean. Lillian, considering it was time to cross the threshold with her Indian, if only the threshold of the parental home, wheedled sweetly, insinuating, I've invited my friend home for tea. What could dear mother respond? She twittered and melted into the grubby beige painted walls of our unimposing vestibule, as Lillian passed with the dark and charming gentleman. For *what* else could one call him? I mean, he really was a gentleman. When

I met him over his chipped teacup half an hour later and was introduced by Lillian as *Only my sister,* as if I had to be around but didn't necessarily have to be noticed, he flashed his teeth, rose from the cracked leather armchair, took my hand in his and raised it to his lips. Just like the brassiere man had done with Lillian on the undies counter in Selfridges! So that was what it felt like! I almost swooned standing there faced with all that charm and the shock, like Nell, of seeing a turban actually inside our living room and of being touched, if only fleetingly, by all that mysterious darkness. I felt squeamish inside me and was only saved from swooning because Emily suddenly put in an appearance.

I have said often that Emily had a ferret's nose and an uncanny talent for sniffing out juicy titbits. Glued to her front window all day, she had seen it all from the coffee set in smithereens to the arrival of the dark and beautiful man, so close beside Lillian. Now she breezed in and, purposefully ignoring the *exciting* stranger, crossed straight to Nell and asked patronizingly, Is our poor Smokey safe from that dreadful woman next door? Bristling, she was, with victory because she had always been just that little bit envious of Nell's relationship with Maud and now at last she could see that the incident between dog and cat might well have put paid to it. Without waiting for Nell-overcome-with-emotion to reply, she stopped short, twitching her ferret's nose, pointing her skinny muzzle enquiringly in the direction of Lillian and the *fascinating* stranger. This is *Only aunty Emily*, Lillian made her introduction. For the first time ever, Emily and I had been relegated to the same status, to the status of *Only*. We didn't quite make it. Just not on a par with Lillian. Outclassed. Not in her category. And with my indignation on the point of exploding and with my web of conflicting dark emotions about the equally dark stranger, I escaped to the kitchen where I was rapidly joined, under the pretext of replenishing the teapot, both by Nell and Emily-who-had-just-had-her-hand-kissed. That was the first time, amidst our suppressed giggles and inquisitive grimaces and Nell's florid confusion, that Emily and I minimally penetrated each other's worlds.

Emily, the conspirator.

What *is* he going to do to her?

What does he want coming here like this?

What shall we say to her when he leaves?

You two leave it to me. I'll talk to her. This sort of thing is better coming from an outsider.

Emily wouldn't rinse the teacups for fear of washing away the imprint of dark lips.

He didn't stay long on that first visit, just long enough for two cups of tea and he went away with his turban, all of us lining up to have our hands kissed again. Lillian proud. He took his aura away from our house, leaving it bereft of its transient glamour, leaving it to sink away behind its old beige walls and to cringe back to normality with Nell's nods and sighs and the burping she'd started doing of late, and Emily's nasal whining of truths, and my turbulence, and Lillian's rosy full-bosomed complacency. She was secretive since she'd met her Indian, she would fall into long silences weighty with honeysuckle caresses and the misty dews of early tender passions. Lillian was blooming and besotted by the dusky enigmatic thrills from her new companion. As usual, I felt excluded from her life, her plans. She would occasionally lower herself to confide in me, a transitory comment flung through the shadows of our night vigils, Of course, he's a *real* prince. He was born in Madras, don't you know where that is? with insufferable pomposity. Plenty of land, you know. Elephants too, apparently. Anyway, I shall see it all soon. He wants me to go there with him to live ..... You're mad! was the only reasonably intelligent thing I could say to her. All her dreams were too much for my London suburbia crust. I didn't have it in me to shed all that, the way she had. I considered her brainless and unfaithful to her past, ungrateful to mother and father. I mean, she really was mad. One didn't throw all that away in a dark jiffy: the peasoupers, the bangers-and-mash, the yellow teeth, the undies counter, little Nell, Smokey and Maud's wounded tabby, Emily's ferreting, and Me-only-her-sister. You didn't cast all that aside to go and live in Madras with elephants. You're mad! I reconfirmed to her and to myself in the shadows, thinking uneasily about those dark lips on the back of my hand and on Lillian's cleavage. She's mad and undisciplined. It was reassuring to think that. Harsh words like that kept the disquieting sensations at bay. They stifled any surreptitious admission that he really was charming, the Indian prince, handsome, exotic, even remotely a possibility as a brother-in-law, and that perhaps, after all, Lillian was daring to entrust her emotions to this fascinating but surely subversive force. On several occasions he returned to our house. On the times when they weren't *gadding about*, at dances and operas and dining on princely money, he paying, Lillian floating on cloud nine, accepting her fortune, taking, taking, always taking, in return for what? And the dark lips brushed the cleavage again. Sometimes he would drop Lillian home after work, driving up to the front gate, suave and controlled in his shiny black limousine. The neighbours goggled. Maud was beside herself with some sort of lewd envy, Cyril grunted disapproval behind his pipeful of acrid smoke. Emily began to feel proud of Lillian again and to goad me into choosing someone *fascinating* too. Her remarks taunted me.

Emily, the taunter.

Our honeymoon had been short-lived.

All this was happening, *going on* around Nell and father. Steadfast and sedate and utterly commonplace, they had never asked for all this excitement. Lillian's reverend-author had been enough for them. When he'd finished his book which was never published, he sent her meekly home again to find another job and she had gone to offer her charms and efficiency to the Assistant Accounts Manager in Bush House. There she was in her element, not with the accounts, but with the glimpses-down-passageways of celebrities, the tasty morsels of gossip about star lives. She was always imagining herself a star of some sort. Never content with her lot, she had sought out her Indian partner from the bevy of beautiful males at one of the Bush House *do's*. There he'd been, freshly plucked from Madras to advise on World Service radio programmes for India, and there he was towering in ebony style, a royal purple turban sheathing his fine head, a white silken Indian collar adorning his lithe neck, towering distinguished above unruly British curls, worsted ties clinging clumsily to rucked shirt collars, unkempt grey jackets, baggy trousers, the bevy of Bush House males. They thought they were fascinating, any girl's dream, but beside the dark and debonair Indian prince they were wrong, they paled, literally dribbled, into synthetic pallor. He stood out above their unruly curls shooting dark-eyed suggestions at Lillian, youthful, comely and sufficiently conspicuous beside the batch of Bush House hens, buxom typists with buck teeth clothed in frump and dowdiness and giggling behind thick-lensed glasses. True, Lillian had the *come-hither* look about her and was not above showing her cleavage on such occasions. As to a magnet, the Indian was drawn towards it. And I think that their friendship was hot and fiery. Lillian, at any rate, often appeared in the house with her cheeks flushed and her eyes ablaze, exuberant with her bizarre choice, that was Nell's word, *bizarre* for it was then that she realised that her elder daughter was attracted to things bizarre. She, Nell for one, couldn't keep up with Lillian's *taste for the bizarre*. Of that, more later however. Lillian and the bizarre, I mean. There was really absolutely nothing bizarre about the Indian prince. More was it within his rights to consider *us* bizarre. Quaint, ingenuous too.

But he couldn't last. Lillian was young and her eyes were everywhere. True, he added a dimension of mystery to her life. She enjoyed his *difference,* revelled in the glamour of the relationship, yet she had an unstable streak which in time clashed with that deep oriental gaze. For the depth in those dark eyes was too much for Lillian. It pleaded, trying to pull her away from the light-headed joys of spring. She wasn't ready for so much depth, she needed vital change, easy laughs, not the strong pulling undercurrent of sincerity, the disturbing motions of deep calm. Lillian needed her bottom pinched from time to time and the Indian prince was too refined for that. Her gay smile and voluptuous bust amused him for a while. He entranced her. But the gap widened as he began to see into her shallows. His land and his elephants lured him homewards to the silent beauty clad in the sari. And Lillian fell, almost thankfully because she had been getting out of her depth, into the round of cheerful party-goers, the bevy of Bush House males where there was plenty of bottom-pinching and daily doses of giggling about nothing.

In her enthusiasm for male contacts, she found a boss for me, Only-her-sister. I was finishing my studies and had started to look around for work, to earn my own keep as it were and if there was any left over, it would be for Nell and father. At first, I was dubious about working in the same place as my sister, particularly since I was *only-her-sister.* The idea was belittling, but it must be remembered that we were in a depression, jobs hard to come by, a girl had to accept what she was fortunate enough to be offered. And be thankful. Even the men were losing their jobs. So I had no option but to accept Lillian's help with a smile and swallow Emily's enthusiastic praise for Yer elder sister's generosity. I wished Emily would stop piping up in my life,

Interfering Emily

leave me in peace to make my own decisions. I told Nell that and she commiserated behind half-hearted support for the ferret. Her relationship with Emily was of the prickly kind. But Nell was poorly, as I have already said, and she was grateful to leave some of the life-organising in Emily's capable hands. Although Emily's capability was, in my opinion, over-rated. She used her guile to play at being capable and sucked both Lillian and Nell into a vacuum of gullibility. I remained, The Sceptic, on the edge of the vacuum. On this particular occasion, she tried to suck me in too. You count yer lucky stars. Not everyone has a sister like that who helps 'em along. You ought to get down on yer knees and kiss the ground she walks on! I stared at her with mute disdain and, although I knew she was right, I *was* lucky, I would never have admitted so to her. Nell burped agreement. Her flatulence was chronic and was getting her down. Irritating the old man, too. They were complicated times for Nell with the burping and the Indian prince hovering around Lillian. In fact, it was Nell's predicament which inspired me to accept Lillian's offer quite apart from all Emily's supercilious goading. That was how I went to Bush House. A good place to work, it was, although I avoided the *do's* like the plague. I was never one to participate in the dancing and the bottom-pinching. I just went there every day, with my plain fringe and serious face, did my work competently and came away. Lillian used to stay on, working overtime in the evenings, getting around the boss. I used to go home and help Nell wash the clothes, rub and soap them, slap and twist them against the wooden draining board, rinse them, wring them, hang them out to dry. She wasn't managing anymore. She let them mount up and if somebody didn't help, Horace and father would have been ranting for clean underwear. They weren't ones for doing their own dirty washing, with three women in the house, it wasn't done in those days. Women had some tasks, men others, all neatly divided. We all knew where we were then, none of this women-wearing-the-trousers and men-namby-pambying. True, I did more in the house than Lillian who hated washing and cleaning for fear of breaking her nails, how she typed with those crimson talons, I can't imagine! Neither did I ever see because she worked in an office on the floor above me, beside a window with a view. From behind my typewriter, I could look out onto the iron railings of the stairway which lead to the ladies'. Even in views, she was luckier than me. She told me she used to daydream gazing out onto the street watching London roll past down below in red double-deckers and matchbox cabs, all that hasn't changed even today, and the city strollers, the hasteners, the loved-ones entwined in and out of each other. Lillian was an incorrigible dreamer.

For three or four years I worked amongst the files of the Bush House administration department, *Admin* they called it, typing letters, filing invoices, answering other people's telephones, they never gave me an extension of my own. Not as glamorous a job as Lillian's. She actually shared an office with only one other secretary and had her own telephone which she answered for more than business calls. I worked at a table in a large room with ten others, It's very good experience, you know! she used to encourage me. Experience for what? For the fulminating career I never had? For as fate would have it, I turned my back on the *romance of commerce* as Lillian, and later on, Horace used to denote it. I discovered that romance with a man was more appealing than romance with commerce. That was at the time when Roland came into my life. Tall and sleek. Dashing he was really. I was only about half his height. He used to call me *Titch* with the greatest affection and twitch his moustache down towards my eyebrows, or at least towards where my eyebrows should have been, I had plucked most of them away because I was ashamed of their bushiness. By plucking them, I could pencil in a finer substitute. Not that I spent hours in front of the mirror like Lillian. She was a fanatic over her looks, always colouring her hair with henna. That was a veritable trial, like a thick mudpack on her head and vile-smelling too. She literally took over the bathroom for three hours every Saturday afternoon for the session with her henna and would emerge each week transformed, either red-haired, chestnut, slinky black, patting and preening her thick locks. They were her preparations for the Saturday evening dances or parties. Because after the Indian prince had retired to his elephants and saris, Lillian hopped from one to another. She alighted on any man who would have her, like a butterfly on spring flowers, fluttering her skins in nervous delight, shaking off the subversive sobriety of her Indian, laughing, joking non-stop, plunging her neck-lines ever lower. I was pleased then that Nell was too preoccupied with her health to be much aware of Lillian and her Saturday evening escapades, and father was normally out at the pub, so Smokey and I were her only witnesses. Horace had gone away to sea, where he spent several years prior to giving up his life to insurance.

After Lillian had left the house, Roland would come and visit me. We used to sit chatting in the cracked leather lounge chairs. Roland's legs were so long, he had difficulty stretching them without his feet knocking against another piece of furniture. But he was a serious man, dashing as I've said, like Lillian's Indian, only whiter. He did something very special to me. Even though I was the shortest girl in my office and probably the shortest in our street too, he made me feel the tallest, the tallest in the world. He even made my fringe feel pretty despite Emily's scornful remarks about it. It was my turn to blossom now, not that I did so quite in Lillian's fashion, but at least I blossomed enough for Emily to notice and stop calling me *plain Jane*. Miracles wouldn't cease, for Emily actually approved of Roland, although hinted that he could do better for himself. I fumed and she laughed, stinging, and Roland laughed, politely, because it wasn't done to answer back. Some Saturday evenings she would hover in the sitting-room with us, playing chaperone.

Emily, the chaperone.

Keeping an eye on us. At Nell's request, I think. You see, Roland was my first love, my first and *the only* love of my life. There was never anyone else. I could never have imagined myself with anyone else. While Lillian flitted from one to another offering her wares and take, take, taking, I stuck tight to Roland and only gave him a kiss-a-week on the Saturday evenings when we said goodbye if Emily, that is, turned her ferret-face away. I would accompany him to the doorstep where we would linger awhile, until Emily would exercise her chaperone powers and call me shrilly inside. Normally I controlled my sentiments, but one night when my blood hithered and thithered about my loins and I was thinking that I wanted to spend the rest of my life with Roland, I lost my temper with Emily.

Lillian is out much later and you don't know who with. You never say a thing against her! I spat hard.

Yer don't know when yer lucky, she retorted, she was always telling me I was *yer lucky,* a nice feller like that and you fallin' all over 'im out there in the night.

And Lillian?

You never mind Lillian. She's older than you and with a good 'ead on her shoulders.

And a good bust on her body, I felt like saying, but didn't. That night I stormed to my room and when Lillian arrived home just half-an-hour later, I heard the lying Emily say to her. Bet yer don't know what that sister of yours gets up to on the doorstep with lanky Roland! I stormed downstairs again, You're a liar and I hate you.

The hated Emily.

I would have given her another piece of my mind if it hadn't been for Nell, groaning with her nauseas. Roland's always very correct, I added. As an afterthought to quell any lurid thoughts Emily might have been having.

Poor you! jeered Lillian, simulating sympathy.

That's more than can be said of all your Bush House cavaliers. You threw away the best one, or he ran back to India to get away from you!

Now Elsie, don't be nasty ter Lillian!

What's the problem? Can't she defend herself? You always have to chip in for her, poke your nose in everywhere. That's what I call it! Poking your long nose in everywhere!

Never had I spoken my mind so bluntly to Emily before. But it quietened her steel-edged tongue. After that little altercation, she became quite subdued with me, even let me stay another five minutes out in the night with Roland on Saturdays. However, I had had enough. I was nearly twenty-three and the home fires were beginning to burn me up. The doctor told me that Nell would recover more quickly if I were to leave and she had no-one to depend upon. I wanted to close the chapter on Emily for evermore. She'd become a perpetual hindrance in my existence.

Emily, the hindrance.

And I was sick to death of Lillian, her lies, her prevarications, her weaknesses, with members of the opposite sex. I contemplated going away but didn't really know where to. I wasn't a traveller at heart and couldn't conceive of branching out in search of my Madras. When Roland finally suggested that we marry, I saw my solution clear and luminous before my eyes, marital Bliss with Roland, even though he was half my height again. But he was the kindest, gentlest man in the world. Horace called him *sloppy, Too soft for you!* he used to remark. And Lillian would back him up under her breath. But I didn't care what they thought. Roland was for me, for ever, that was the only thing of which I was absolutely certain. Love, it was. True Love.

So they dressed me up in white and Roland in black and we met at the altar on a cold January morning. My knees knocked as I walked up the aisle clinging to father's sturdy arm, walking up, way up towards the Christ on the Cross and towards Roland my Destiny. That moment was only marred for me because I caught sight amidst the crowded congregation, not that they were all invitees, some just butted in on wedding ceremonies for something to do, others because it was cold out in the street. Because I caught sight of

the musteline Emily

twitching her weasel's whiskers, poking her ferret's nose out into the aisle. Horror of all horrors!

Emily, the horror!

There she was in her musquash coat propping Nell up over her hymn book. That was too much for anybody's wedding. I remained composed however and directed my gaze and step ever forward towards my handsome knight in black tails and as I passed Emily, I detected a whimper. From her? Or from Nell? Mendelsohn blared and Lillian heaved her bosom, packed discreetly for the occasion into the high neck of a grey woollen dress, she would have looked almost demure except for the enormous gilt broach clasped to her cleavage. Father's breath smelt faintly of whisky, one to *get him on his feet,* I suspected. He'd promised to go to the church suitably dry. Mendelsohn proclaimed my arrival at the altar and there was Roland, shining with Brylcreem, gleaming with steadfast devotion, waiting for his bridal Titch and her fringe, the fringe I'd tucked back off my forehead under my head-dress just for that day. The happiest of my life.

* * *

Elsie's ageing eyes clouded in reminiscence. She swallowed very hard indeed and remembered that her pot of tea had gone cold. It was late afternoon, the light was dimming, inexorably silent, and she had been writing since Kathleen had left that morning when the sun had shone brightly upon her belongings. She was tired and stiff. She needed a gin and dry. The telephone rang, I bet that'll be Lillian. She picked the phone off the hook. I thought it'd be you ... Doing? Nothing much. Just about to have a gin. And you? ... Tomorrow? with feigned surprise, What time? I'll meet you at Waterloo then Begrudgingly. What time? Right you are. Have a good journey. Give my love to Horace. Elsie was almost amiable over the telephone. But as soon as she had crashed the receiver down, Damn it! I knew she wouldn't last out down there much longer. Back she comes then to creep under my skin again. Well, she's not going to stay tomorrow night. Only at weekends. Enough's enough! A malicious thought suddenly crossed her mind. I could always get rid of my spare bed, then she couldn't stay! The gin helped Elsie's machinations along their befuddled path. She wavered and teetered between Roland's husband-hood and her projects for making Lillian as uncomfortable as possible in her bedsitter. She sobbed a tear of two into her gin and remembered the fine figure he cut waiting for her beside the minister at the altar.

She would go on writing about it tomorrow, But of course, Lillian was arriving at Waterloo, There'd be no time, Lillian, turning up like the bad penny, irrupting into her time and thoughts with her flighty, febrile foolishness, Roland pulling his pints had many-a-time mumbled oaths against Lillian into the froth of each glass, he'd hated having her under his feet and he'd packed her off willy-nilly back to Australia thankful that Australia was the furthest country in the world away from England, that way she wouldn't come back again in a hurry, Alas, he was wrong, back she came, always rushing in on our marriage, and I hated her for that, instead of allowing Roland and me to enjoy those latter years alone together, god knows, we'd worked hard enough and had put up with the family trials and tribulations, I looked after the old man until he was nearly a hundred with his long, long ears and crusty old ways and when Nell died, much earlier that was, Lillian was off in South Africa, never around to face the music so to speak, she'd always run away from the uglier things, because there were other trips, not just Australia, But no! She had to be there to ruin the autumn of our days, *be there*, not ferreting exactly like Emily, but *there*. *There* all the same. Of course, Roland really *did* look dashing on our wedding day, everybody said so and I thought so.

Elsie was becoming maudlin, already on her third gin and the tears kept coming. I never minded I suppose, When the first thing he would do before opening his eyes in the morning would be to reach for a cigarette, instead of reaching for his Titch curled up beside him in her nylon nightie, Elsie had a *faiblesse* for pink nylon nighties and petticoats with lace across the bust, the expensive one he'd given me on our wedding anniversary, I never minded either, When he spent every weekend of his life glued during his free time to the box over his cricket or football matches, a *one* for sport Roland was, When he spent money gambling on the horses, the dogs, on whatever, I never really minded. She was kidding herself, for during Roland's lifetime she'd complained bitterly about his weakness and misguided actions, complained to the point where she almost had to admit, at least to herself, that Horace may have been right when he'd called Roland *sloppy, too soft for you!* I mean, he had as much of a right as anyone else to relax, didn't he? And that was his idea of relaxing, the tele, even on the very rare occasions when we could get away for a long weekend, Roland would lock himself in the hotel room watching sport all the time and he would only come out when it was time to have a drink or a meal. Of course, that wasn't healthy, was it? When he wasn't relaxing he spent his hours amongst crates of beer and bottles of alcohol, all his life, every day from six in the morning, downstairs in the cellar he used to be, counting the crates and the empties, down there at six in the morning before washing himself, already on his fourth cigarette, such a tolerance for smoking he had, but it finished with him in the end, I mean, if he hadn't coughed so much with his hernia, he might have pulled through instead of spluttering his way through those last awful weeks in the hospital, I couldn't believe it, watching him wasting like that, witnessing that dashing good-looker I'd married seizing up so slowly and painfully, on second thoughts I think he'd been ill for a long time, when I remember those sweating fits, beads of sweat lining his forehead and he used to go florid, puce, even when he wasn't under any strain, the poor darling, and he became irritable, something he normally wasn't, I mean he was renowned for his even temper was Roland. He never enjoyed his accountant's job, threw it in he did for pub life, dragging me in after him and at first we liked it, a sort of a challenge it was to us to see if we could make a go of it, an early success of our marriage, against everyone's advice, when Emily piped up about a publican's life being a *cheap way to spend yer days,* I was fired with a flame of revenge, I'd show her I would and Roland said he'd show her too, he still hadn't got his own back on Emily for her telling him he didn't know how to choose a woman, choosing *me* that was, so we flung ourselves into the pub with the fervour of our newly-wed days, we ordered crates and crates of beer, we cut rounds and rounds of white bread sandwiches, we pulled pints and pints of Guinness, we laughed with the clients and they liked us, they kept coming back for more, the newspaper workers on the printing machines, the tips of their fingers ingrained with printing ink, the office workers for a lunchtime lager, the shop-owners for a *quickie* between sales, all the business layers of the City used to drop by our pub, the commuters too, one for the road before catching the train home to the missus, and, the clients rolled in and the tills jangled gaily. In not so many years Roland and I were making the success we had dreamed of, hard work, back-breaking work it was in those early days until we earned sufficient for me to have my little Irish cleaner to help me out, that was after Polly, my baby daughter in white, was born, I'd always wanted a baby daughter in white and Roland gave her to me, now there was nothing Emily could reproach me for, a successful business and pretty Polly and, of course, Roland,

Emily, the reproacher.

We worked like bees in a hive so that Polly could have a good education, we worked up from nothing, happy together Roland and I, the way people accustomed to little in life do and it would have all been alright if Roland hadn't been drawn to gambling.

Elsie sniffed self-compassionately and stubbed her cigarette out on the wooden table. She couldn't find the ashtray which she'd overturned involuntarily with an unsteady hand. That had happened when she'd interrupted her reminiscences and had laughed at something on the tele, for the tele had been on, she'd put it on herself, as indeed she did every evening, when she poured her first gin and dry, and so the ashtray had fallen to the floor as Elsie had laughed for one hearty moment at the *Two Ronnies*, laughed caustically to herself causing the abrupt movement of her hand which sent ash and stubs flying and scudding and ashtray rolling out of sight under her chair. But by the time she lit her next cigarette, which was almost immediately after overturning the ashtray, and had poured herself another gin and dry, she had forgotten the incident and went on flicking her ash into the imaginary ashtray by her side. The gin was making its presence felt in a warm lapping way, a gentle flooding of the mind, a slow inexorable permeating of the limbs, the mellow inebriation of the solitary silent drinker, alone with his thoughts. Elsie burped for comfort's sake and, relieved, she smiled a little stupidly into the deserted room around her, her bottom lip quivering slightly, a barely perceptible tremor which was a sign that she was lapsing into Un-control. She had forgotten to eat. Neither lunch nor supper had she eaten. She found it a bore to eat alone and only made more of an effort to prepare herself food when she was accompanied by Lillian or, very occasionally, by Kathleen her *friend*. Otherwise, accompanied only by herself, she would swallow her food in unpalatable lumps, grimacing as the stuff descended her oesophagus and penetrated her innards. If she had her own way, she wouldn't eat at all. There was no pleasure in it for her now that Roland *was* no longer, to appreciate her culinary efforts. The tiniest trickle of saliva escaped from the right-hand corner of her thin lips, from beneath the sparse sturdy hairs which formed her octogenarian moustache and, unaware, she allowed it to continue its silvery trail down to the edge of her chin where it stopped and dried rapidly in the tobacco-stained air of her bed-sitting room. She raised a finger to rub at the sensation of stiffness on her chin and misfired with her finger, reaching instead into the hirsute growth of her upper lip, fondling with a certain tenderness the wiry down which would accompany her to her grave. She forgot the sticky sensation and decided that she should make her way to bed. Early it was, but she had to be at Waterloo tomorrow, why was that? oh yes, Lillian was arriving, she'd been away, hadn't she? where was it? to her erstwhile boss's home in the country? For just a minute, Elsie was satisfied with that reply to her question. Things were blurred. Life had a furry edge to it. She pushed herself to her feet. Swayed. Tottered a little. Got things into perspective. Remembered that Lillian had been to Horace's, not to her erstwhile boss's. Lurched towards the television and switched it off obliterating a Dimbleby brother in the middle of a sentence. The sudden silence crashed into her room and caused her to hiccough and trip slightly on the fringe of the loose rug that lay under the tele stand. She grabbed onto the arm of the chair Lillian used on her visits, ooh sorry! inadvertently thinking it was occupied, it was after all rare that Lillian was not sitting in it at this time of the evening. She must get to bed. But I really ought to go to the bathroom, Elsie was a stoic at holding her water, could last out a whole day and the next night if necessary, but it was all the same prudent to use the bathroom before settling for the night, a full bladder provoked dreams, Which way? Ah yes, I know, over there! An uncertain grappling with chairs and table edges, walls and door handles and she was ensconced, relieving herself of her excess liquid, a long determined stream of gin and dry which left her lighter in body and mind. Now she wended her way to her bed and with an erratic jerking and pulling and a clumsy unfastening of zip and buttons, she shed her garments and climbed between ice cold sheets, letting out a long sigh as her head collapsed onto the pillow.

Life swirled and there was Roland again, he always came to her at night, when she *hit the hay* that was, He would be there, tall with his beginnings of a stoop, years of bending down to listen to people smaller than himself, Roland, with that gentle wagging of his head, a nervous tick it was really, it came over him when he was trying to concentrate hard on whatever it was he was being told, he was too sensitive and shy a man not to listen his very hardest to people's gossiping, give them a helping hand, commiserate with his wagging head, lend money to the spendthrift, poor Roland was no judge of character, he was easily taken-for-a-ride lending cash from his till, cash he never saw again, cash *I* never saw again, too free and easy he was really with his earnings, maybe Horace was right, Roland *was* a softy, could never refuse a favour and the happy spenders got to know him and got to know how to milk him too, his was a mixture of good education and weakness, he was weak with people, always giving them the benefit of the doubt even when Rogue was written all over their faces with a capital R. His weakness with people used to irritate me, I'd watch them do their grovelling, sucking him in, getting around him and I'd nudge him on the hip Or dig him in the ribs Or tread on his toes to prevent him sliding down into the quagmire of pawning, he was like a pawnbroker but a loser on every score, never accepting a thing in return for his generosity, all his loans turning into gifts because they were forgotten, not that I ever forgot, used to try to jolt his memory, although it wasn't his memory that failed him, it was his courage, incapable he was of reminding them that they owed him. Occasionally one of them would say: 'aven't fergotten, guv, they all called him *guv*, 'aven't fergotten I owe yer. I'll pay yer at the end of the week, as soon as I git me wages. That's alright mate, no worries, Roland would pacify, instead of demanding his due, hopping mad I used to be, a bunch of rogues they were, that was it, Rogues with a capital R, they were. The money just slipped through his fingers. If he wasn't lending it, he was frittering it away on betting and gambling, incorrigible habit, or on jewellery and even fur jackets for me, musquash and ocelot at first, fox fur and mink later on, and I told him we had Polly to think of, she needed clothes too and, more important, an education, I never wanted all that luxury, well it was nice I suppose, while it lasted, I have to admit I enjoyed dining out in my furs at the Top-of-the-Tower or in the RAF Club, or that smart Italian restaurant-what-was-its-name with the good-looking waiters who always smiled such charming smiles, dark-haired they were, too dark for Nell's liking the poor little soul, she would never have been able to swallow her dinner on their account if she'd lived to dine there with us, No Roland never thought about the morrow, when he knew we had sufficient to send Polly off to boarding school, off she went, and to buy a new Vauxhall car, streamlined in those days it was too, then anything over slipped easily through his fingers, I suppose he never thought that life would deal him the dirty blow it did, Death I mean, so early, Only in his mid-sixties when it came with its axe to cut him down, stone cold, leaving me widowed, couldn't believe it when they told me I qualified for a council flat, my income was so deficient, Roland was in debt up to his eyeballs, Weakness, out of weakness it was, he borrowed to lend and gambled to lend and borrowed to gamble and gambled to buy until his debts caught up with him, or rather caught up with me because where he's been for the last seventeen years there's no such thing as debts. Yes. After all, Horace was right. Roland was soft. Look at Horace, gave up smoking he did, like a rod of iron that will of his, after watching Roland die, Roland died stifled by smoke, he choked his way to the grave because he couldn't give up smoking, even those last weeks in the hospital I used to smuggle them in to his room, he pleaded with me you see and although I knew it to be no good for him I couldn't bear seeing him deprived of his favourite habit and did it matter at the end, the nurses said nothing to reprimand him, they must have known he was at the end of the road and that a few more puffs wouldn't make any difference. But it horrified Horace who used to sit with him by his hospital bed watching him cough himself blue in the face. Horace went white in the face, with fear, and threw his last carton of un-smoked tobacco away, said he had no intention of dying in so undignified a manner.

Yet I've never been able to give the cigarettes up, couldn't imagine life without them, I don't know what it is, a comfort they are really, somehow I don't feel so lonely, company in the evenings I suppose, I've reached my eighty years on them, so it doesn't matter now does it, but if Roland had given them up he might have had a more gracious death. Too weak, he was. He wasn't only weak with his customers, he was weak with Polly too, that child would have been spoiled to death if it hadn't been for me, I mean I tried to discipline her, patch up all the damage he was doing. He gave in to her on every count, said he couldn't stand her whining when she was a tiny tot, then when she was older, a teenager all dressed in white to go out, he used to stare at her, drooling, I hated that, kept on about how pretty she was, how the boys would go for her, run his fingers through her fine chestnut hair, tell her, he did, that no boy would ever love her the way he did, he was jealous, that was it! jealous and possessive, envious of his own daughter, men can get silly like that with their daughters, can't bear the idea of another fellow taking over in their lives, I can't remember my father being like that when Roland stepped in to take me away, but of course he drank so he can't have been in full command, he wouldn't have been jealous of me anyway with my fringe, Emily would have seen to that, father was besotted by Emily and took notice of everything she said, she stirred him up

Emily, the stirrer

she would have made quite sure that if father was to be jealous of any one of his daughters, it would be Lillian. Lillian! Where is she? Ah yes, at Horace's! Not for long though, she'll be back again soon, when is it? Tomorrow?

Elsie paused in her reflections. She let the night silence hang around her. Somewhere outside a door slammed, passing laughter under the neon glare in the street, a drunken lout called in lurching tones into the black and empty streets, a car droned in the distance. Silence again. Only the neon glare. Elsie sighed and turned her frail old body and the withered flab of her arms towards the wall, pulling the sheets up around her neck for warmth and comfort as she did so. Her eyelids were heavy, sleep encroaching, gently hauling at her consciousness, easing it away towards somnolent depths. What was it about Lillian that disturbed her so? She loathed the weight of the responsibility she felt to be incumbent on her at this time of her life, just when she ought to have felt as free as a bird. There was something useless and pathetic about her sister which stirred Elsie's sense of protectiveness. The moment she felt protective, however, the rebel would surge up in her, the old octogenarian rebel with grey tobacco-stained curls, a hirsute upper lip, wispy eyebrows and a mouthful of caustic remarks, the rebel who would rear its ugly head, demanding explanations, justification for the softness she showed towards her sister. Soft and weak I am, like Roland, she jeered at herself.

How complicated it all was. Tenderness mingled with outright impatience. Dislike, almost as soon as it sprang to the fore, allayed by a strange sense of need, a pathetic sort of sympathy. It was a ceaseless battle between blood and reason this game of playing sisters.

VI

LILLIAN'S MEN

Lillian often reminisced during her train journeys and as her London-bound carriage hurtled along over the rails, she imagined that Elsie was sitting in front of her in the train carriage and remembered, in tune to the gentle lurching.

Smothered in salt, he was. An absolutely unique case. Don't you remember how the doctors called the medical students in to study his corpse? They'd never seen anything like it before in all their years at the hospital bending over sick bodies and corpses. Encrusted in salt the way Harold was, Never! He looked as if he'd spent a night out in the frost. Even I could see that through my tears and mourning eyes. Only minutes after the breath left his body, the salt started to appear, at first like a fine white powdery film around his gills, on his temples, tracing his hairline. It was frightening to watch that happening.

The regular thumping of the train carriage across the railway lines seemed to deepen her reverie.

Of course, you weren't there. You and Roland and Horace and Mavis, you all turned up later. I remember sitting there by his hospital bed, holding his dead hand and thinking that he was more beautiful dead than alive, though missing him terribly. Then the salt started to break out of his body, pushing out through the pores of his dead skin as though it had been imprisoned and had been released by his death and as his body was still warm, it gave me the uncanny feeling that he was still alive, only pretending to be dead. The salt thickened gradually, clinging around his bushy eyebrows, crystallizing there, he was growing into a snowman before my eyes. Fine and powdery I said it was at first, but it thickened in layers and in uneven patches and on his more prominent parts, his nose, his forehead, his cheek bones, it took on a shinier hue, a smoothness like icing sugar. Where was the husband I'd taken and left, and taken up again in marriage, behind this crust of virgin white? I sat there with him for what seemed like hours before the doctors turned up, before you all turned up, you and Roland and Horace and Mavis, to do your commiserating. You did commiserate, it's true, but half-heartedly. Underneath all your manifestations of sympathy, I knew that you were secretly relieved that he had gone, that the *boor* had gone, you all called him that because you considered him vulgar and in bad taste. I know he was never any match for my Indian prince of years back, but all the same he was an opera-lover and then there was the theatre which we had in common, we both loved the theatre, used to hang around backstage after performances we did, in the hopes of catching a glimpse of the actors.

Harold was drawn to that world, to the theatre world, even though he didn't act professionally himself, although he could have been an actor, he used to have me in stitches with his impersonations but they never gave him a chance when he was younger did they, and then in those days they looked for stars before they made them, you had to be innately glamorous, be good-looking before they plastered you with make-up. Harold was not good-looking, even though I thought he looked beautiful after his death, so I suppose that he wouldn't have had a look in at any audition. But he could act all the same and he did a lot of amateur theatre with the Scotland Yard dramatic art group. He worked at Scotland Yard on important cases you know. He'd spend hours in the evening going over his lines, making me give him his cues, he pulled the funniest of faces with his thick, rubbery lips, sometimes cruel faces too. You all said, you and Roland and Horace and Mavis, that he had a cruel streak in him, that wasn't fair, it was only on the odd occasion that he used to taunt me, then when I cried and threatened to run out on him, he would stroke my hair and cuddle up to me, tell me how much he needed me, you never saw him like that, when his face and rubber lips would break into the most heavenly of smiles and straight away I'd forget that he had upset me and forgive him because I knew he was often under strain in his job at Scotland Yard. He had a very important position you know Elsie, a taxing position it was, in the criminal department. Some of the files that went through his hands held information of the strictest confidentiality, not for any eyes you know. They trusted him and often asked his opinion on how to deal with one case or another, he used to tell me that. He told me that even the top-notchers, the really big bosses, would come down to his office to talk their problems over with him, why they didn't give him a better office I can't imagine, when they considered him so important, stuck away in a back room, amongst the filing cabinets in the basement he was, without a window, would you credit it, working all day at his important papers, small print under electric light and with the noise of the boilers next door all through the winter. No wonder his health went so quickly. I often considered complaining about his working conditions, somebody of his calibre stuck down in the bowels of the building, but they wouldn't have taken any notice of a wife. Wives didn't count for much in those days, did they?

But Harold was under strain, there was no doubt about it and none of you, nor you nor Roland nor Horace nor Mavis, understood that, understood the strain of a highly responsible position, I mean Mavis had only done nursing before she married and Horace, what did he do when he returned from his sea-faring? A simple clerk in insurance and then you and Roland in that pub, pub life is no strain, it's all social chit-chat, having one-for-the-road with clients, watching the coins mount up in the till, no strain attached to that. Unlike Harold who had to investigate some of the most complicated crimes in Britain and bring home a worker's salary at the end of the week. It took toll on him, that strain, *stress* they'd call it today. And I had to go on working, how could I give it up in the circumstances, being married to a man they were exploiting, he was loyal to Scotland Yard because what he was doing was so important, he couldn't have turned his back on them when they thought so highly of him. So you see, he threw his spare time into amateur dramatics to shake off all the tension he accumulated during the day and sometimes they even gave him quite big parts. And we made friends, a lot of friends that way, a lot of young men used to come to our flat or invite us to parties, often they would invite Harold alone. That was when he started coming home very late and had me worried about him. I never knew, he never told me, what he was doing into the early hours with those young fellows. One day I noticed a gold band on his finger, when I asked him where he'd bought it, not that I dared to question how much he'd paid for it, he was so cagey about money, he brushed it off saying a friend had given it to him and looked surly at me, it was a *friendship ring* he said. We never pursued that further, but years later, at his deathbed, a young man I'd never set eyes on before turned up to see Harold-encrusted-in-salt, at first I thought it was just another medical student sent to study his condition, but no, a *friend* he said he was. Don't you remember how rude you were, Elsie, when I told you that, told you it was the first time I'd set eyes on the man?

I don't know, perhaps it was a good thing we were never able to have children. Though, god knows, I wanted them but, unlike your Roland, Harold would have been an impatient father. Behind all the love I felt for him I could see that. The times he was impatient with me and his face would turn dark, black like a tempest. I used to run out of the room when I sensed his tempers coming on. At times he seemed uncontrollable and he really frightened me and then our tiny flat was never big enough, even a mansion wouldn't have been big enough, to escape from him. Those tempers altered his face completely, his thick lips twisted in an ugly way, the nostrils of his already wide nose flared, pushed outwards over his cheeks as it were, until his nose became the salient feature of his face, then his eyes would shoot venom, Elsie, I'm telling you, dangerous shooting sparks they were under his louring brow and frowning forehead. Really terrifying, Harold's tempers were. Sometimes they came on all of a sudden. Sometimes they built up after days of irritability. He'd be there in the evenings as though something was niggling him inside, morose and cowering he was then, as though the whole world were against him, of course, I knew it was those important cases at Scotland Yard, he'd bring them home, chew over them, so he could give the big boss an intelligent reply when he was questioned, because he never knew when he was going to be questioned about a case, if they couldn't find a file they would always ask him to look it out and to give his opinion on the side whilst he was looking to see if he remembered correctly, you can imagine, in the event that that happened he had to have all the different cases in the files imprinted on his brain, I mean if the big boss asked him about a case and if he couldn't produce the details just like that they would have lost their confidence in him and might even have invited him to leave, give him the *golden handshake*, and so he memorised everything, Harold's was the longest memory imaginable. But just thinking about all that crime made him irritable. Then he wouldn't speak to me, however much I tried to cajole him. Just snap occasionally saying his ulcer was playing up because of my cooking. If you could have seen the trouble I took over our suppers and, god knows, I was tired myself after a day's work at the office. But I tried everything to please him you know, nice pieces of white fish especially cooked in parsley sauce - his favourite - nourishing beef stews I did, appetising chicken breasts and apple charlottes and fruit pies, you know I used to cook well, but no, when he was in one of his moods, nothing was right for him. So if I couldn't deal with him, no child we might have had would have been able to either. Maybe it was better that way, better to be sterile and not complicate life with children. But I did so want them, Elsie, my heart ached to have them you know. Before I went to see a doctor about it, I used to blame Harold, inwardly that was, I never dared suggest that it might be his fault, but I was secretly positive that he was responsible for my barrenness. Some nights he wouldn't even look at me, turn his back on me under the bed covers even though I had put on my sexiest nightie to try and entice him, he'd just look at me indifferently, when I took it off altogether to show him what was underneath hoping that would stimulate him, he'd just turn off the light and smother himself with the blankets, almost as though I repulsed him. Mind you, that was only when he'd had a hard day with his crimes at Scotland Yard, I knew it was that, the poor darling, I mean, any man would be the same, wouldn't he, with his wife?

So I used to forgive him if he didn't feel like having me some nights, but if it occurred too frequently then I would start my blaming, silently under the sheets, How could we ever have a child if he wasn't prepared to do his part? And Why did we want a child if we didn't have the money to educate it properly? he would spit at me if I ever broached the subject with him. Who'd look after it, old Mrs Bloggs down the road, if I had to go out to work because three could never exist on his salary? But I didn't care about things like that, I just knew I wanted a child and I sobbed into the sheets when he was indifferent to me. Couldn't understand it either, because I didn't have a bad body did I, Elsie, you remember that don't you? So I put it down to his *stress* at Scotland Yard. After we'd been together four years and I still hadn't managed to become pregnant, that was when I confided in a friend at work and she advised me to go to a gynæcologist, she would accompany me, she said. And she did. That was the worst day of my life Elsie. When they told me I was sterile, that I would never have children, there was always adoption, they said. I came away from that doctor sobbing my eyes out, my heart wrung through it was with grief and what's more, full of remorse for the bad thoughts I'd had about Harold. All his fault I had always imagined, four years telling myself it was him to blame, my poor over-worked, under-paid Harold who couldn't perform in bed because he was too preoccupied with his Scotland Yard crimes. And although I'd never let on to him that I'd considered him to be the guilty party of the two, how could I break the news now that we could *never* have children, even if one day they were to promote him, raise his salary, give him an office on the ground floor, which was quite on the cards. What I didn't realise on that black day was that the very knowledge of *my* sterility was going to release *his* libido, ooh what we used to get up to after that Elsie, no bed was big enough I can tell you. But at the time, I was distraught, in agony I was, and I lost so much weight, pining for the child I was never to have. You remember, I had to tell you about it because you and Mavis and Emily kept on at me, What's the matter with you for goodness sake? each time we met, although if I recall rightly, you didn't worry overmuch for me, involved as you were making a mint at the pub with Roland. You were insensitive, only asked me about it so you could gossip to your customers, You wouldn't believe it, my sister's just found out she can't have children, just imagine, I couldn't bear life without our Polly, That was smug and hypocritical Elsie oh yes, don't deny it, I heard you one day as Harold and I walked into the pub.

My nights were really terrible then. And my days. But at least I had my job and there were people around and things to do and there was a fellow who gave me cuddles behind the filing cabinet because he could see how upset I was, one day we went a bit further than cuddles and after that it was every lunchtime behind the filing cabinet when the office was deserted. I never told Harold and it's the first time I've told anyone, but I needed something to help me get through those terrible nights. For months I didn't tell Harold he was never *never* to be a father, even if they promoted him and he earned more and he was given a better office. It took me months, all those lunchtimes behind the filing cabinet, all those terrible nights of pining for my unborn baby, before I could bring myself to spill the beans to him. We were really estranged at that time, he morose with his files on crime, me with my problem of sterility. We hardly noticed each other during those months, he certainly didn't say how thin he thought I was or was I sad about something or why wasn't I eating. Then at night I was glad he didn't touch me, exhausted I was after the filing cabinets and red-eyed after weeping in the bathroom, he'd just turn the other way as if I didn't exist. Months of that, how many exactly, I can't remember now, but Months.

When I did eventually muster up the courage to tell him, and when I no longer had need of my lunchtime consolation, you can't imagine his reaction. As though a weight had been lifted from his hunched shoulders, he straightened his back, unfolded his spine as it were, before my eyes. Quite incredible, Elsie. As though someone had peeled the layer of misery from his face to reveal a new light-hearted husband to me. Quite incredible, it was. From that day on, his embraces were frequent and ardent, no longer did he snap off the light when I stood before him in my sexy nightdress, on the contrary, he urged me to show myself to him. He was rapacious, half mad with passion. I was confused, didn't know how to accept this altered person. I mean, would you? So sudden it was, all his fervour for me. He seemed to be rejoicing because we couldn't have children and whenever I confessed to him that it saddened me, he would pull me to the bed and make me do all those things with him. The sadder I was, the more he took interest in my body. I could never understand that. I'm sure I told you at the time, never an affectionate word did he have for me, only passion, forcing the passion out of me as though he wanted to extinguish the very breath in my body. And all that time, I'd blamed Scotland Yard for his moods. What was really responsible for them was his fear of becoming a father. Poor Harold.

After that we began to go out more. More and more to the theatre, to the opera. Oh, how we loved the opera, Elsie, all those bright costumes and glamorous faces and the singing. You all said he was a boor without a soul. That was sheer cruelty. If you could have seen him at the opera, transfixed with the music and the spectacle of it, I used to see his breast heave with emotion, I even caught the glint of tears in his eyes on more than one occasion. How could a boor have all that soul in him? And the theatre. He used to take me to watch our young men friends acting, he used to whisper to me, what do you think of him? don't you think he's attractive? whisper things like that in the darkness of the auditorium, fondling the bare skin of my thighs up around my suspenders, fondling in the darkness and whispering those things at the same time. Then he'd repeat the same questions about those boys when he was having me in bed afterwards. If I replied that I didn't know or I didn't think so, he would force my arms above my head until they hurt, forced me that way he did to bend to his will. I think that was when I imagined I saw the first signs of madness in him. Well, perhaps not out-and-out madness, but some sort of mental derangement. It was about then that he started making me dress up in male underpants and parade in front of him before we went to bed at night. There was a weird touch to him Elsie, you know. He became brutal with me too. I often wondered if he actually enjoyed hurting me with his acid comments and physical excesses. I'm sure it was delving into all those criminal files that did it. But he was so important at Scotland Yard, I could never have asked him to leave there. All I wanted was for us to be happy, believe me, Elsie, I'd have done anything to achieve that. The trouble is, everything I did seemed to annoy him, whether in or out of the bedclothes, in or out of the kitchen, inside or outside his theatres, whether alone or at parties. That was the worst thing of all, those parties with all our friends, you don't know how much he tried to belittle me, pulled me down, he did, constantly, in front of our friends, even told them I *enjoyed* dressing up in men's underwear, I ask you, when it was he who used to force me into that. Then he would start scorning my job at Bush House, when I was working for one of the top men there, old Fibbit, you remember, scorned my job he did when I was earning almost as much money as he was. He would ridicule my work in front of the others. All that hurt me, more than any of you can imagine, because I loved him I suppose. It isn't true that he was a boor, the way you all said. On the contrary, he did what he did because he was sensitive, extremely sensitive. You and Roland would never have understood that sort of extreme sensitivity, too busy stacking it up in the pub you always were. You were all always against him, you and Roland and Horace and Mavis, until the day I ran out on him and you told me then to return, Go back, Stick to your marriage, Marriage is for life, You've made your bed, now lie in it, Don't disgrace the family, How will poor Nellie take it? Oh, I know you blamed me for Nell's death, don't worry, you've done nothing but accuse me of that all your life, fancy breaking up your marriage - even if it was to a *boor* - with poor Nell on her deathbed, well I'm telling you this now, she would have died anyway and, divorce or not, not one of you wept more than I did when she died, but the fact was that I couldn't stay by Harold's side a moment longer. It's all very well for you to criticise, you wouldn't have put up with him for five minutes with your impatience. At least I did try. *Try* to understand his tempers and look for reasons behind his foibles, but with all that criticism he was making me ill. My friend at Bush House, the one who'd accompanied me to the gynæcologist, *she* told me to walk out on him, she told me I wasn't working properly anymore, told me I was like a scraggy rat, not eating or sleeping properly, god knows, with all the acrobats he forced me to get up to at night on that bed, I could never have put on weight, and tired I was too, tired out all day long and then behind it all, the image of the baby I was never to have. That took me years to overcome, so you can't blame me with all that pain inside, for taking refuge in Ferdy, can you?

Ferdinand Rollins. Now that was a man who understood women, if ever there was one, an eye for women he had, swaggering masterfully through life in his check jackets and wellington boots. It was one week that I kept bumping into him on the bus, mornings and evenings, he got on at the stop after me and got off at the stop before me. You know how it is, Elsie, although I know you've never been unfaithful to Roland, but then you were never up to much with the men, were you? Anyway, the fact is that even though you can be tired and fed up and unhappy, subconsciously you go on looking for happiness convinced somehow that you'll find it somewhere, I suppose it's what keeps us going through the bad times really, this perpetual search for happiness and I just knew at that time that happiness for me consisted in finding a man who understood me, someone who would care about my barren state and give me some affection despite it. You know what it's like on a crowded bus, Elsie. You bang up against people, surprise touches like the unsolicited gifts we write on the parcels we send through the post. Then when your shoulder hits a man taller than you are on his chest, it's inevitable that you look up into his eyes, for forgiveness isn't it, to say how sorry you are. Well, that's what happened the very first time with Ferdinand Rollins. I said Sorry and he said Any time darlin' with such a mischievous charming wink. I found myself blushing, all embarrassed. The next day we didn't bang against each other, unfortunately, but he searched me out from the other end of the bus, across the medley of heads and beards and moustaches and hair-sprayed beehives, with his hot eyes and I suddenly realised that I'd been looking for him, unawares of course because I was a married woman, but relieved all the same when I set eyes on him. Then we both smiled at each other across the beards and moustaches and hair-sprayed beehives, smiled full on and that same evening he pounced on me in the bus queue and said he liked the jumper I was wearing. Afterwards, he told me he'd waited over half an hour in the queue in the rain, letting bus after bus go past, waiting for me. Waiting for *me,* he was! I mean, how can any girl refuse a request like that, husband or not, barren or not. On the way home we chatted gaily, the way I never used to with Harold, and as he got off, he said See you tomorrow, and squeezed my arm, leaving me warm and soft and conquerable. Every night and morning that week we took the bus together, on each occasion more and more eager to see each other, until on Friday evening he said he'd have his car back the next week. When he said goodbye on that Friday, Black Friday I thought it was, he looked long and hard into my eyes and said, You're a lovely girl Lillian, you know that! I cried all weekend, howled alone in the bathroom and when I lied to Harold, saying it was because I wanted the baby we couldn't have, he turned his back on me and went out the whole of Saturday night with a boyfriend, leaving me to sob hysterically into my pillow for the love I could have had with Ferdinand and didn't have. All weekend weeping and wondering how I could go to work on Monday morning on the bus without Ferdinand jolting along beside me to cheer me up. I knew I was madly in love with him, yet here I was married, tied down to a sour grape who was starting to find his kicks with young men. What a disaster it all was!

I don't know if you or Mavis could ever have understood those unfaithful feelings, when you know you'd just chuck it all in and run off with the man of your dreams, you and Mavis were both so faithful and uncomplicated, it could never have happened to you. The way it happened to me. Was *destined* to happen to me. For come Monday morning in the bus queue, heavy-eyed and sodden-hearted from love-sickness and weeping, I was just about to clamber onto the bus when I heard a frenzied hooting and someone call my name. That was the beginning of it all with Ferdy, the beginning I suppose of my *real* downfall, the beginning of a love affair in the back of his shambling old van amidst the pot plants and bags of manure for his nursery, he had green fingers with plants and fruit trees and soft silky fingers with women, I can tell you. What that old van didn't see Elsie, I can tell you wasn't worth seeing, the tricks we got up to in it. And it was there that we planned our elopement, about a month before I sent you and Nell that card from Cape Town, remember? You have to understand Elsie, Ferdinand Rollins was my only chance of escape from the misery I was living with Harold.

South Africa was our joint destiny. Ferdy made a success of everything he put his hand to, everything he touched turned to gold Horace used to say, nothing mediocre about him, I can tell you. We had a luxurious life out there in that land of opportunity. It was the first time I'd ever been waited on, I was the lady of leisure with a black gardener and his black mammy wife for a cleaner and I had an Indian cook. Those were the days, party after party it was, with important people too, from the Embassies, barbecues out in the veld, visits to wild life resorts, up Table Mountain and to the beaches, trips to Johannesburg and Pretoria, made our life in Plumstead look as dull as ditch-water, grim in fact. And the clothes Ferdy bought me, and the diamonds, some of the best Cullinan cuts, I wouldn't have missed all that for the world. It was living in the real lap of luxury, it was like living in a dream with the breakfasts served to us in bed, lounging in rustling satin sheets until all hours, champagne for breakfast, exotic seafood lunches we treated ourselves to, I just had to order what I wanted and the cook would bring us lobsters, fresh king-clip, anything at all from the street market in Cape Town. Then at night, we entertained, me with a new outfit nearly every week and I'd spend the afternoons resting, sleeping off the lunchtime wine, manicuring my nails and preparing myself for the evening supper or party or theatre. I tell you, I blessed the day I met Ferdinand Rollins. I blessed it that was. Before I cursed it. For months I blessed it, before I cursed it.

I started to curse it when he fixed his hot eyes on a young blonde newcomer to our group, the twenty-three-year-old daughter of a Dutch journalist and what a beauty she was! I told you Ferdy had good taste, but all of a sudden the jumper he'd liked on me in the Plumstead bus queue, paled into insignificance, into frankly bad taste - though I say it myself - beside the journalist's daughter with her sleazy blouses. From the fateful night she joined our circle, he was after her, sniffing around her like a bloodhound sniffs around a bitch on heat. The charm oozed from every pore of his body and he played his trumps with all the sophistication in the world, South Africa had added a sophisticated veneer to his hot mischievous winks and a few more g's to his gerunds, the money and the life-style helped. And she fell, I mean what could you expect, flattered to death she was at her age with all his attentions, obviously she never thought of calling him a dirty old man, he was almost twice her age. It was then that I began to feel old, old at thirty-five I ask you. I spent hours in front of the mirror comparing myself to that young beauty. And the depression set in Elsie, you shouldn't make comparisons of that sort should you, someone always comes off worst. The one with more wrinkles. Inevitably. Obviously Ferdinand started making comparisons too and saw me wilting away and that was the second time in my life that I experienced cruelty from a man. All through those terrible months which ensued, my thoughts fled back, way back to the charming Indian prince of my childhood, how much better off would I have been with him in Madras instead of with these cruel cold Englishmen, and I felt guilty too about having rushed out on Harold. When I began to be unhappy with Ferdinand, I remembered the good times with Harold, the opera, the sessions on the bed in our little Plumstead flat, the friends we had in common, the crimes he used to deal with at Scotland Yard where I imagined him having been promoted to an even more important position. I compared the two men and realised that, despite his weird streaks, he was a more cultured person than Ferdinand, even though you did all call him a boor, you and Roland and Horace and Mavis.

Ferdinand demonstrated his scorn for me in such a frightening way. He more or less put up with me whilst he was courting his young blonde, kept me dangling as it were, in case his plans fell through. They didn't, she was easy bait and more than willing to comply to his designs. It must have been after the first night of conquest that he started taunting me, realising he wanted to be rid of me, he started pressing large sums of money into my hands, Elsie, I told you that when I ran away from him, all generosity he was one day, but it was a cruel baiting game, for the next day he would demand to have the money back and woe betide me if I'd spent any of it. Mind you, I learnt very quickly not to because he lashed out at me with his belt in fury on two occasions. But you said I could have it for myself, I pleaded. That was yesterday, he would goad gruffly. He pushed me to my wits' end, giving me money and presents and then, leering at me like a madman, ask me to return them. I became scared of him, so scared that I would do anything he asked me. It's only now I can see what a tyrant he was. And I'll tell you, the nursery van in Plumstead was nothing in comparison to the demands he made on me in South Africa, that bedroom became a nightmare, a torture chamber, more like it. He was a real sadist and, what's the other one? a masochist too, he had no end of tricks and fantasies and objects for stimulating himself and me too. I put up with it all because I was terrified not to. After whole nights of satisfying his crazed whims, I'd be all alone because he would disappear for days, weeks on end, on business he said, taking the blonde with him. And I began to be the laughing stock of our circle, I noticed then that the women no longer invited me to their tea parties and I was left out of their supper invitations when he and the blonde were away. I was so lonely Elsie, roaming around that large house and garden, like a waif, even the maid looked at me scornfully as if to say, I know what women like you get up to, you deserve what you've got! My imagination maybe, but she really looked as though she thought that with her black floppy unsmiling jowls. Perhaps Ferdinand told them not to take orders from me, I don't know, but when he was absent, they would surreptitiously disappear leaving me to do my own cooking, cleaning and ironing. How long could all that go on? I put up with it for a year. Being the laughing stock for a whole year, when I could have been living in Madras with the charming Indian had I played my cards differently. No, South Africa turned very sour for me, until I resolved to run out the very next time he placed a wad of notes in front of me. I'd wait my chance and sell his diamond gifts too, if necessary, to pay my passage home. Home to Harold. If he'd have me.

Harold would have me. Of course he would, I kept telling myself during the passage home. I would stare into the wake the boat left behind it, staring back towards Ferdinand and Cape Town, letting all my regrets ripple away, thin out like the choppy v-formed wavelets behind us, all those regrets would merge anonymously into the whole of the sea which was fast becoming my life's history. Timid I was, initially, in my thoughts about Harold, conscious of being once bitten twice shy. From the stern of the boat I left the wakeful of regrets to flow backwards towards all that blue unhappiness in the land of plenty and made my way towards the front of the liner. I stood high on a deck where I could just catch sight of the prow heaving proudly out of the water, slicing down into the froth, pushing the depths aside, surging on through night and day, carrying me, back to Plumstead and to my Harold. I felt valiant and cleansed in the strong salty sea-breeze, my hair blowing back, my bust swollen forward in a peace offering. I felt like Harold's mascot. Brave out there in the midst of the ocean. And there were eyes on me too, plenty of eyes, all suggesting and washing away the doubts about my thirty-five years. Of course, it was natural to take advantage of them, have a bit of fun, just a last bit of fun before offering myself anew, *re-virginised*, to Harold. I mean, any girl would have. Even you would have. I convinced myself that I needed a boost to my self-esteem which had fallen down around my ankles after all the suffering I had done in South Africa, I mean, heaving about on the waves, the *bosom of the ocean* the poets call it, is an amorous exhilarating experience in itself, it incites secretions in the love glands, the sea is made for love Elsie, I suppose that's why you and Roland always went anywhere you went by air, no time for temptation there. Unromantic. Like you and Roland. But the dances at night on the ocean waves, the exotic drinks they mixed for you, the suggestive glances, the dressing-for-dinner, the lounging-on-deck eyeing the swimming trunks pass by, I mean, you'd be silly not to take advantage of all that, wouldn't you. Besides, it took my mind off my worries. I knew Harold would take me back but then again, maybe he wouldn't. Ooh, it was romantic in those creaking cabin bunks, tightly squeezed together. I could have taken up any of the offers they made me, but no, I'd made up my mind to be faithful to Harold, well, as faithful as possible in the circumstances, you understand. You see, I can see now from my eighties that being thirty-five you are still only very young and innocent, young enough to do lots of silly things and to enjoy doing them. I suppose, all things considered, that the sea journey did a lot of cleansing and curing, brushed aside my humiliation in quick briny breezes, it renewed the wounded epidermis, those beatings that Ferdinand had meted out to me on more than one occasion, when he left me black and blue, all that was soothed in the sea air, in that watery no-man's-land. It was good, refreshing, to feel carefree and I never gave another thought to Ferdinand, I mean, we'd hardly had a cemented relationship, had we, it'd been little more than a *shack-up* agreement, there was no true commitment there, after all. Not like Harold and me, a true marriage, that sacred contract of wedlock. Harold respected those things, whereas Ferdinand Rollins didn't respect anything or anybody on god's earth. Harold was a good Samaritan. He would take me back. Of that. I had no doubt.

Or did I? As we left the indigo blue waters of the southern Atlantic and steamed our way up the west coast of Portugal and Spain, we were cast to misfortune near the Bay of Biscay, all hell let loose it was Elsie, with the waves smashing up against the railing of the top deck, the Spanish sea was angry, revealing its cavernous hollow troughs of dark liquid, I can tell you I was terrified of us being swallowed and sucked down under into the depths, I mean you wouldn't have a chance in a sea like that, would you, easy bait for any lurking sharks. Many of the passengers were as sick as dogs, in front of your eyes, they lurched over to the side of the railings and threw all their discomfort out into the waves. The entire boat creaked and groaned, it was just like a cork, bobbing about on all that water, I'm telling you. And that night, the wind didn't subside, it just kept on howling and I was lying in bed, unaccompanied for once, all alone in that creaking bunk and frightened I was too. And it was then that I began to feel the oppressive greyness of England, the encroaching closeness of Plumstead and, tremulous, I remembered Harold's fits of temper and ugly eyes shooting sparks of venom. That storm worked its way under my night-time skin, needling sharply into my mind, bringing with it evil memories. I suddenly recalled that I had been the one to walk out on Harold, not him on me. *I* was the unfaithful one. I became swamped in remorse and guilt. He had no reason at all to forgive me, after all. I was mad to even consider returning to him. I could take refuge with father. But of course, I hadn't been there when Nell had died and he would never forgive me for that. He wouldn't want me. Neither could I go to Horace. He and Mavis had enough to cope with rearing their three children and not much money to do it on. Then there was you and Roland. But you both had the pub, and Polly, and I sensed anyhow that you weren't sympathetic towards me. You'd only written to me once in the whole year after Nell died, not that you were much of a one for letter-writing, and even though I wrote back, you never answered me. No, I didn't want your sympathy then, I decided. So where could I go? To return to Harold was the only option.

The storm subsided leaving the water somehow oily and sinister, swelling and immense around us. Hostile. Through the drizzle I could just make out the white cliffs of Dover and my heart flipped at that moment I suppose in a second of patriotism and gratitude that England was my home. We ploughed on through the waves to the Thames estuary and as we docked at Tilbury, I remember feeling sad that those carefree weeks had drawn to a close and envious of those passengers waving and shrieking out to friends and relatives awaiting them. Nobody was waiting for me. I would have to make my own way to the Plumstead flat.

And I did. As you know. I couldn't let myself in because I had thrown the key away in spite and anger and when I arrived the caretaker was out and Harold away, presumably at Scotland Yard. I was overcome with fatigue, weary from the long sea voyage and the flat grim reception of a London where no-one was waiting for me. I felt hemmed in after the freedom of weeks at sea, by walls, superfluous obstacles, claustrophobic in this great city full of human masses and teaming with cars and strident with noise and as I sagged my body against the wall of the Plumstead flat and let myself collapse to the ground, I half-heartedly asked myself why I had bothered to return to the inhospitable London grime. I could have run away from Ferdinand to another part of South Africa, I reflected. Why come back to this pit of gloom which was my erstwhile abode and which reeked of sad memories. But I had come back, back to stay, in spite of myself, and suddenly the caretaker popped up from nowhere and broke into my unhappy reverie, Well I never! Welcome back Missis Lillian, nearly falling over his bandy knees and pigeon toes with delight. Now that was really nice to hear, almost brought the tears to my eyes, it did. Mister 'Arold will be pleased, I'm sure. Between you and me, and I remember he lowered his voice, it's a godsend you've returned. And, on second thoughts. You 'ave come to stay, 'aven't you? Mister 'Arold needs lookin' after you know. Not at all well, he isn't. The caretaker let me into the flat with his master key, the key to all doors but not to all happiness. You'll never know the strange feeling it was Elsie, to walk into that flat. The place had a smell of death about it, yes Death with a capital D. Not easy to explain that, it was something that hung in the air, a smell? No, not a smell, but a feeling, a sensation of sort of, sort of ..... pending doom. Elsie, do you understand? It was nothing, like say a perfume, which was directly identifiable. No, it was a mustiness without the place being musty because the windows were open in each room. Harold wasn't dirty or untidy, you know, he'd kept the place in order, spic-and-span it was. But as I went from the hall to the sitting-room, to the bedroom, to the bathroom, to the kitchen, the Doom was there. Everywhere in the flat. Was it in my mind after what the caretaker had said, Not at all well, he isn't. Was it my own guilt, that by running off I'd aggravated his ulcer, and that meant that his moods would be worse, oh god, perhaps I'd better leave, run out again while I could.

Yet it was strange, Elsie, I tell you I was assailed by guilt and repentance and, above all, by a fervour of curiosity to set eyes once again on my ailing and erstwhile husband, as though I wanted to witness for myself the damage I'd done by running out on him, the more damaged he was, the greater must his love for me be, I mean, if my departure had been a relief to him, he wouldn't have been ailing now, would he?

Things were still in their place, very much as I'd left them eighteen months ago, seven exuberant months ago, eleven nightmare months ago, a whole lifetime ago, in another paradisiac world, did South Africa really exist juxtaposed against this musty, ill-fortuned apartment? The weeks on the waves had evaporated in a mist like the top of Table Mountain, evaporated in the grim light of reality. And as I eyed the objects of my past, the poor sticks of furniture, no lavish leather here, no plush hangings, no maid, no gardener, no garden even, I was prey to panic. That's what they say, isn't it, Elsie, when your stomach turns and your intestines knot and your lungs constrict and your chest tightens and you catch sight of yourself in the old bedroom mirror, marked and yellowed because it had been cheap and second-hand and god knows how many faces had peered into it in the past, and in it you catch sight of yourself but it isn't yourself because you don't recognise the cringing paleness underneath the already forgotten sea-breeze tan, the lips stiffened with a sort of inner horror, the eyes wide, wider than ever because you know my eyes were big and wide, the men used to say Like pools of mystery, and the tautness in the lines on your forehead, and the absolute weariness at having just landed off a boat which had brought you from exotic climes back to this grey mundane world into which you've been born and have in your blood and it's so hard to rid yourself of. You know what I mean, Elsie, London's a part of us, isn't it, whether we like it or not, whether we try to escape and run away from it, we can't, can we? I suppose you wouldn't know that, you've never tried. But it has us in its clutches like the old sticks of furniture, the old walnut bedstead chipped around its top edge, the worse for wear, like the calico bedspread fraying at the edges and looking tired of living, pushed away and spurned it had been too many times to give way to all our antics, if the walnut bedstead could talk, Elsie, it'd have many a tale to tell! A smile brushed across my face, the one staring at me from the second-hand mirror. Most of our stuff was second-hand, but second-hand or not, that bed had served its purpose, the details I'll leave to your imagination, though on second thoughts, maybe you're too prim and proper to let your imagination run away with you. I left my bag unpacked in the bedroom and roamed aimlessly around for a while trying to relive, to recapture, the past. I must admit I was scared, filling in time before Harold came in from Scotland Yard, my soul felt bleak, if you know what I mean and I was cold and miserable just staring through the windows at the grey drizzle outside, and waiting in the silence of that flat, too scared even to turn on the radio, and I started to feel really frightened, remembering Harold's moods, those rubber lips contorted in anger, worse than Ferdinand's goading they seemed to me at that moment. I sat on the edge of the old sofa-for-two trembling, waiting, listening to time, remembering, fearful of what he might do to me when he saw me there, like an intruder now really, I suppose I was. If I think back I could have used those hours to prepare Harold an especially nice supper, something appetising like white fish in parsley sauce, his favourite, but I didn't have the heart somehow and anyhow, he might not have come home and if he was ill he might not have wanted to eat it. I wandered into the kitchen, listless I was, not knowing what to do with myself, not knowing how to fill in the time, I realised I was hungry so I opened the larder, not much to cook with, the minimum, three cooked sausages sat forlornly on a plate under a fly-net, a tin of beans beside them and a tin of Campbell's mushroom soup. That'd help to warm me up, calm me down. While I was eating it off a chipped plate, it suddenly occurred to me that Harold might have put it aside for his supper, what would he do, coming in, first to find me, second to find I'd eaten his supper. Stop it, you're getting paranoid, I chided myself, he won't mind and, No matter, we can always go out for supper the way we used to in South Africa, always out to supper there, but then maybe not, Harold didn't have Ferdinand's money, did he, or he wouldn't be living in this down-and-out hole, would he, this squalor which was his home, which had been my home. Was it to be my home again? I dissolved into tears over the remains of sausages and beans and the congealed scrapings of Campbell's mushroom soup. Then fell asleep on the sofa.

Was it really Harold sitting in the armchair opposite, reading the paper? The *Evening Standard* behind glasses? He'd never worn glasses in his life. He was like a stranger to me. His hair, brown before, was streaked with grey, almost white at the temples. Thinning too, no longer the lush curls where I used to bury my lips. His forehead was near disfigured, deep troughs of wrinkles Elsie, I'm telling you, frown marks too, you know, those two vertical lines above the nose, all that concentrating over Scotland Yard files. Some people say that lines add character, history to a face. Maybe they do. But they change a face. It's also true to say that. Harold was suddenly ugly to me, not distinguished like some older men, but aged and disfigured. And worse than those lines which criss-crossed his forehead and decorated the tender skin around his eyes like a heavily-marked cobweb, worse than the furrows outlining his mouth, worse than that Elsie, were his sunken cheeks and sallow complexion. He looked really awful, ill, I can tell you, all hollow and gaunt like that. His face was like a papier-mâché face, like an old puppet, if you know what I mean. And his shoulders were hunched. Even as he sat in the chair, I could tell that his jacket was hanging, as if on a peg, nothing to cling to, no bones or skin, just a rickety old skeleton. I remember taking all that in as I opened my eyes. I rubbed them to ascertain that this man sitting in the dim light a few feet away, wasn't an hallucination, that he was in fact my Harold, my erstwhile and future husband.

My stirring, perhaps it was the sound of my thoughts - I'm sure he used to read them sometimes Elsie, you know – caused him to look up from his *Evening Standard*. You won't believe what happened next ..... In just a second, all my anxiety was dispelled. Harold let his paper drop to the floor, removed his glasses, leant forward stretching out his arms towards me and those old rubbery lips widened into a smile, a real smile of *welcome home* it was, I couldn't believe it and in a second I was in his arms, locked in embrace the way it always used to be, You fled the nest my little bird, he murmured to me, what did I do to make you flee the nest? Here was Harold blaming himself, taking the blame automatically off my shoulders and piling it onto his own. I hadn't bargained for that, had I, I mean I'd always considered myself the guilty party, rushing off to South Africa like that. And I felt guilty that he was smothering himself with guilt. If you think about it, we women are always looking for something to feel guilty about in life. Silly really, isn't it? But I only had to look at Harold to see how he'd suffered in my absence. The caretaker of the flats was right. He was all *grey* Elsie, grey and sort of *consumed,* as if life was eating away at him like a dog gnawing on a bone, all twisted and agonising he was, and there was I all brown from my sea trip, well-nourished on South African seafood and champagne, bursting with health despite the sadistic masochist, the masochistic sadist of a Ferdinand Rollins. Wasn't really fair that, was it? And I'd seen the World, whilst he'd been poring over his Scotland Yard files, gradually getting more and more stooped. It was all that responsibility they piled on his rapidly hunching back at the *Yard*, as he called it. I often thought that he would have been better off if he hadn't been so talented, if he'd had a lesser job, less of a strain you know. Being clever like that Elsie, does have its burdens.

Well, that was my homecoming. Back to London, back to work, back to washing clothes and cleaning up our flat like any black-faced Mammy with drooping jowls, and South Africa safely tucked away in a far corner of my dreams, the good times in South Africa that was, the bad ones I eradicated quick smart, I wasn't going to be weighed down any more than I already was by the pressure of my own errors, life had to go on. And it did go on. Every day it went on with Harold moving closer and closer to the grave. You remember how sick he became, oh he was so ill, the poor man. I had my time cut out looking after him. First with his evil humours, that temper had become worse than ever and after his outbursts the moroseness was frightening, last for days it would when he'd take no notice of me whatsoever, just as if I didn't exist. He used to carry on as though he was all alone in the flat, eating his meals in silence, taking refuge behind his papers, not a word Elsie, I assure you, turning his back on me at night. I forgave him always because I knew how ill he was and I suppose, well, I felt guilty and repentant, didn't I? I'd sort of vowed to care for him, even though he'd never openly blamed me for running out on him, because that's what I'd done, hadn't I, run out on him? About eighteen months after my homecoming and our second-time-round-nuptials, he started to deteriorate very rapidly, couldn't keep a thing down, the doctor made him give up his job at the *Yard* and then he seemed to know it was the end, having to renounce all his criminal files, they said he wasn't concentrating properly. I really had my time cut out then, you wouldn't know Elsie what it's like to care for an invalid and keep your job going at the same time, anxious all day at the office, rushing home in the evening, boiling up invalid pap, washing and ringing soiled clothes by hand, patience, patience, always patience whatever his comments, whatever his moods, however exhausted you were, listening to doctors, making him take his pills, don't forget this, look after that. It was a burden for me, you know. Months of it, too. Harold clung onto life like a leech, I used to tell you what a tenacious person he always was, Well he was tenacious to the end. I didn't admit it then, not to anybody, but I used to wish he wasn't so tenacious about living, wish that his end would come before he killed me off in the process. I was so tired. Worn to a frazzle, the girls at work used to say to me. But exhausted as I was, never once did I think of running out on him again, maybe because the doctor confided in me that the end wouldn't be long in coming.

That awful, salty end. Poor Harold.

*   *   *

Those we most fear speaking the truth to are precisely those who most provoke thought within us. For Lillian would never have accused Elsie openly of anything, nor would she have entrusted her with her innermost thoughts and self-recriminations. She would have liked to have said it all to her, loud and clear, not because of anything her sister might have to say in response, but because she had a stinging need to affirm herself in front of Elsie, to crush the feeling of inferiority she experienced with her younger sister. In her old mind, she held Elsie somewhere on a plane up above herself, Elsie floated, superior, beyond Lillian's reach. Just beyond. Theirs was not a relationship based on equality for Lillian was perpetually crushed to ignominious non-existence. The lesser of the two, she both feared and adulated Elsie's pragmatism and she flagellated herself almost as much as others flagellated her. It was a problem, this weakness, this lack of self-esteem, this over-dose of stupidity, Born daft, that was what she'd overheard Horace say about her once, around about the time she returned from Cape Town to care for her ailing Harold. To still her self-annihilating thoughts, she took refuge in holding long conversations in silence with Elsie, it was a way of making certain that she always came out on top, it calmed her frustrations, it almost convinced her that she really was capable of holding her own with her sister. These conversations invariably took place on her train journeys down to Horace's from London or up to London from Horace's, it was a way of preparing herself for the onslaught of Elsie's jabs which she would be certain to receive no sooner had she clambered down onto the platform at Waterloo, clinging anxiously to her overnight case, clicking and staring nervously at the *hurriers* who pushed past her. She would dawdle and let them go on their way, looking about her, a fragile wisp in the wind on shaky old legs, her wide eyes watering with the effort of looking about her at the scurrying bits of life haring past, purposeful, business-like all of them, leaving her behind to wage her path towards the ticket barrier and her younger sister waiting on the other side of it.

VII

WAITING FOR LILLIAN'S TRAIN

Why she ever married that *boor*, I can't imagine! Dreadful type. If there was ever anyone crude in this world it was Harold. Free and easy with his tongue in front of us and no respect at all for Lillian herself. She used to stare at him with stars in her eyes, sitting on the sofa together tight against each other, On the sofa, I ask you, in front of Roland and me, in front of Horace and Mavis, Even in front of father and Nell, sitting there on the sofa full of bad taste, she pecking at his lobes, Harold had repulsive, outsize lobes on his ears, all droopy and fleshy, I used to stare at them and Mavis sometimes giggled at them right in front of Harold, Mavis could never control her giggling and the more in front of people she was, the more she giggled at them. Nervous giggling, that was Mavis' problem. What we all had to watch with Lillian pecking at Harold's lobes! I remember Roland used to blush under his moustache and wag his head and whisper, They're at it again, to me, and Horace, who was really quite prudish, decorous in his conduct despite his sea-faring, used to shift uncomfortably from one buttock to another and stare up at a picture on the wall saying to Nell, It's raining again. I mean, if he hadn't felt uncomfortable he would have looked *outside the window* and said It's raining again, wouldn't he? The lobe-pecking used to go on in their courting days when we were all a bit young and silly. Though never as silly as Lillian. And don't think it stopped at the lobe-pecking, because there was hand-holding and tongue-tickling too in front of us, that tongue-tickling when Harold would respond to Lillian's lobe-pecking by letting his tongue protrude just a little bit through his lips and she would do the same and lean towards him until their tongues met. All in front of us, Mavis giggling, Nell tut-tutting but too embarrassed to say anything, tell them to do their dirty business elsewhere. She was a *one*, Lillian, I mean, really a *one*. Fancy falling for that! The lobes were bad enough, but his lewd comments were worse. When she held his hand and cuddled up to him on our sofa, he used to say, And she really thinks I love her, Look at her, She's daft, Silly as a wagonload. Fancy saying that about her in front of us, I swear I would never have married Roland if he'd said that about me. And worse things too, if he wasn't in one of his good moods throwing his facetious jokes about, then he'd be in one of his bad moods which was more often than not and he would sit on our sofa not saying a word, cryptic silences those as though he were sitting inside himself, revengeful of the world, from the moment he walked in, not even a hello or a goodbye. Boorish fellow. And we all trying to make conversation with him and it was as if we hadn't spoken for all he answered us. He lived in a world of his own, a selfish world, as though no-one else existed. How Lillian had to fix her eyes and aspirations on a man like Harold has always been a mystery to me, with the number of boyfriends she had, she was never short of male company, always on the doorstep with one specimen or another, that Indian prince and the Selfridges bra-seller had only been the first of a long line of them and most of them had their lobes pecked on our sofa too. And Nell just used to sigh, probably asking the Lord in silence what she'd done to be given a daughter like Lillian, a *loose* daughter. That just goes to show how unfair life is, and god is, I mean, if he took people's feelings into consideration, he would never have given our little god-fearing Nell, all sweetness she was, a *loose* daughter like Lillian. Tough for her to cope with that.

That was all at the beginning, in the early days with Harold. Later on. They married. Of course They Married. We all Married. That was done in those times. Although Nell only regarded Lillian's as a half-Marriage, not a convincing Marriage, because Harold refused to take her to the altar all dressed in white as Roland had done with me. Perhaps because he knew she wasn't a virgin. I was when I Married, so I deserved that white wedding, didn't I. But Lillian ..... Not that she wouldn't have liked it. She'd spent all her adolescence dreaming about the white wedding dress she was to have, but Harold said No, he wasn't going to stand before the altar of any god he didn't believe in, and Lillian would have to go without her white dress and marry in an ordinary suit and better if it wasn't white. To Nell's dismay, it was a registry office affair, a *civil* Marriage, and Harold with an evil leer on his lips that day and I think it was the first time he was cruel to Lillian, but she had too many stars in her eyes to notice. Cruel of him it was, forcing her to marry in that way. I think that it secretly spoilt what she'd hoped would be the best day of her life. You know, the day that every young girl dreams of, but Harold took it upon himself that day to be in one of his vile moods. There were no facetious jokes that day, in fact, he didn't utter a word to any of us. Haughty and ugly he was at his half wedding, his registry office *commitment.* I felt like warning Lillian to un-marry herself straight away, but it wasn't done, was it, to marry for only ten minutes. As it was, she married him twice, the second time around after she returned from South Africa, from that shameful escapade which I think was responsible for sending Harold to his salty grave. The second time she married, it was to a half-dead man. Quite illogical. Though logical for Lillian I suppose, because she was an illogical person.

But it wasn't just the facetious jokes and the vile moods. It was the sweet-sucking too. Harold used to steal sweets meant for Polly or for Mavis' and Horace's children, steal their sweets, those treasured and rationed post-War delicacies, when they weren't looking. Now *there's* something really hard to credit, a grown man stealing sweets from small children, difficult years they were, years of rationing, so any little luxuries like chocolate or sweets we relinquished ourselves and gave to the kids. I mean, that's what being adult is all about, isn't it? Being able to go without. Yet not

Harold! Thank goodness he and Lillian never had children or they would never have set eyes on a sweet, their father would have guzzled them all. We often used to visit Horace and Mavis altogether, Harold and Lillian, Roland and Polly and I that is, we'd travel together on the train to Horace and Mavis' house for a Sunday lunch or a Saturday afternoon tea if Roland and I could leave the pub in capable hands for a few hours, not easy to get responsible barmen, men who wouldn't clean the till out for you in your absence, and we'd save our sweet rations for the infants, that was the way it was during those hard years, none of the affluence there is today. Well I'm blowed if Harold wouldn't wave the sweets Lillian had saved right in front of the kids' noses, unwrap the wrapping paper slowly, temptingly, watch the children's eyes light up, then whoop! into his own mouth would he pop the sweet and his cruel raucous laughter would hurtle through the house as the small pummelling fists and screams of Uncle Harold's taken my sweetie, cascaded after it. I couldn't believe how anyone could be so cynical. Cruel and cynical. Downright cruel and cynical. After that I told the youngsters in no uncertain terms, You count out your sweeties, don't leave them around for that gobbling wolf to steal, Clutch onto them hard. But of course they dropped out of the jolting pockets and fell from the grasp of little fingers eager to play and were forgotten in ashtrays and on side tables by infantile minds and duly pounced upon by the waiting vulture. If ever I caught him red-handed, I'd give him a piece of my mind, but he used to just laugh at me and say things like We can't all be good Samaritans in this world, Some of us are born wicked.

How Lillian put up with him, I shall never fathom out. She drooled over him, convinced of his importance when he was nothing but a two-penny-halfpenny clerk at Scotland Yard, filing away the musty old papers of long-forgotten crimes into dusty filing cabinets. They didn't even give him an office above ground. He worked *underground*, can you imagine! As though they'd put him away in the basement to keep him out of sight, the ugly toad, with the papers he filed, Out of sight Out of mind, they say. If he'd really been intelligent, they would at least have given him a respectable office where he could be seen. But Lillian used to go on and on, grind on like a cracked record, about how intelligent, how *lettered* he was. How *essential* he was to Scotland Yard, Don't you believe it! Horace would retort, Nobody's *essential* at Scotland Yard or anywhere else, everyone can be replaced, there's always someone else who can do the job better. Lillian found that hard to swallow. She was obsessed by Harold's intelligence and supposed sensitivity, lived in a sort of dream world about him, she did. It boosted her own importance, thinking that she'd married a man of brilliance. The only bit of brilliance about Harold were his shoes on the days he bothered to shine them. If he was clever, he never displayed that quality to any of us. In fact, we never extracted any sense from him at all, we were the recipients for his scowls and silences or for his lewd jokes, no wonder Lillian used to ask us all the time whether we liked him or not, I had to tell her a hundred times that we didn't. That Nell was scared of him. That father disregarded him completely. That Mavis said he gave her the creeps with his lips like grey marshmallows. That Horace couldn't abide him because he wasn't a *man's man,* or if he was, he wasn't in Horace's way. That Roland agreed with this and said that Harold wasn't one to have a drink with the boys. That I couldn't stand him because he was rude and cruel to the children. That Polly was frightened of him. Then Lillian would gather herself into a corner and sulk and say we were unfair. That we didn't give him a chance.

It used to revolt me too, the way he hung around all those weird theatricals, worshipping the very sod they trod. I mean, that isn't a normal thing for a fellow to do, is it, Hanging around the stage doors of theatres to see the young actors come out. That's the sort of behaviour you'd expect from adolescent girls, stage-struck and romantic. Later on, when she told me he used to be out late at night and bring men friends home to the flat without so much as asking her permission, I wasn't surprised. A strange streak did our Harold have. And it was as though he was doing it on purpose, trying to exclude Lillian as it were, going out with his men friends to make her jealous, bringing them home to the flat, lounging around all over the carpet into the early hours, pushing her out of the conversation. She reached the stage when she'd tell me everything and it was pretty obvious to me, for reasons unknown to any of us, that he was trying to rid himself of her, or did he simply reap satisfaction from hurting her? He was a macabre piece of work. She even confessed to me once that the more she tried to seduce him, the more he rejected her. What goings on, I ask you! How peaceful life was beside Roland ..... Then the way he reacted when she let him know that they couldn't have a child. Poor Lillian. I even felt sympathetic towards her then, he took advantage of her weakness to satisfy his own lustful habits. She was a fool to put up with it as long as she did. He never cared two-pence about them being a childless couple. On the contrary, he appeared to prefer it that way. There was so much she just couldn't see through, all of it going on under her nose and she was blind to it. In a sense that dreadful Ferdinand Rollins was a saving grace, got her out and away from her misery, but it didn't take her long to go crawling back, seeking out that awful *boor* again. I always thought he was cruel to her because he had a chip on his shoulders, an inferiority complex because he was incapable of extricating himself from those musty old Scotland Yard files.

But Lillian annoyed us all as well. It wasn't all sympathy. No! When she got herself worked up, she'd accuse me of being unsympathetic about her sterility. She said, How could I possibly understand with the easy life I led. Easy! She had no inkling of the hard work entailed in running that pub, not any idea did she have of the way Roland and I slaved through our days, she just thought Because they have money, their life must be easy, never seemed to get it into her head that money doesn't grow on trees, yet she should have realised that, having to work all her life the way she did, not like Mavis who was fortunate and managed on Horace's income. Still, apart from Harold she'd always chosen boyfriends well stacked, men with plentiful bank balances. That's probably why she had to label Harold with intellectual prowess, because he didn't have any bank balance to speak of. But she offended me to the core, although she never knew it because I never let on to her. She offended me, saying that I didn't understand her suffering sterility. Of course I did, I simply had other things on my mind, that was all. Things on my mind and Nell on my plate, Nell who was suffering much more than Lillian, suffering with her failing health and old-age-before-her-time and disillusion with a husband, father that is, who drank and had never understood her, and a *loose* daughter who kept making the wrong choices. Sad, sad were Nell's last days. Apart from helping Roland in the pub I had to spend my free time in between opening hours running to and fro between the pub and Nell-bedridden, consulting the doctor, administering the medicines he prescribed because father couldn't be counted on to do that, some days he never knew if it was morning or afternoon, twice a day I used to go, in the mornings before we opened and in the afternoons after we'd closed and at night it was Emily who would come and plump up her pillows

Emily, the nurse

and keep father company, hold his hand and tell him not to worry, self-interested commiseration hers was, it was then that Emily really got her stake in on father's life, making him her special apple pies with currants and cinnamon the way he liked them, because she said that Nell couldn't feed him properly anymore so she, Emily, would be the provider

Emily, the provider.

Of course, right at the end, Nell was taken into hospital, but I still used to visit her every day, whereas Lillian went on Saturdays only, said she had to work during the week, before that is that she raced off to South Africa and, poorly as Nell was, she seemed to realise that Lillian no longer visited her on Saturday afternoons, ill as she was, tiny and pale and shrunk and wizened in that big hospital bed, she always knew, like a clock, when it was Saturday.

And so I was obliged to tell her that Lillian had gone away. Poor Nelly. Her lips trembled then and the tears rolled down her emaciated cheeks. She didn't even ask me why Lillian had gone away. She knew without asking. She also knew that she would never see her again. After that, it was really the downhill slide, it didn't take long for her to die, as though with the family breaking up, with Lillian breaking the family up, that is, with her departure across the seas, that was the signal for her to take leave of us all, put Plumstead and father behind her, leave the way open for Emily to put an end to her spinsterhood,

Emily, the assuager of widowers,

Nell had to put an end to her life if Emily were to put an end to her spinsterhood, not that she *took* her life, she just *gave it up,* gave it up to the Lord, asked Him to take it for her. She told me that she'd asked Him to do that, after Lillian left for South Africa. And I watched her die through my tears. I was never a one for crying with my metallic nature, but the tears came and flowed freely as Nell went up to the Lord. All that time hurt deep down, so you see I was too exhausted, wasn't I, to worry much about Lillian's sterility and her problems with Harold. Not that I ever believed she was faithful to him even before Ferdinand Rollins. She could never keep her cleavage to herself and in those days when Harold wasn't taking any notice of her, too busy cavorting with his boyfriends, I don't believe that she kept her cleavage fully under cover during all that time. Lillian was uncourageous and she would never have had the courage to walk out on Harold if she hadn't been sure that some other man would caress her cleavage for her. When Nell died, I wrote her a letter. Several weeks later I received one from her in which she said how miserable she felt, how she Wept every night for Nell, Wept into her pillow with remorse, Wept because she hadn't been there to hold her hand at the End (not that she had ever held it much all through from the Beginning), Wept because she felt guilty that I'd done all the caring, Wept because she felt guilty for having run off to South Africa, she hadn't only run out on Harold she said, but had run out on Nell and on me too, Wept in choked sobs into her pillow so as not to disturb Ferdinand Rollins' snoring.

So Nell had died, her little bird-like body was laid beneath the soil, her soul would have gone up to the Lord she'd loved and served. He was her strength and hope, He was her true Masterbuilder, not father, He was the object of her love and striving more than we were. I suppose Horace and I had more or less moulded our lives to Nell's aspirations, church-going aside, but not Lillian. Where Emily praised Lillian nonstop, Nell spoke little of her, as though trying to silence her *loose* life. She was always embarrassed, worried about what neighbours might say, what Maud and Cyril might think. Really Nell had little confidence in herself and scant understanding of human nature for all her prayer-chanting, I mean, she worried more about what people would think of Lillian than about the harm Lillian was doing to herself. That's one of the reasons I could never share her faith, a faith that didn't make you strong isn't very worthwhile after all, is it. Not that Nell was hypocritical the way I've since discovered many bible-bashers to be. Not hypocritical, no. But somehow, innocent, believing everything the flabby-jowled whisky-swiller of an Irish priest told her, yet not understanding how to apply her belief to every-day life, her belief wasn't strong enough to help her over the jolts, so to speak. She receded, on the contrary, into herself, had a sort of running dialogue with the Lord, I used to hear her on occasions, muttering away there in the kitchen, Oh Lord God, why do I always come off worse, why did I marry a man who drinks, why did you give me a daughter who is easy with her body, blaming the Lord in petulant mutterings, instead of asking him for the strength to rectify, to deal with life's jolts. No, I could never envy Nell her faith except perhaps for the ease with which she surrendered up her life to the Lord. Although, come to think of it, that was strange too, strange for her that acceptance of death at the final count, because she had spent her life fearing death. Where father was nonchalant, I don't care what happens to me when this is all over, he'd bluster, blindly self-assertive, They can do what they like with me, Whoever it is in charge, Nell used to quake with emotion when she spoke of death, titter nervously as though confronted with a hurdle she knew she could never hope to jump. Apart from Nell, we all scorned the idea of death, it still doesn't concern me greatly, the closer I come to it, for all I know it might be just around the corner, *come over me in the bathtub, take me off* whilst I'm counting out the shillings to pay for my bottles of gin and vermouth, *harvest my legs from under me* whilst I'm waiting here at Waterloo for Lillian's train to arrive, any time now it could come along, Death not the train, with its great scythe, slit my throat or beckon me politely to follow into the dark hole of oblivion. Perhaps after all it wasn't even scorn that I felt for death, perhaps it was mere indifference. I think I was really too pragmatic a person to let anything as invisible and intangible as Death worry me. What was the point? I always considered that the priest tried to knock fear into us to make us be good, telling us all about hell fire and damnation. What did he know, any more than anyone else? Setting himself up on a pedestal, distinguishing himself from the *commoners.* A commoner himself, what authority did he have to talk about invisible things like Death when he had never died and lived again to tell the tale afterwards? I mean, one thing is to have a tangible, visible queen with a vested interest in the nation and a proven affection for her people, no harm in putting *her* on a pedestal, kings and queens are in their rightful place on pedestals, or thrones rather, but then they deal with the solid things of life, not with the vain promises of heaven, that black wilderness stretching out the other side of life. I never trusted the authority of the parson or of the clingers-on to sects, Quakers, Jehovah's Witnesses, the bible-bashers trying to infiltrate into your home with their unproven promises, their faith coated in honeyed words. I was never one to believe in anything I couldn't see. Too pragmatic, as I've said before. I love the queen and I believe in her because I can see her, she's there for us all to see, decked out in her finery for ceremonious occasions, walking in gumboots through the mud in the fields around Balmoral, a scarf tied under her chin like any other housewife of the nation, I mean if you reached out it's as though you could touch her at those moments. She's of more comfort to us, her subjects, than any priest could be, disrespectful they are with life as it is, as we know it, telling us the real life comes after death. I ask you! I always think that the flabby-jowled priest made Nell dislike her life because she began to wait for death as though it were the promise of greater things to come if she believed fervently enough. So she despised life for a long time before she actually died, turned her back on it as it were, letting Emily do all the bustling and bossing.

Emily, the bustler.

Emily, the boss.

Fervent belief and despising life, it was with Nell. I've often despised life, but not in the aloof way she did. I despised it, but I've always been prepared to fight back despite substantial odds, not cling to an imaginary life somewhere outside this one. That seemed a senseless theory to me, putting all your eggs into a basket which hangs too high above your head for you to reach .....

But the queen is different. You can see her on television. You can even see her, *bump into* her, if you're lucky, in the street. I was lucky enough to be nearly run down by one of her escort cars once, near Admiralty Arch it was, and she came quick sharp behind in her glamorous, shining limousine, gleaming black and so absolutely British and there she was, our very own queen, smiling and waving to her subjects, elegant in her wide-brimmed hat and long white elbow-length gloves, I was still breathless after my *near miss* with the escort car, but I rallied round and smiled and waved and I'm sure our eyes met and I nearly melted on the spot in a paroxysm of patriotic pride. That was a chance meeting. Yet there were many occasions which were planned *outings* when we'd spend hours, literally hours, squashed into the morsel of space in the crowd, to watch her or any member of the royal family pass. That was when we were younger, naturally, I couldn't stand those crowds now.

But youth puts up with any discomfort to achieve its heartfelt desire, at least it did in those days though I'm not so sure now, comfort seems to be a number one priority of today's youth, if a bit of illusion and desire are thrown in for good measure, all well and good, but *striving* for the desired object against all odds is unheard of now amongst youngsters. Of course you can only blame the *welfare state* for that, they've lost the magic of bowing down to a queen, to a bejewelled fantasy, the *welfare state* has pushed romance out of young people's lives, on the *welfare state* they have it all too easily, too quickly, they don't even appreciate where it comes from, out of the crippled taxpayer's pocket, that's where they get their perks from.

Elsie had never stopped to consider who was paying for the Council flat she inhabited. It was *hers, My flat*, she would say. If the State had not rallied round she would have been left impecunious in the gutter when Roland died after his life of extravagant gambling.

It isn't healthy for youngsters to have it all at once, they never learn how to struggle to keep the nation on its feet. Weak. That's what they are today, too weak to stand up for their Royalty and Nation. Not too weak to grab what they can from it, mind you, without contributing. If I had my way, I'd take them back to my early days when you struggled or you sank. Every day was a struggle then, nothing was easy and all we received for our labours were rationing and salary cuts, but we accepted whatever they meted out to us, accepted it for our loyalty to Queen, or king in those days, and Country. Citizens of the World they call themselves nowadays, joining hands and singing international songs with beads around their necks, flowers in their hair, all shacked up together, like Lillian and Ferdinand Rollins only in groups, and all they talk about is cutting down the army. They want that money taken from the nation's defence to foot the bill for their dole. Shameful it is. I know what Horace would call them, The Scum of the Earth with a capital S, and Lillian would agree with him without knowing why, too scared to disagree I expect. Poor little Nell, if she could come back now and see it all, this deteriorated race, hybrids we are now too, little of the true blue British blood left, a load of hybrids all jumbled up with mothers and fathers and children of all colours with the temerity to call themselves British. Outsiders take one look at us now and call us *The Brits*. I fume inside myself every time I hear that disparaging expression, as though we were anything but what we are.

And if Nell could have come back shortly after her death and witnessed Emily installing herself beside father, wheedling her way in beside him,

Emily, the wheedler;

if she could have seen that, she would have wanted to die before she did, efface herself in the face of Emily's wheedling with her apple pies. Father drooled over those apple pies, the currants, the cinnamon, the pastry-to-perfection, crusty yet melting in your mouth. Grudgingly I have to admit they were tasty those apple pies, turning up the way they did every Sunday with Emily. Mind you, she wasn't very imaginative because scrumptious as those apple pies were, it never occurred to her to do anything different, say like blackcurrant crumble or custard tarts. Perhaps she thought father would have rejected those. He could be difficult. When Nell was ill, Emily started going twice or three times a week in the evenings with her apple pies to feed father and to cook him a hot meal, usually stew and dumplings if it was a weekday and roast-something if it was a Sunday and invariably followed by the pie, the apple pie prepared with solemn and affectionate meticulousness, placed tenderly inside a circular metal container with a lid, transported carefully across the road for posterior consumption by father, apple pie for the Apple of her eye it was, with poor little Nell ailing upstairs in her bed with starched linen sheets scratching her wasting body and Emily poking her ferret's nose further and further into the household affairs, not to mention into father's whims and fancies. He only thought about his own comforts at that time. His wife sickly, somebody had to care for him and Emily was like a stick of furniture in the house, had been for years, like the mainstay, the centre leg of the dining table, straight and stiff and breast-less as she was, rigid in deed and word, the only relieving protrusion on her cardboard body being the long twitching nose, which poked forth from her sharp glinting eyes and turned blue in winter. Mean as the ferret she resembled. She only *did* and cooked for Father for the comfort she obtained for herself, to get a firm foothold. I suppose that if I hadn't detested her so strongly, if she hadn't been the bane of my life throughout my youth, I might even have mustered up a spot of sympathy for her in her loneliness. It was her loneliness too which forced her to gate-crash and build herself into something ultimately indispensable to father. When Nell went to hospital, she tripled her attentions, spending hours in the house organising, *taking over* on a perpetual basis, cajoling Nell with sugary phrases which were greeted with indifference, telling her *not to worry*, father would be fine in her capable hands, she'd look after him for evermore, at least until her own death which didn't look as though it was just around the corner, and I remember Nell just stared, glared, at the white wall making no response at all. But Emily was insensitive to Nell's glare, she only knew that she owed it to herself to obliterate her loneliness, those sixty odd years of putting up with herself and herself alone. Born an only child, she was rapidly destined to become an orphan. Lonely and cold and miserable she said she was, huddled on a street corner one winter's evening, snivelling her misery into the darns of her skirt, she was *picked up* by a horse and cart, tossed in with other snivelling waifs and orphans and *carted off* to a whole home full of snivellers and it was There that she learnt how to whine and deceive and ferret her way into others' affairs, it was There that she learnt to defend herself, with scratching and fisty cuffs if necessary, it was There that she learnt to eat pap and slops and semolina if she was lucky, and dream about golden apple pies, sniff out the cinnamon and currants in them with her adolescent nose which was stretching with the years, long, thin, to shape her ferret's muzzle. It was There that Emily learnt to defend herself by pushing and insulting and being mean, defend herself from other human beings, assert herself throwing the teenage weight of her breast-less body around. Hers was a fighting, scratching youth, an adolescence of hating the world, of bearing grudges. They taught her how to read and write, how to add up and subtract, but at fifteen, her childhood coming-of-age, she was packed off as an apprentice to sweep the floors and clean the windows of grimy office buildings. Anything to be rid of her, to prevent her making trouble with the other waifs.

Emily, the waif.

Emily, the trouble-maker.

True, Emily never had our sort of opportunities, no secretarial college, no rendezvous with Indian princes or the likes of Roland. But she worked hard with her cleaning and in time earned enough to rent herself the two front rooms of the old house across the road from ours. I used to go there with her sometimes when I was small, against my will of course. I used to go there to run errands for her, fetch and carry her bits and pieces, run *up and down* the road between her house and the store on the street corner, run *across* the road between her house and ours, fetching her bits, carrying her pieces, bits from her wobbly old welsh dresser with its three long legs and its one short one, pieces to help patch up father's loneliness. I hated that welsh dresser, propped on its three and a half legs against her grubby cream wall. It was an eyesore, an offence to anybody's good taste, jammed full as it was of the stringy portents of Emily's existence, drawers Where the wire hairpins she used to keep her bun in place shared space with the hat pins she collected for the hats she coveted in shop-windows and could never afford to buy, Where scraps of paper from her purchases poked untidily through the slits between drawer and dresser, Where cotton reels from her sewing entangled themselves in the strands of wool from her darning, Where the spoons for her apple tarts jangled rebelliously amongst a medley of knives and forks, an ungracious heap of tarnished metal, Where chipped crockery lined the higher shelves, a sad array which shuddered every time she opened a drawer or every time a train went past on its rails near her dwelling. She used to say it sounded like *Them trains is comin' right inter me livin' room.* She dropped even more "g's" than usual when she was flustered or angry. That dresser! It was a dismal reminder of the mundane traipsing of Emily's days. I hated it. Every time she would beckon me over and open one of its drawers, I remember wondering what she would take from it next. Never anything nice, that was for sure. Nothing pretty or in any way appealing to me ever emerged from its dark hump of a body. It occupied too much space in her living room, it stole light from the window which was already far too small. It was plain ugly and because of it, I have considered welsh dressers odious ever since. For me, they evoke the claustrophobic air of Emily's living room. Heavy, ungainly pieces of furniture filled with useless, unattractive oddments woven about with the hoarse whispers from Emily's breast-less chest, the wheedling remarks of *How was Nell today, I mustn't forget ter bake yer father's apple pie, 'is Sunday wouldn't be a proper Sunday without that, would it?* And Nell always in the background, as though disturbing Emily's dreams, bountiful righteous Nelly, standing *in the way* of her scheming.

The times I listened to Emily's confidences beside that dark stained dresser! Confidences I was then too young to understand but which flit now in and out of my mind as I put two and two together, gradually piece together the jigsaw puzzle of our lives. She was besotted with father, besotted from an early age. She confessed to me how, as a young woman, *When I was like you is now,* she would spy on his building site, *accompany* him as it were in his toiling over bricks and mortar, *watch over* him as he poured water slowly, purposefully, from a rusty clanking bucket into the circle of cement and sand. She was there with him, like a watchful spirit, as he bent his then youthful strong body over the spade with which he mixed the cement, kneading it affectionately with the tip of his spade, turning and churning it together with solid human effort, efficient forerunner to the cement-mixing machine, lifting it up, slopping it down into the rapidly liquidised mass, a grey whirlpool of unfulfilled dreams,

Emily, the dreamer

where Nell's face would always appear, Nell in the centre and Emily just out of reach whirling around the edge with her spite and envy. Emily yearning for father's youthful torso, tanned by the summer sun, strengthened and glistening his muscles after winters of hard labouring. Emily, meek and attentive on the side-lines of the site, hankering after a dream which was not to come true. Summer and winter she would pass by the wire fence which separated her from the workmen, linger after her bouts of office-cleaning, hoping for a glance, a word, a smile flung with nonchalance towards her, a token which would nourish the deadening hours of her next few days. More than half her time she spent hanging around building sites where father was sweating and straining his limbs, needling her way into his life with her sharp presence, watching his hands roughen through contact with the jagged ends of bricks, the open cracks on his fingers suppurating in the icy winds of winter, tender curing sparks from her eyes and father with his grinding labour in the mounds of sand without sea, building up castles for people to live in and building up a family before Emily's envious stares. No easy machines then, only makeshift pulleys and precarious planks for scaffolding and able fists, walls rising, souls sinking, brick-laying with care and talent cementing solidity into the soul, the knowledge of a job well done with each layer of bricks. Emily heard voices roughened by the wind, saw gestures coarsened by the crude battle to earn a wage. Emily watched and was edified by the effort father put into his work; Emily faithful to her unattainable ideal. She would have liked to work on the building site with father, mix the cement beside him, climb onto the scaffolding with her putty, father hauling her up by her wrists. Touching her. All day long beside him, puttying around windows. She'd have put up with any inconvenience, with the cold and the mud, the dust and the grit, just to be by his side. She was convinced she could be a builder, like any man. But the men wouldn't like it, having a girl interfering, snooping and sniffing around their putty. Women were meant for kitchens, not for building sites. On building sites they were a disturbance, a ripple, a ruffling to men's minds. Furtive glances upon a cardboard, breastless body were a danger to the competent laying of bricks, they would leave prints of frustration engraved forever in the cement. And so Emily contented herself to watch from the side-lines.

Those were the days before the apple pies, before she resorted to her wheedling with the oven. She was tenacious and obstinate and convinced that her dream, the dream of holding father to her nondescript bosom, would sooner or later eventuate. Father was innocent with his Nell and his children and in return for her pains only threw her the occasional glance through scaffolding and barbed wire, or raised a cement-sculptured hand to wave an acknowledgement to her presence, wave at her from his gumboots, ankle-deep in mud, lance his innocent smile, replete with Nell and children, Horace and Lillian and me, that was, in our smallest versions, across to her on the other side of the barbed wire. And Emily would smile a bitter smile to herself. A knowing smile: Nell's health was dicey. And she would fold father's glance up into her jealous heart and take it off with her to her hired front rooms, tuck it away into a secret drawer of her welsh dresser, pull it out for me to taunt my youthful imagination in her hints and her confidences beside the dreaded dresser.

Never, not once, did she invite me to sit down in that room, the room of her resounding whispered, hoarse-whispered, confidences. I recall how her breath smelt of fags and stale tea-leaves, stank across the gloom which separated us, across the surface of the welsh dresser, no dust on the surface, no, because Emily was a cleaner by profession, although this outer display of cleanliness had little in common with the dirt which lined the drawers and objects of her dresser and encrusted her soul, her soul waiting to pounce, to make her breast-less body lunge out in offering to father. In Emily's front room, I felt perpetually uneasy. It was as though the gloom louring there seeped into me like a peasouper. It was as though you must never raise your voice within the cream confines of her grubby walls. It was as though all life outside those walls suddenly became non-existent: Vanished Nell and Lillian and Horace, Vanished the Brown School, Vanished Sunday roasts. And there was I, like a recluse, listening, or pretending to listen, to the broken whispers of confession from the lips of a crone.

Emily, the crone.

I would nod and smile nervously in the appropriate places and stiffen if she grasped my arm because although I didn't fully understand what I was hearing, something in that gloom made me feel a traitor. To what, or to whom, I can only now, today, devise. It was Emily letting me inside the reason for her existence, inviting me to step inside a forbidden room and instead of appreciating her for that, I despised her, despised her for making me accomplice to something which was not my concern. Why hadn't she chosen Lillian, I used to think, to run her errands and to do the listening, why choose me, the least-loved of the two sisters? Didn't she want to besmirch Lillian with her dirt?

In that room, Emily lived. In the other, she slept. That I knew because she told me as we would pass it with a wave of her arm, not because I was ever admitted into the sanctuary of her sleeping hours. Her two rooms were connected by a dim passageway which also led to the bathroom and kitchen she shared with other members of that motley Plumstead household. The door of her living room creaked on its hinges as she opened and shut it, it gave me the creeps, yet Emily would shrug her shoulders with a nervous un-girlish giggle and point her sharp muzzle in the direction of the squeaking hinge each time as if commanding it to be quiet. It did not occur to her that a dab of oil would have done the trick, for Emily cleaned and schemed, but thought little. Opposite the welsh dresser stood a circular table with three un-matching chairs and directly beside the small rectangular window, or rather *under* the rectangular window, was a rickety armchair covered in dismal-brown-corduroy-velvet-worn-at-the-edges-frayed-along-the-bottom. I remember, as a child, how ugly that armchair seemed to me, ugly like the rest of the room, ugly like its inhabitant.

Emily, the inhabitant,

Emily, the ugly inhabitant.

* * *

Elsie jumped out of her reveries about the past and stared into her present, which glared at her with uncompromising exactitude from the station clock. Ten past three. Lillian's train was due in fifteen minutes. Fifteen more minutes. She had already been waiting half an hour. She always arrived early for appointments, whatever they were, whether to meet or catch a train, whether to have her hair done. Elsie had always *had her hair done*. I can't come down tomorrow, she would say to Horace, I'm going *to have my hair done*. And she would emerge from the hairdresser's with her smoke grey curls trussed and trimmed into a fine net to protect them from the vindictive gusts which hurtled down London's alleyways. The white of Elsie's hair was yellowing now, like the parchment of Time, wisps tinged with cigarette smoke and her hairdresser was confronted with a hard battle to restore life to the brittle strands of winter hair. Elsie went to the hairdresser in subconscious defiance of the dreaded childhood dousing, the dousing which had made her incapable during her life of washing her own hair. She still remembered with vivid pangs the soreness of her scalp as her mother, Nell that was, had pulled at the persistent knots, the dripping threads whipping around her shoulder blades, cold rivulets trickling inside her liberty bodice, and she had no intention of inflicting a similar martyrdom on herself. With her metallic nature she would probably have tugged at her knots with such a vengeance as to pull out the very roots of her hair. Hairdressers were gentler with their soothing, massaging fingers, you could doze off under the hairdryer, they relieved you of the whole onerous business. Besides, Elsie's arms were too short and they ached if she lifted them above her head for more than a few seconds, she could never have tackled rollers and knots, she could only tackle things which were below her head, like Lillian's mishandling of her life.

There she was, advancing gingerly down the platform towards the ticket barrier. Here she comes, muttered Elsie into her whiskers. Back to London to taunt me again, dithering along as usual. Look at her! Elsie's sight was poorly. No matter. She could *sense* Lillian approaching with a sort of sixth sisterly sense, Lillian, stepping cautiously out of the horizon bumping her bulky body against others, staring at the taller passers-by, She looks like an ingratiating mole, thought Elsie, in that dark brown coat, peering about her in the daylight without properly distinguishing anything. Look at her! Wending her way along the platform, back again, Into my hours, my days, my nights. No, my nights, no! I shall sell the spare bed tomorrow. I won't have it, putting up with her snores all night long. I had enough of that beside Roland when he was alive, the poor fellow, but snoring is part of the marriage contract. Quite another thing is having to put up with it from a sister. No, she'll not sleep with me anymore. In fact, I'll tell her tonight not to unpack her belongings at my place. She's to go home to her own flat. Elsie let a sigh escape her thin disgruntled lips. She knew she didn't have it in her to *oust* Lillian. Not in the way that Ferdinand Rollins had done with his nasty behaviour.

Elsie was metallic, but she wasn't cruel.

With a pang she recalled that Lillian had had a lonely life, all things considered. Of course, she'd brought it on herself with her flitting and infidelity. She never knew how to choose men, always on the lookout for glamour and good looks, lured dangerously towards the bizarre, the momentary fling. An unsound nature, Elsie mused. And she let them all dominate her, the way she lets Horace dominate her now, something masochistic there, allowing them to use her in strange ways. Kinky that. Always nestling up to the wrong body as if she were searching desperately hard to be cared for and to please. My insecure sister, teetering, look at her, on her skinny ankles and block heels. Still imagining they'll turn their heads to stare at her legs perched up on top of those heels. I've told her a hundred times to get herself into flat shoes, she'll fall and break her neck one of these days. Not that that would matter, she's veering close to her end anyway ..... Elsie checked herself, momentarily abominated by her own tell-tale display of callousness. For a second she suspected that Lillian might even think the same about her, yet brushed such a contemplation rudely aside as being unlikely, stupid even, because Lillian thought very little. Just as Emily had thought very little. Two of a kind really, they'd both kept mental activity to a minimum and Lillian because she'd always been too occupied in her search for dominating males. She could go and stay permanently with Horace then .....

Ooh! There you are! I was wondering if I'd find you.

Yep! Here I am. Elsie braced her sedate little body for the fray. How was the journey?

Alright really. A bit tiring though.

And Horace?

Oh, him! He's alright. The same as ever. He sent you his love, you know.

He did, did he? That's nice. I send him mine too. Any chance of him coming up to visit us?

You must be joking. You ought to know by now that he won't be budged. Lillian put in her first spoke of faintest scorn. Already on the defensive before being attacked by her sister. She was feeling courageous after her absence, feeling a little *special* having made the lengthy journey all alone without mishap. But Oh so tired! How pleasant it would be to nestle into her younger sister's flat, take refuge for a while in being cared for, not having to feel responsible as she always did with Horace because he was drinking so much.

He's on the bottle again, you know Elsie.

Was he ever off it? Her reply was a sneer.

In this vein, they made their way to Elsie's flat. Lillian teetering on her block heels, Elsie marching sturdily in her flat soles. Like a pair of debilitated battering rams, they struck out into the wind, their abrasive permed curls flaying against the stiff northerly. They clutched onto one another for something like moral support against the common northerly enemy. Not that they were in the habit of embracing each other, or of exchanging affectionate taps and pinches, that play of caresses was not their style. When in each other's company, they kept themselves as physically far apart as was possible. Now in the rushes of bitter air, Elsie munched against her coarsened gums and yellowed canines, the soft pink of her inner jowls velvet soft against her false molars, whereas Lillian pursed her lips tight fast against the translucent blue of the teeth which had seen her from infancy through seven subsequent decades. Proud of her teeth, she'd always been. They'd been a talking point in her favour when she was younger. When everyone else complained about visits of hair-raising agony to the dentist's, Lillian would smile smugly, flash her perfect set of pearl white teeth, I haven't a filling in my head, she would boast with pride. You all eat too much sweet rubbish, and Elsie would flair, I've never eaten a sweet thing in my life, you're just lucky, that's all.

May as well take the bus, don't you think? You know I can't stand the tube.

Indeed, the *tube* was a source of panic to Elsie who, like Horace, suffered from claustrophobia in cramped spaces. She hated the long escalators which rumbled and clattered up and down for evermore, descending with their human load into the bowels of London. The echo and the grime and the blackness of the tunnels were disagreeable to her as were the unpleasant gusts of air as the trains rushed headlong into the stations smelling of life in the sewers and mercilessly lifting her *hair-do* on end, not to speak of the crowds, the seething masses who encroached like flooding waves on the doors as they opened, packing themselves into the stuffy compartments, still smelling of the beds they'd just abandoned or the musty office files they'd laid low for the night, or the rancid smoke of pub counters. Elsie never associated Roland's pub counter with this unpleasant smell. The *tube* was a suffocating world to her. And Lillian agreed, although she didn't really because she was quite unaware of the things her sister complained about. What concerned her were the nasty men who stared at you, almost ate you up with their lascivious eyes some of them, or the bag snatchers or the purse lifters or the ones who rubbed themselves up and down against some poor innocent female, although Some of those young hussies ask for it, flashing their eyes the way they do. Lillian was obsessed, secretly fascinated by those who obtained their sexual kicks in crowded undergrounds and, what's more, she was haunted by the idea of being followed down the long deserted passageways at night, I might even have been raped, she said with a mixture of terror and wistfulness. You couldn't be much more than you already have been, Elsie retorted in no uncertain terms. Lillian sank even further inside her brown mole's coat.

So they waited in the queue for the bus. Elsie unfailingly prevailed upon Lillian to mount the stairs. It was a challenge to her, proving to herself that at eighty-two, she could still clamber up and down the steep steps of a double-decker bus in motion. Lillian, three years her senior, had doubts about all this exercise, she was scared of falling, but she followed her younger sister obediently, panting meekly behind her and collapsing thankfully into her seat, breaking one of her long, corny fingernails as she did so.

I really don't know why we still sit up here, she hazarded timorously.

I do! Elsie chirped. You can see better, can't you! Besides, I can't do this downstairs can I? she queried, lighting herself a Players.

I suppose you can't, mooned Lillian thinking it would be better if Elsie gave it up but not daring to make that comment for fear of the habitual reprisal, Well I've got to eighty on 'em, so I'm not going to give 'em up now.

They jolted along, side by side, on squeaking springs, communicating now and then in between the lurching plunges of the ungainly vehicle. It was not a long ride: across Waterloo Bridge, past the Law Courts on one side, the Pen Club on the other, surging up Fleet Street towards Christopher Wren's louring dome, Lillian, by the way, could have descended from the bus by now, could have returned to her flat behind the Law Courts, but she sat cosily on, complacently receptive of Elsie's begrudging hospitality, hugging her knees with enthusiastic gnarled knuckles. As the bus continued its pitching path, Elsie signalled to the yellow daffs in the gardens by St Paul's and, in one fleeting flash, felt pride at being a Londoner, at *belonging* as it were to her beloved metropolis. Lillian only saw the yellow of the daffs without feeling pride, or any particular sense of belonging. Pretty those yellow daffs, aren't they? At a comfortable distance from the Law Courts, Lillian uttered with an expert dose of remorse,

Ooh, I could have got off back there, couldn't I?

Yes, you could have! Elsie never beat about her bushes. She was thinking, ferocious inside herself, that she hadn't sold the spare bed on time. Well, she would get around to it in the next few days. There was plenty of time really. But she couldn't put up with her sister for too much longer. Why should I? she thought with vehemence. Lillian suddenly exploded into an unexpected giggle.

Well, there's nothing funny about it, is there? snapped Elsie, imagining that Lillian was ridiculing her unspoken thoughts.

Look, I've just seen that car. It looks just like old Aly, do you remember?

Relieved, Elsie forced her lips into a synthetic smile which almost hurt.

Oh! That car you had years ago. Broken down old thing, shunting along the way it did! she commented with disparaging affection.

Shunting! Kangaroo hopping, if you ask me! Lillian almost choked between her spurts and bubbles of mirth. It had been her first car and for that reason she remembered it affectionately. Like a box on wheels it had jolted and jumped and farted its way along the road, it had cellophane flaps for windows and a number plate featuring the letters A L Y. Hence, she christened it. Occasionally, if the jolts were too rough, the door of the passenger seat would fly open. Fortunately, she rarely had passengers beside her for she was an erratic, scatter-brained driver and most of her friends preferred to take the train than to veer around corners on the wrong side of the road or to be delayed whilst *Aly* spluttered and stalled and had to be re-stoked with oil or water. The only passenger who delighted in riding beside her was Horace's mongrel. Black and white and proud, he would sit in canine faith on the rubber cushion of the passenger seat, erect and observant, alert, ears pointed, a parody of gratefulness to Lillian. If he growled or barked at any object which attracted his attention, she would jump, clutching instinctively at the wheel, veer, twitter, tut-tut, because Lillian had begun to twitter and tut-tut shortly after Harold's death, when she had been haunted by wavelets of remorse at having run off with Ferdinand Rollins and of having caused, inadvertently of course, Harold's salty departure from this world and from her life. And she would more than likely make Aly stall. Now you mustn't bark like that, old feller, she would cajole the mongrel back to its characteristic calm. Aly took Lillian on many a ride around the English countryside. It spluttered and backfired its way down the Oxford country lanes, past the lazy Cotswold cottages, the rolling downs of Devon, through Cheddar Gorge and Somerset cider villages and even as far as Newcastle up in the north. Quite a record for a car on its last wheels, Horace remarked facetiously and Lillian instantly felt proud of the purchase she had made which everyone had criticised at first. Yes. Aly had been a good companion to her after Harold's untimely disappearance, whatever the rest of the family had to say. Aly gave her a measure of freedom, an independence she had hitherto not experienced, attached as she'd always been to the whims and irksome fancies of her male companions. She'd dominated Aly better than she'd dominated her males. Although, those in Australia ... she mused quizzically.

Come on now! Off we get. Quickly! Elsie's harsh voice, smattered to smithereens by Players, broke into Lillian's daydreams before her reminiscences had a chance to return to Australia ... Those big bronzed muscular men with blond ...

Get a move on. Down you go! urged Elsie with a violent shove which sent her old sister almost headfirst down the bus steps.

You are rough with me, you know Elsie. You shouldn't push me like that. You've hurt my arm. As they alighted onto the pavement.

Well, you should get a move on then, shouldn't you? The bus won't stop for ever, will it?

I think I was better off travelling in Aly.

Go on with you! That old charabanc! You must be mad, Elsie scoffed.

The two of them climbed cold inhospitable stone stairways up to Elsie's lodgings. Cold and inhospitable, with whiffs of the trout Mr Wadham was cooking for his high tea.

That know-all Kathleen isn't about, I hope? asked Lillian.

You're referring to a *friend* of mine, warned Elsie with a bitter strain twanging at her voice.

Not much of a friend really, is she? Lillian bitched.

Well, she is to me.

Her snappy reply put an abrupt end to their interchange as they continued climbing out-of-breath past the trout whiffs up to Elsie's front door. Lillian was panting and flummoxed after the surge of activity. As for Elsie, she put the key in the door, pushed it open and headed straight for her cocktail cabinet. After all, if old Wadham could have his trout, she was entitled to her gin.

Put your bag down near the door, she said to Lillian, with hope in her heart that she could later inveigle her into calling a taxi to take her home. But Lillian picked up her overnight bag and took it straight through to the spare bed.

I think I'll stay here tonight, if you don't mind. It's a bit late to go home now. Elsie plunged her whiskers and frustration into her glass of gin and dry. Oh well, she muttered to herself, she'll have to go tomorrow then. I'll *make* her, the first draught of gin imbuing her with acid strength.

VIII

AUSTRALIA AND A WEDDING

Australia! The Land of Opportunity, they called it. Do you remember? It might have been that for some, but it wasn't for me.

I seem to recall you didn't do too badly out of the place. At least you managed to save some money living as you did in Horace's house and working for that cricketer in his sports store.

Ooh! ... That's right. Old Evans. Yes, he was good to me, but his beastly son wasn't. How that boy used to push me around Elsie, tell me what to do when Evans had put me in charge of him. Jealous he was, downright jealous of me. And brawny too. Like most Australians. They're a brawny race, really, aren't they? Always out doing their surfing.

Well, most of them spring from us.

It must be all that hot weather and outdoor activity which makes them so muscular.

It was the drawling voices which used to get on my nerves. Like a load of cats yowling, they never seemed to know what to do with their vowels, I mean, who did they think they were to alter our Queen's beautiful English?

We used to have some fun at those office parties though ..... Lillian's eyes lit up as brightly as the yellow-veined whites of them would allow, in fact, they positively *goggled*. She'd never been cured of office parties. They'd started in the Bush House days of her Indian summer and continued all through her career as secretary-typist-shorthander-boss comforter. For Lillian was renowned for the way she comforted her bosses in their moments of administrative anguish. She opened her arms to them, caressed their greying side-levers, sat on their knees as they drank the evil brew brought around by the tea lady. Comforted the worn patches of their commercially harassed souls. ..... And the Australian ones were ..... impressed by her qualities as secretary-very personal assistant. She liked the firm brawn which coated their knees, Harold's had been frankly less substantial, skinnier, bonier to sit upon. Full of good healthy relaxed fun, those Australian bosses were, as though they hadn't a care in the world. That was the good thing about Australia, people were happy, optimistic, brightened by the sunlight in their lives, not puny and pinched and pimpled as they had been in Britain, always hankering after the sun and the warmth which evaded them in perpetual favour of southern climes. And Australia was a southern clime Where Lillian could bask on beaches, stretching out the full length of her breasty body, her spinal curvature, her short bird legs, Where she could become a sun-worshipper, letting the surf and the sun lap up her British cares, her erstwhile miseries, Where she could luxuriate on golden sands, softly, willingly, obliterate the Plumstead purgatory, now far behind her, dimming into the recesses of her fickle past, consoled by Australian muscle and brawn and tan.

The office parties were plentiful and raucous, Any excuse for a drink mate, It's old Stan's birthday. Let's celebrate! Lil's been with us a month today. Let's celebrate! And beer bottles were placed on desks, typewriters and papers pushed aside in a frenzy of hilarity. Let's celebrate! Relax, with our feet up on swivel chairs. Sexy knees crossed against filing cabinets. Didn't know they made 'em like you in the Old Country. And Lillian beamed into her new fair dinkum surroundings, giggled and spluttered over her first strong ice-cold Australian beer, You'll be one of the diggers soon, luv. For they were the true Fair Dinkum Days, when things were Beaut, She'll be right, You'll be right, they all said to each other, those wonderful problem-less days, blue azure, eucalyptus green days, making Lillian forget the fifty years of her past. People, men particularly, still wanted her, she was still sought after, she was the life of the party. The life too of many of Horace's parties.

That was when Horace and Mavis *entertained*. Horace's friends were drinkers. Boozers. He sought them out amongst his office pals, the older ones with the florid noses and glazed eyes, the younger ones with early morning indigestion and feverish gills, sought them out and invited them home to his large company house perched on top of forty steps with a harbour view, the house Lillian thought was like an hotel the day she arrived crisply British into this land of shark-fearing, god-forsaken buddies. She arrived with her untainted patriotic pride into this gaudy Land of Plenty, her feet penned up in fifteen denier nylons and cramped into narrow high heels, to this open air Paradise where gritty golden sand clogged and oozed, oozed and clogged between her toes, where waves thrust their surging froth against her ankles. Lillian mistook Horace's house for an hotel because the whole of her life in Australia had a holiday flavour about it. It wasn't just the hall carpet with its floral pattern, nor the imposing stairway with its streamlined metal banister, but the parties at home, the parties at work, the gleaming weekends which enhanced her Sex Appeal, bronzed the skin of her cleavage. Mavis, who was breaking down nervously under the strain of her menopause, used to say, not without envy, that Lillian had It. She's got It, Mavis whispered confidentially to her wide-eyed thirteen-year old daughter, What's It? asked Mavis' daughter and Mavis averted her eyes from those of her piercing Adolescent, she cast her gaze downwards and mumbled, embarrassed and trussed up inside the straight-laced-jacket of her post-Victorian upbringing, Well, you know ... It ... That ... with men. Stumbled. At a party ... I mean ... you know. Mavis' Adolescent didn't know, but her imagination was spiced and afterwards she would study Lillian carefully, waiting for It to manifest itself. Could It have something to do with a bronzed cleavage? Lillian revelled in the crass stupidity of the parties, revelled in the bottom-slapping, arm-pinching comments about nothing, glad that it wasn't too late to start all over again, doubled up with easy mirth over lewd jokes about jackaroos and wallabies, possums and kangaroos, *'roos* they were called, like they called her *Lil*, never Lillian. She hooted bent double as they introduced her to the abbreviated Australian Way. The heat and the cicadas chanting all night on the opposite side of fly-screened doors, the sensual slithering of iguanas under garden bushes, liberated Lillian to a point which she had imagined she could no longer recuperate. She became re-moistened. Australia was a *new start*.

She went inland. Away from the beating surf into the Outback to purge her soul and lavish her body in the red dust of Bourke, where she watched three thousand sheep being rounded up by a savage with a wide nose pierced by a stick of wood and as many cattle stampeding over the brown plains of pulverised earth. She'd never seen so many animals. She watched it all, sipping civilised tea from a wide wooden veranda. Watched from a distance. Safe. Retaining her British-ness although her English rose complexion had fast waned in the cruel Aussie sun. She watched. From a distance. Safe. The deep hanging purple twilight. She heard its mysterious silence. She felt uneasy at the strange and surreptitious night rustlings and she huddled, minute, inside her Englishness, trying to retain an iota of the Plumstead identity, unconsciously trying, grasping at it in the Bourke star-studded night, yet letting herself drift deliciously away from her Plumstead prudery. Australia was a place where you could open up. Heart, arms, legs, the lot. Australia was a generous land of bountiful wide open people with nut brown faces which broke into a thousand good-humoured wrinkles, Australia in the Fair Dinkum Days was a stress-less place where food was healthy and plentiful and where wine and beer flowed in abundance and parties abounded, where New Australians emerged from the crust of their Mediterranean poverty and began to feel the benefit of their expatriate struggles, Greeks in their coffee shops, Italians in their delicatessen, and where the English Queen was still revered from afar and Lillian loved that. Lillian loved the Australians, Old and New, for that. She even wondered, in the Bourke dust, whether the Aborigines also loved the Queen of England. Funny looking fellow, that one, she commented to her hostess during her slow veranda evening, as she watched a jackaroo settle for the night in his shanty way up on the Ridge, the Ridge which wasn't high, which barely obscured the red-purple black-hilled horizon. Bourke was flatness, uninterrupted flat plane except for the Aboriginal's Ridge and the shanty where he slept which looked in the dusk like the hump of a cow or a sheep. Once she saw a kangaroo hopping with a baby in its pouch, its hind legs kicking up marsupial mounds of russet dust. That was the day her hostess, who allowed her pet dachshund to sleep on a mink coat, her affluence having little in common with Plumstead poverty, drove Lillian around the wide-ranging boundaries of her property, acres and acres away from the homestead; Lillian jolted in an open jeep across the flat ruts and ridges of Bourke, and the gullies which were wide but not deep, in a level and monotonous land. At night she heard the clean cold moonlight call of the dingo-wolf and it chilled her blood in the night. She imagined it creeping close, spying stealthily on the sheep, awaiting the sacrificial lamb, she imagined the dingo, lithe on four slim legs, slinking, flee-bitten, nosing around under the wooden stilts of the veranda, close, intolerably close, to her sleeping and her sleeping was perturbed by shudders down her vulnerable spine. Lillian, oh Lillian! Where have you come to drown your sorrows?

She returned from the big brown Outback to the city diggers.

Did yers see any 'roos? they asked her. What about the Abo's and their wild dogs?

The dingos, you mean?

Good on yer, luv. Yer a little Beauty.

Ooh, they're lovely things, said Lillian with stupid misplaced courage.

They're not much like yer Pommie dogs, are they? sneered a city digger.

And she smirked embarrassedly.

Let's celebrate Lil's return ..... Let's have a party.

She was the life of it.

Lillian again the life of all parties. If Ferdinand Rollins could have seen her then he might well have shed his blonde, if he hadn't already done so.

She worked in the sports store, in a book shop, in an import/export firm. She comforted one boss, tired of him, flitted unfaithfully to another. The only place she didn't flit from was Horace's and Mavis's. There she anchored herself, picking with smutty tactlessness at Mavis' menopause and criticising Horace's chaotic habits. The boozing habits. She did it all with a critical eye. No right to be so critical after the goings-on in her life. Mavis suffered her insensitivity with the cold shivers and hot sweats of her days and cringed away from Lillian's It, and shed tears over her disparaging remarks. Horace's hide was tough and he remained indifferent. Her criticisms were to him like bird-droppings. Lillian was Horace's sister. But she was not Mavis' sister. Gradually, the vituperative accusations began to impinge on the party celebrations too and the Australian bosses weren't so much fun, after all. Even Elsie and Roland were better value than Horace and Mavis' menopause and their London pub more welcomingly grotty than the artificial Australian company house perched like an hotel on top of forty steps. Lillian was about to flit again. London called. She left Sydney, tossed around the Australian coastline, across the Bight to Perth, and way way back across the seas in a cargo boat in which only twelve passengers were allowed, *exclusive* passengers according to Lillian. She tossed and rolled beside the cargo and drank and giggled and gave her body to as many of the *exclusive* passengers and ship's officers as had sufficient need to turn to the crepe skinned cleavage, in much the same way as she had rolled and rioted back to London from Cape Town. Adventure, with years, has a similar taste. She visited exotic countries and immediately forgot where she'd been and what she'd seen. London was awaiting her. And London loomed out of its grey cushions. Its spires and domes and skyscrapers, Lillian's landmarks, were wreathed in drizzle, as Lillian pushed open the heavy door of Roland's saloon bar,

Cor blimey, look 'oos 'eer! If it ain't yer ole duck uv a sister, Elsie!

Lillian gulped as she remembered the diggers and their nut-brown smiles. Not much of a welcome, this. She stayed the night with Elsie and Roland.

She stayed a year with Elsie and Roland. In and out and around London again. But cold. Always cold. Always craving for the lapping warmth of Sydney waters, talking, talking about them to Londoners. She partially smothered her cravings in light opera and musicals, wiping the smouldering tears for her absent Harold from the corner of her eye with the corner of her handkerchief, her breast heaving in the darkness, gulping back the waves of emotion which assailed her. Getting Harold out of proportion. Again. She needed girlfriends to soothe her misdemeanours, with a whisky, or a coffee, or a chat. Her memory was always playing her up. Lillian had a curious sense of perspective, always remembering the good, forgetting the bad and wanting to go backwards. *You can't go backwards Lillian. You're only given one opportunity, one chance to make the most of it, to do it properly, you have to get it right the first time.* They were right when they said it was no good all this crying over spilt milk. She contacted a *friend* who sang in opera. Marlene. Marlene sang in the crowd scenes, crowed her way through the operettas without an aria to herself, although Lillian imagined she was a top-notcher, as Harold had been a top-notcher in Scotland Yard, sought after, always working. The truth was that Marlene did an excessive amount of *resting*. Her mother gave her money so she could always afford to lure Lillian out for a *night on the tiles* so that she might forget her pinpricks of conscience and

Lillian revelled in her theatrical friend and the thrown-in acquaintances. The parties started again and Roland looked at her, listening politely, wagging his head, disbelieving at all the big names she dropped. Disbelieving and disapproving, Roland the Freemason was only glad she went to those parties to keep her out of the house, out of his pub, out of his life. As she had with Horace, Lillian eyed Roland up and down with a critical despising eye, accepting his hospitality in return. If they met in the passageway in the flat they shared above the pub which was Roland's and Elsie's home, he would grunt at her begrudging the time of day and wishing her far away. Sometimes even wishing she were dead, off to join Harold in his grave. She clicked and tut-tutted at him in annoyance, Momentarily, only Momentarily, conscious of his black look, Momentarily feeling unwanted. But the feeling faded and she stayed on, outstaying her welcome.

Until Marlene was called away *on tour*, a year tripping the lights around the States it was to be and life in London felt very glum for Lillian then, because Marlene's theatrical acquaintances fell away, refusing to recognise her. She was only a secretary, after all, not in the Theatre, not One of Them. Elsie was bad-tempered, overworked and a bore to be with and Lillian found herself thinking with fond memories, mistaken memories, of Mavis and her menopause, of the solidity of Horace her brother, of that warm family life back in Sydney.

She could always return there. After all, what was stopping her? She'd saved enough for the fare. She could live initially with them again. They wouldn't mind. Then move out to a place of her own, her Own Real Sydney Pad. The idea was enticing. She wrote a beguiling letter not to her brother Horace, but to her sister-in-law Mavis, a diplomatic letter which would wend its way around Mavis' menopause, an endearing note promising that she would find her own place as quickly as possible, the very moment she had found an income which shouldn't be difficult because Australia was the Land of Opportunity, just as South Africa had been for her once upon a time. She took a large passenger liner this time, a white queen of the waves, a heaving streamlined thing with numerous pockmarks to port and to starboard which were portholes and a strong cream-coloured funnel which shrieked vibrantly into sea mist. Lillian felt excited and novice in her small cabin which creaked newly as the massive liner steamed its way towards the southern hemisphere, ploughing through water and salt, salt and water. She matched her strength against willing gents on deck with games of quoits, she bathed in the gurgling swimming pool letting herself float back and forth, back and forth, with the slopping slapping waves which moved in tune to the Indian Ocean outside. She revelled and rivalled on the dance floor at night, pitching and swaying to the rhythm of the ship. She was cavorting Down Under towards the great promised Land, holding out her arms to Australia and to the men on her way there. She was insatiable. As insatiable at fifty as she'd been at twenty. At fifty her insatiability had an incurably innocent strain to it. A pathos. She never tired of having her crepe stroked. Was there nothing better for her in life? Suddenly the false ceremonies of romance paled to tattered endings, the promises from uniformed males emptied out into the waves, males who had unwittingly searched for their absent wives between Lillian's belly and her breasts, as the Aboriginal Land eased its way towards them out of the horizon, its white-cliffed heads mocking them out of the depths of the Pacific. A second Coming, not home-coming. Lillian steeled her sagging body against the blue-grey steel of Sydney's bridge, that *bloody coat-hanger* to Melbourners, Would the ship's funnel hit it or not, she breathed a sigh of relief as the funnel sank lower and lower, slid silently beneath the Bridge and the majestic queen of the ocean turned its prow, weary now, towards its Pyrmont berth. She leaned over the railings of the ship, touching a uniformed sleeve and giggled a last sea-faring carefree giggle, then shot her eyes into the mass of bodies hustled against one another on the quay. Would Mavis be there to meet her? Horace? They'd said they would. It was after all an occasion, meeting a ship with a month-full of salt encrusted on its stern. As the liner floated, glided submissively to its berth, Lillian spotted Mavis in lemon and white. She crowed and shrieked and gesticulated from on high, but Mavis didn't spot her.

I've just come for a few weeks, you know, she cajoled them as she took renewed possession of her bedroom overlooking the harbour in the house/hotel perched on top of forty steps, Just for a few weeks until I can find a place of my own. Mavis' Adolescent was now fifteen and she eyed Lillian suspiciously, one eyebrow prematurely raised, You remember you used to have It, she blurted, Well that means SA. They told me that at school. Lillian giggled around that one as best she could secretly wondering if the school was some sort of St Trinian's. I forgot to tell you that the last time you were with us. And Mavis retreated to the kitchen. She really hadn't expected her Adolescent to be so tactless. But after four months had passed and Lillian had found herself a job with another Australian boss, but not her Own Real Sydney Pad, Mavis' Adolescent spilt the beans in no uncertain terms: We all thought you were going to find a place of your own. It's alright, but it's really a bit of a nuisance having you here. Again, Mavis retreated to the kitchen. Horace changed cheeks in his chair and cleared embarrassed hoarseness from his throat rather more loudly than was necessary. He accused Mavis' Adolescent – she was only His Adolescent Too when she behaved – of speaking rubbish and out of turn. Lillian squirmed at the biting evidence and earnestly promised her brother that she would find A Room of her Own, not that she realised what she had said because she'd never read Virginia Woolf. Neither had Horace, so it didn't matter.

She promised earnestly and glared at Mavis' Adolescent, swearing inwardly eternal battle with the impudent child. After another year had passed Mavis' Adolescent had forgotten her counselling and Lillian had forgotten her earnest promises, but an abrasive exacerbation arose between the two of them. Mavis' Adolescent was passing through a religious fervour. She had offered her life to Christ, been taken in, gullible Adolescent, at a Billy Graham campaign and she acquired a smugness when gazing upon Lillian. Lillian spat about her when she was alone in the toilet, going to the toilet made her mutter to herself. She would get her own back, she hated smug adolescents and didn't understand youngsters anyway. Her barrenness had taken care of that. Once when Mavis and Horace were away, Mavis' Adolescent was violently ill, retched her heart out she did all over the toilet floor. Then reeled against the toilet walls for sympathy and groaned at the remaining bile in her belly. Lillian was in the kitchen fumbling to prepare a supper, she'd rather lost the knack since the days when she would cook for Harold, Harold the Healthy, Harold the Invalid, lost the knack so that even Mavis' Adolescent now denigrated her attempts and longed for the day when her parents would return. Mavis had a menopause, true, but she still cooked well. Lillian fumbled in the kitchen with utensils more than with ingredients and she heard the bile rumbling in the adolescent belly from afar. It aroused her disgust instead of her sympathy. The smell of vomit, recently ejected, was seeping across the hall and living room towards the kitchen and Lillian screwed up her nose and sneezed into her fumbling supper. Wretched child. She isn't going to spoil my supper. My supper at least will be consumed hot. What a moment to be sick. She can clean it up on her own. On her very own, indeed. Cruel Lillian. Torturer of adolescents. The moaning for sympathy rose in insistent waves and the smell, whether of adolescent bile or of Lillian's supper, was nauseating. Lillian mustered herself and marched, decidedly purposeful for a fumbler, towards her ailing niece, Mavis' Adolescent. Mustering together her years of frustration at having been *done out* of child-bearing, she flung the beastly words at the Niece bent double over her spasms and her vomit.

You'd better clean that filthy mess up and come and have some supper!

That filthy mess is because of *your* filthy suppers.

The Adolescent hated the Aunt with a vengeance at that moment and sobbed with rage into the filthy mess. The Aunt went off, huffed and hurt to the core, Momentarily at least. She would find a Room of Her Own, her Own Real Sydney Pad, she resolved, Momentarily at least. Whilst Mavis' Adolescent gritted her teeth, now soured by bile, and hated and hated and hated, I *hate* her she shrieked inside herself.

The stage grew to be the bitterest pill between them for when, two years hence, Lillian had recovered from her Momentary resolve to branch out alone and had decided to stomach the Adolescent because Mavis' cooking was better than her own, because Horace, her beefy brother, was staunch to lean on, because being Alone was a cold way to be, the Adolescent decided she wanted to be an actress, she'd been told she was *reeelly* good at her school and she believed it and believed that a life on the stage was the only possible thing she could do, I'm cut out for it, she would state categorically, a hint of affectation creeping into the tone acquired at her drama classes. She'd left her life in Christ's hands several months after Billy Graham had departed, for Him to do as He wished with, decided that acting was her line instead of religious counselling, she was gradually turning Left, without realising it, unwittingly protecting the Underdog which made Lillian bite her lower lip in fury because she, as an Underdog herself, admired her Bosses fervently, they were Top-dogs. However, the real difficulty over the theatre, the history of theatre classes, the voice production classes, the movement classes, Mavis' Adolescent had learnt to say *mou*vement, pouting her lips in the French way, was that Lillian was jealous. Embittered at having been shaken off so abruptly by Marlene's theatrical crowd after Marlene had left for the States, Lillian had become sorrowfully aware of her own shortcomings as a valid member of that crowd. Now that had really hurt. A painful coming to grips with one's shortcomings, the lacking which kept one fastened to a permanent state of mediocrity. Truncated aspirations were mortifying to bear. Lillian giggled a lot but she had very little true sense of humour, at least, not sufficient to eye herself up and down with an amused glance now and then. And so the theatre had become a bitter pill to swallow and oh so much bitterer now that the horrendous Adolescent wanted to burst out onto the boards, had actually got as far as inveigling her mother to pay for acting classes and was learning more about the viscera of the stage than she Lillian ever had. She could only retaliate by saying that Of course, the really *great* professionals would never have done it that way, she knew them, they'd told her how they wept on stage, none of this Really Making Yourself Cry. It all had to be acted out, pretended, the tears could be blobs of glycerine even if that meant the actor had to actually appear from the wings weeping the glycerine stuck on by the Stage Manager. Mavis' Adolescent pooh-poohed that, declaring she was capable of bringing real tears to her eyes at the drop of a hat, We're taught *properly,* you see, In your day they didn't know, did they? The ground slid from beneath Lillian's feet. It was jab and pinprick and frustration after frustration. She put up with it for another twelve months before she began to see that Australia wasn't really the Land of Opportunity she had imagined at all. The theatre could *never* compare to the London musicals.

It lacks variety. She would provoke the budding actress.

Varieties are appalling, retorted her tormentor, spiteful enough to twist Lillian's words to suit the jibe which dropped from her tongue and trying very hard to sound intellectual. Lillian cringed at her own nonsensical tastes. She'd loved those leg-kicking variety shows and the gay musicals with their slapstick humour and sugared romance. She wasn't into Chekov and Ionesco and Pinter made her skin creep with his vulgar characters stacked like dirty plates around the kitchen sink.

Lillian missed London, for the truth of it was, that after seven years on and off in Australia, she was at last beginning to realise that she'd made a mistake about the Land of Opportunity and that, in her heart of hearts, she was a Londoner. London was becoming *essential* to her, stuck as she was twelve thousand miles away from it. A pining set in. A sort of long, low moan within for the theatricals who'd rejected her, for the autumn colours, for the winter frosts and November mists, for spring bluebells. She was pained in this brash Land of Opportunity where Opportunity had passed her by. Plumstead became paradise and Lillian had no other emotional option than to book her return passage. Yet again. Horace hoped, but doubted, that she was doing the right thing. He warned Roland that she was on her way. Mavis heaved a massive sigh of relief and her Adolescent just stared dramatically after the receding stern of Lillian's boat, secretly wishing it was she who was wending her way across the world to perform in London.

Ah well! Lillian had missed her Opportunity yet again. Australia was another failure to add to the list of her failures.

If you call that place a land of opportunity ...! Elsie scorned.

Perhaps you don't remember it properly, mused Lillian. After all, you were never there for very long.

Of course I do! How could I forget that dreadful heat? Lying in bed sweating in anguish and exhaustion because I couldn't sleep and knew I had to be up the next day. A silence. And then. Was it work or play you used to go to with all those parties?

I don't know. Lillian giggled. A bit of both, I suppose. We did have a good time. Wistful. I suppose it just wasn't the same as London for me. After all, I was born and bred here.

So was I and I think you were crazy to spend so much time in Australia, though secretly she wished that Lillian had remained there for good, had married an Australian with a substantial bank balance, one of those big sheep farmers with a *station*, had lost herself in the Outback. Anything, except what she had done which was to return to London and plant herself on *me and Roland,* this time putting her roots right down below surface, firmly embedded in the London soil and the cellars of *our pub.* Intolerable years they were with Lillian as an appendage to us, like a leech sucking our blood and money, dithering around our days. At least Roland and

I managed to escape to Australia ourselves for a couple of holidays. Not that we could have left her in charge of the pub, I mean you couldn't leave Lillian *in charge* of anything, could you? She would have ruined our takings. She wasn't a Top-dog, a Manageress, she was an Underdog, needing to be pushed, or mauled, around.

Of course, we really went to Australia because Polly had gone out there at first to work and then to marry. She'd chased her Destiny across the seas. Australia was *her* Land of Opportunity. There she found independence and stability, away from Roland's obsessive control. She escaped in Sydney from her father's morbid possessiveness. Of course, it hurt him, coming to grips with her absence far across the seas and that was why we went to Australia. To visit Polly, Roland to *spy* on Polly, survey her boyfriends. He'd always been adept at that. As if he had any say in it ..... Polly was going her own way and had no need of paternal advice. Secretly, I think Roland was still jealous watching his Polly so sure of herself, bronzed and attractive in the Australian sunlight. I mean, what father permits his daughter to shed the family shackles with ease? Unknown it is for a girl to climb without effort from the family fetters, there's always a father overshadowing her attempts to flee with the hefty weight of his unchallenged authority. But Polly managed. She was lighter, happier, in Sydney. Less spotty. Better nourished, though I say that against my will. She found a job in a department store called Farmers, a buyer's job which fitted her personality like a glove. There again, Roland was disappointed. He'd always wanted her to creep along in his footsteps, be a barmaid, in a decent establishment let it be understood, maybe even own her own place one day. Only too glad I was to see her out of that life. I used to imagine her working in one of those beer-swilling pits on Castlereagh or George Streets. The Aussies used to down their iced beer with a vengeance, with a facility which would lift the heart of any pub owner. I remember Horace's son telling me about their competitions: one beer in every pub in Castlereagh Street, see who could reach the end of the street without keeling over. Reeling they used to be! And they drank their beer freezing cold with an icy haze on the glass. It shook an Englishman's liver to pieces that did. Ruined the taste of the beer, into the bargain. It was an assertion of Australian independence from Britain, a manifestation of thanklessness to the customs and generosity of the Mother Country. Ungrateful I call it. Unjust to the brewers. But then nothing was the same *out there*, was it, nothing was the same as it is *over here*. Different insects they had, those biting ants and lethal spiders, not like our harmless daddy-long-legs, centipedes to triple the length of any I've ever seen *over here*. *Out there* they would appear out of the plug holes in the bathroom, enough to make any god-fearing soul screech. And the gardens full of lizards, those big ones, goannas, sent shivers up my spine and unnerving ripples through my sun-blistered skin. I used to go pink, puce more like it, under those strong rays of sun.

I never knew how you put up with all that sunbathing.

Well you never had much of a skin, did you? I mean, you need a good quality skin to take the sun, like the Mediterranean people.

Tough skin, rhinoceros hide, I'd call it! Thick-skinned like all their droppers-in. Their Neighbours. I've never seen so many uninvited callers all angling to get a quick coffee, a quick drink, out of you. They shamble in and out of each other's houses at any time of the day or night and don't even bother to dress for the occasion, stand on the doorstep nattering, until you had no option but to invite them in for whatever, on the doorstep with their rubber thongs, no stockings the women, nor socks the men. Casual uninvited people who never respected their neighbours' hours and privacy. I couldn't live like that for any length of time and I don't know how you put up with it, I'm telling you, for so long.

They were good scouts, really Elsie.

That's about it. Good scouts, lacking in respectability. Nosey lot, if you ask me. Renowned for their hospitality, Mavis always said. She was too innocent to realise that their hospitality was a way of making sure they poked their noses into your affairs. Bored those women were, without a job to do in the world. Boring too. What could you expect, tucked way down under at the bottom end of the earth, miles away from everything and anything.

They did cling to the Queen, you know. They did respect England. They even used to call it Home.

Well, that shows you, doesn't it? Fancy being born in a place and calling Home another place!

Elsie could see nothing positive about the country which had received her daughter with such welcoming generosity and which Polly had embraced without a qualm and without the slightest feeling of nostalgia. Australia's adoption of Polly, Polly's adoption of Australia, was a problem of considerable dimension to both Elsie and Roland. It meant that they were obliged to spend their hard-earned cash and holidays flying out there to visit her. It also meant that for them, Polly had insulted her true home-land. She'd relinquished her birth-right, betrayed her heritage, Roland's pub, for a mere buying job at Farmers. Elsie and Roland were *disappointed* in Polly to say the least. That didn't seem to worry Polly though. She took to Australia like a duck to water. She even learnt to swim there, something they'd never taught her properly *back home*. Elsie and Roland accused her of being light-headed like her Aunt Lillian because she loved the Australian *way*, she loved the carefree, happy people with brown freckly skins, she loved their easy smiles and the way they welcomed her, unquestioningly, into their lives. If they called her a *pommie*, she laughed it off. She enjoyed the beach parties and the barbecues, told her mother not to take any notice if she saw a goanna peering at her from behind a rock, she revelled in the warmth and the steamy summer weather, she felt free up on the Heads staring out into the wide Pacific, none of that cooped up sensation she'd had in London and particularly in her father's pub. Of that, she had only unpleasant memories and certainly no intention of returning or of making herself a similar life on the other side of the world. Studying Elsie and Roland it was hard to understand how they had produced this *new* youngster, modern in outlook, disrespectful of tradition in a way her parents could never comprehend, independent-spirited and with a sharp eye for a well-padded nest. She accepted her parents' criticisms with an ample humour for one of her age, with the relaxed nonchalance proper to youth. She did not allow Family to worry her one iota. She did not even *hit it off* with Horace's three children, so she stayed away from them and made her own friends. And all the time Polly was growing further and further away from Home. Eventually she married an Australian, a dynamic blond male who sported masculinity at its most muscular, a male who marched his way into Elsie's and Roland's life with brash self-assurance and a minimum of tact for Home traditions. What a blessing they were destined to live so far apart. Elsie and Roland put up with him on their cursory visits and he only bettered in their eyes when he aided Polly to produce their first grandchild. Born on Australian soil. A long, long way from Home. Nothing was ever perfect in life. By that time, Roland had completely given up hope of bequeathing his pub to any of his own lineage.

You seem to forget what I had to cope with back Home whilst you were doing your cavorting in Australia.

Forgot what? You only had the pub to worry about and you were used to that, anyway.

Yes, you've forgotten already. Convenient, isn't it, this business of forgetting!

Well, your own memory isn't so good nowadays, is it?

Perhaps it isn't, but I'll never forget the palaver surrounding father's marriage to Emily.

Emily, the bride.

Roland and I tried to convince him not to marry again. We felt that Nell would have hated the idea. To me it was sacrilegious. But father never considered anyone's opinions and certainly didn't consider what Nelly might have thought from her grave. He'd barely ever considered her alive, when she dared, that was, to voice an opinion of her own. Yes, you were cavorting Down Under whilst Roland and I had to get father and Emily to a registry office. Father had taken it into his head that Emily was the woman who would best accompany him to the threshold of his grave. Nothing I could say about her canny wheedling nature would influence him. She'd become the Apple of his eye, like the pies she'd cooked for him over the years. It was really the Pies he was after, more than the nights and days beside Emily. After all, he was nearing eighty, not a lot more to look forward to apart from gratifying his stomach. Bit late to worry about marriage again though! What he really wanted was a Pie on the table every day and if that meant that he had to have a Ferret in his bed every night, then he would put up with the Ferret. He was adamant. Far from me was it to cross him. Marriage it was to be. He'd forgotten Nell, the unsentimental old devil. We had to help him to dress. He hired a special suit for the occasion and the trouser-bottoms flapped short around his ankles, but he liked grey and the only grey suit was short in the leg and that seemed to worry him less than a suit which fitted perfectly but which was navy blue. For some unknown reason, navy blue grated against Father's limited aesthetic sense. He normally had no sense of colour whatsoever, calling reds browns and yellows oranges. We chose him a maroon tie, bought him new socks and undies and a new pair of black shoes. I even washed his hair for him. He looked quite smart. Proud of himself, as we drove him to the registry office in the Vauxhall, a white carnation in his buttonhole, skin shining and taut on his rosy old cheekbones. Old for a bridegroom, true, but proud all the same. If you'd been in London then you could have helped me with all the running around for his clothes, helped to organise the ceremony afterwards. There were about twenty of us in all, cousins with their wives and husbands and kids, hangers-on who come out of anonymity for weddings and funerals, just appear on the scene for any droppings they can scavenge, then disappear afterwards until the next family *occasion*. Roland and I prepared for it all in our special saloon at the pub, the one we reserved for ceremonies, whether for the freemasons or otherwise.

It was a lot of hard work, Elsie snapped Lillian's head as good as off. And tiring, you know. But what crowned it all was having to suffer Emily. *Me* having to suffer Emily. There again, you would have done that better than I did, you were always her favourite. If you could only have seen her waiting at the registry office, there in that bureaucratic foyer. All alone. She had no-one to accompany her on her Big Day. She'd managed to reach seventy-five without a friend in the world. I remember she was peering about her anxiously eyeing her watch, scared father might stand her down at this her very first marriage. As thin and harsh as a sharp-edged lathe, all steel and metal she was, said Elsie who was also metal. Her weasel's eyes were starting out over her ferret's nose, glinting beadily with nerves they were from behind the navy-blue netting which made a demure attempt to cover her face. Too demure at seventy-five. I thought father might have been put off, save the day and not go through with it, when he saw the navy blue of her netting, but he was too absorbed by the ghost white powder with which she'd plastered her nose, grains of ghost white powder clogged against her lurid red veins and the open pores of her skin. She'd painted her withered lips with vermillion, more appropriate to a girl of twenty.

Ah! Presumptuous Emily.

I suppose, if I could have mustered up any sympathy for her, I might have called her forlorn, a forlorn little figure on the registry office horizon. I mean, all those years of detesting Emily, being *against* her because she'd been *against* me, suddenly faded when I saw her vulnerability. It was sad at seventy-five never to have known conjugal bliss, seventy-five years of solitary longing had been the story of her life. Yet here she was on the brink of it now, on the brink of goodness knows what, and it was as though she was standing there in that bureaucratic foyer on the very edge of a cliff, frail, and about to hurl herself into the abyss below. Terrified she was that Father would stand her down, leave her in the lurch to finish her days in the selfish misery of Oneness. I could see it all as we approached the registry office, her face puckered with fear, as well as a certain self-consciousness. There she was beneath the two pheasant feathers which teetered, almost jauntily, above her brow, red and brown pheasant's feathers which were quite incongruous with the navy netting on her hat. They looked as though they'd been stuck there at the last minute, an unfortunate addendum, an attempt to give the utterly mediocre hat a touch of *flair*. The two feathers sat awry on top of her head, shuddering stupidly in little spurts and starts, as Emily fidgeted from one foot to the other, evidently assailed by a sense of doom. What if he didn't come? She really did seem *out-of-tune* in the registry office foyer, I mean it's hardly normal for one to marry for the first time at seventy-five is it? And I felt genuinely sorry for her.

My sympathy was short-lived, however. For the very moment she caught sight of us approaching, slowly, hesitantly, me and Roland and father-on-my-arm, that was, she tripped towards us, her sloppy shoes sagging on the extremities of her pin legs which were striped bluely with varicose veins. Hardly the legs of a bride. Immediately she lashed out in her shrilly voice, more piercing than ever because of her nerves, whipped her tongue across her lips and gave us a piece of her mind for keeping her waiting. Father looked guiltily up at the ceiling, feigning curiosity for the ugly chandelier hanging just above us. He looked painfully bewildered. I protested that we were on time, which was true, there were still ten minutes to go. But she insisted, shrilly and accusing, that we'd kept her waiting and if that was any indication as to how their marriage was going to be, well it just wasn't good enough.

Intolerant Emily.

She didn't seem to realise that half the fun of being old is that the little time one has left is to be used as one wishes, unhurried, unpressured, yet here she was already trying to jostle and harass Father. What was he getting himself into? The angry white tip of her nose poked through the clogs of powder and sniffed at the navy netting which moved in and out in time with her jerky breathing.

Calm down Emily, suggested Roland with a diplomatic and characteristic wag of his head, Calm down he said, seeing father looking *put upon.* The quarrels come after your marriage, not before it. I don't need any advice from you, young man. Take heed of that! She snapped Roland's head off in a flash of defensive spite. And glared at me into the bargain, as though we were responsible for perpetrating the delay on purpose. It was then that disgust replaced sympathy. I still tried to smile at father, even though dislike was oozing out of me, encourage him to wage on into battle if that was what he wanted. *Was* it what he wanted? Did he really know what he wanted? I often think he only re-married, apart from the Apple Pies of course, to try and recapture something of the old spark. Whatever the reason, marriage seemed a drastic course to me. But Roland and I had organised the wedding breakfast and other guests were already arriving, so there was nothing for it but to wipe the bitterness from our faces and continue to play out the ridiculous farce. Emily drew herself up, drew her cheeks in, as if to savour her last breath as an inveterate spinster, the pheasant feathers tottered and the navy netting stuck to her nostrils making the white tip of her nose look as though it was caught in a fishing net. Father also drew himself up, looked proudly, if bewilderedly, at the guests and pointed his nose in the direction of the ceremonies room. Bride and bridegroom they entered. Husband and wife they emerged.

Emily, the wife.

Father, more bewildered than ever at the reception, looking about him wanly as if searching for someone who wasn't there - perhaps it was Nell - eventually drank himself into a coma. Emily spent the entire gathering, which was in her honour as a married woman, bitching about the fact that we hadn't made more of an effort, a reception properly organised in a nice hotel. She bossed and criticised her way through the event. Do I have to tell you what a relief it was when it was all over? Particularly for me when Emily said in her usual cutting manner, What a pity Lillian couldn't have been there for her day, Lillian would have brightened things up, wouldn't she? I remember gulping.

The ungrateful Emily.

But Lillian wasn't there, was she? Lillian couldn't be found... She was in Australia. If you ask me, you did some pretty convenient trips in your time.

You accuse me as though I was away on purpose. How was I to know Father would want to re-marry whilst I was in Australia?

But you could have returned home a couple of months earlier than you did.

You didn't tell me about the wedding in time, did you? Otherwise I just might have been able to organise my trip home before I did. As it was, I had to give a month's notice, couldn't just walk out on them like that, could I? Elsie tut-tutted disbelievingly. She stared hard at Lillian with a mincing look, literally as though she could chop her up into very tiny pieces.

It wasn't only the wedding, you know, she snapped sharply. It was their marriage after that. Because after the wedding, straight after it in fact, there was no honeymoon. Father was too miserly to take his new wife away anywhere, or perhaps too ashamed to show her in public, and they spent their wedding night in a room in our pub and bumped into Roland at breakfast the next morning, to his disgust. He said that Emily looked fearfully crotchety, he'd never seen her in an unwashed state before and to see the seventy five year old newly-wed was too much for any good man, as she shoved past him into the toilet, her pink vyella nightie crimped around her emaciated thighs revealing the varicose legs and the knobbly knees, her eyes heavy with sleep, so heavy that one eyelash was stuck down fast giving her a cyclopean air. And he said she burped and her breath smelt, the breath of an old married lady, thick and clammy, it mingled with the odour of beer which was constantly present in every nook and cranny of the flat, wafting upwards as it did from the bar, invading our living quarters. We were normally accustomed to it, but it only needed another contrasting smell for it to be thrown into relief and those were the times when I wished myself far from beer and pubs and from Roland too. Anyway, he said he wondered what sort of a night of it Emily had had. She didn't look de-flowered. He didn't believe father capable of consummating the marriage in the condition in which he'd gone to bed. Or in any condition, for that matter. Roland wondered in fact if the marriage would ever be consummated.

Well, as I was saying, immediately after their marriage, father took it upon himself to pester me, and therefore Roland, more than he ever had before. Prior to his marriage, he'd been easy enough to manage, calm enough, making his way over to see us once a fortnight on Friday evenings, no more. Emily had always done his housekeeping ever since Nell died and he'd seemed quite contented with that arrangement, paying her for her pains with a peck on the cheek now and then. Don't think there was ever any more to it than that. And back she'd go to her own place to her two front rooms with the welsh dresser. But since they'd married, her wheedling turned itself into bossing. She insisted, he told me, on ousting his old mahogany side-board and on replacing it with her welsh dresser. She tormented him if he left his clothes lying around whereas before she had meekly gathered them up herself. She criticized him if he spent too much at the local, goodness knows, it was worth paying a mint I would have thought just to escape from her moaning. He confided in me that everything he did now was wrong. His old voice even cracked when he said pathetically that his house no longer seemed to be his own. When Emily had wheedled, it had been him who'd felt sorry for her. Now she'd become a tyrant and we, Roland and I, should feel sorry for him. Don't say we didn't warn you, Dad! Father's visits to us were an *escape*, an attempt to opt out of the distasteful contract he had signed that day in the bureaucratic registry office. He lost weight and began to look livid around the gills. Sunken cheeks. Pale skin. You know. No, of course you don't know! You weren't there to see him like that. You only knew him in his robust days.

I keep telling you Elsie, that wasn't my fault.

Elsie was worked up in the fever of her memories.

I'm not so sure about that, she said viciously. Father was a wreck, a wreck when he died. The only thing that kept him alive all that time with Emily was the Apple Pies. Religiously every Sunday and every Wednesday she served him her Apple Pie. As for the rest of the contract, well it had been an error. Roland had been right on that first morning. Father couldn't bring himself to consummate the marriage. He even whispered to me that there was nothing attractive about her. I answered him curtly, There never has been anything attractive about her and marriage isn't going to change that. He should have known that. He wasn't born yesterday. But I thought she'd *look after* me, *care* about me, he confessed. And feed you on Pies, I suggested. Her apples are still sweet he contested, it's she who's turned sour, as bitter as one of her raw cookers. Emily might have turned sour, To me she always had been, she might have been consuming father, but she was thriving on doing just that. She had come into her own as it were. For the first time in her life she had a man in her grip, her very own man. She'd grasped her marriage contract with an iron clasp and had no intention of budging on any of the issues which she considered to be her prerogative within that contract. She had suffered herself for too many years to let others off scot free, and that included her Only Beloved. In a vaguely conscious sense, she blamed father for her suffering. When she had needed him, he wouldn't renounce Nell and us children. After Nell died, it had taken him years to accede to her, Emily's, wishes. And now that she finally had him in her clutches, the roses had found their way to her cheeks. There was a gloat in her beady eyes, a sarcastic leer in her expression, croaking triumph in her voice. She put on weight as fast as father lost it. She at least was benefitting from the Apple Pies. She gained around the girth which emphasised her spindly varicose legs, she stomped along as if her legs were two sticks which might break under her newly acquired plumpness. At long last, at seventy-five, Emily had grown into her *middle-aged spread*. Marriage afforded her a certain complacency, an authority in society, even if that simply meant better treatment, a doff of the cap from the greengrocer and postman. She must have been without the *curse* for years by then, but it was as though she'd only just settled comfortably into her middle life. The extra weight filled out a few of the wrinkles in her face. She was losing the haggard look of old, the gaunt goading expression. She was blossoming strangely before our eyes. And she lived her marital state every minute of the way, apart from the consummation that was, which never appeared to worry her. She did all the caring she possibly knew how to do. Her caring was bossing, bulldozing, pushing Father around and, more often than not, out of the way. He interfered with her cleaning. She wanted him out of the house and so he came to us more and more for refuge. Took his refuge at one end of the bar counter, sunken in his pale old age. His gaze was wan and many a time I had to drive him back home in the evening because if I hadn't done so, he would never have returned to his shrew. How he regretted having married, he said. He never spoke much of Nell but just occasionally he'd mutter that Nell had cared for him without bossing and bulldozing. At least, as far as he remembered. It was pointless to insist that he'd made a mistake. Let sleeping dogs lie. My job, as his daughter, his only daughter present that is, was to be patient and help him through his last few years as equably as possible. Emily, meanwhile, was blind to the effects of her bullying and I didn't dare to confront her outright about it. I mean, I wasn't brought up to speak out of turn, was I? Nell hadn't educated us to poke our noses into other people's matrimonies, although I think you did a fair bit of that in your time, didn't you?

Oh, don't be so unfair Elsie. All I did was to live with you until I'd found a place of my own.

That took you some time, didn't it? And you criticised all of us enough, as if it was your business the way we lived, Roland and me and Horace and Mavis.

I thought we were talking about Emily, not about me!

One and the same, mumbled Elsie just out of Lillian's hearing. She huffed into her moustache and poured herself another gin. Yet another gin. About time we thought about bed, she yawned, downing the stiff contents of her glass and banging her elbow sorely against the wall as she momentarily lost her balance. Damn!

Well, you shouldn't drink so quickly, warned Lillian.

Oh shut up, silly cow! Elsie was in an evil humour. An inebriated humour. It was the thought of yet another night lying awake listening to her sister's snores. It was the unpleasant memory of Emily and father's last years. It was the gin.

I don't know if I'll go to bed yet. Lillian was comfortably oblivious to Elsie's caustic abuse and fondled her half glass of whisky with a lingering affection. It was the warmest thing she had in life.

Go when you like, but don't disturb me if you're going to sit up and don't wake me when you're getting undressed. Her admonition couldn't have been more explicit.

Oh well. Perhaps I'd better come to bed now. Indecisive and timorous as usual.

Come when you like, spat the acrid sister, spraying Lillian's perm with a light spurt of semi-swallowed gin. But make up your mind and stop dithering.

Lillian downed the remaining whisky in her glass as Elsie had downed the remaining gin in her glass. A bubble appeared, uninvited, at the corner of Lillian's mouth. Her perm was flattened on one side where she'd dozed earlier on in front of the tele and her hairnet was askew. She looked haphazard and agedly fatigued. Weary of it all. The biting back, the accusations, the complications of having to live in more than one place at a time. She'd never mastered the art of ubiquity although she had practised it all her life.

As the two sisters lay side by side in their twin beds, night and silence fell between them and somewhere, nestling far back in Elsie's subconscious, was a parallel with the nights they had shared together as children. Side by side they'd been as teenagers, before Lillian had broken the family harmony, that was. And side by side again as old ladies they were. Like a full circle.

But of course, Father died eventually, you know. As though it was Lillian's fault.

Of course he did. I know that. There was a shield of defence in her tired old voice.

You might know it. But you weren't there to see it! And Lillian could almost see Elsie's moustache bristling with acrimony. She dared to glance in her direction and saw in a flash the disgruntled sisterly mouth lit up vivid green as the neon light from the Italian restaurant flashed momentarily upon it. Green hairs on a disgruntled upper lip. Elsie with green lips. How unpleasant! And she thought at that moment that she really hated her younger sister. She was a torment in Lillian's life. Then she checked herself. What am I doing here with her then? Why do I stay with her? I shall leave tomorrow morning, go back to my own flat and only come and visit her when she's ill.

Would Lillian leave in the morning?

I really do think that Emily forced him prematurely to his grave, she pushed him right to the edge of it with her dictatorial ways and then gave a final spiteful shove, declared Elsie, licking the fur which was already beginning to settle like mildew on her teeth for the night after the generous helpings of gin.

I think it's nasty of you to blame Emily.

How would you know? You've never been able to read through Emily and, besides, you weren't there, she insisted again. This time, Lillian was well and truly silenced. Do you know, that towards the end, when Father became bedridden, Emily used to call for my help every day? I had to spend every morning over in Plumstead with her before coming back to serve in the pub at the lunchtime session. She couldn't cope by herself. She whined that her back ached, her limbs were sore from lifting father about. He was heavy, admittedly, despite the fact that he was rapidly wasting. Do you know, during his final weeks he wouldn't even eat her Apple Pie. Lost interest. Totally and utterly. With life and with Apple Pie. As for Emily, his pale sunken eyes looked right through her as though she were invisible, a nonentity. She kept on telling him she was there for him, but he must have thought that he'd take silent revenge on her after all her dictating and wheedling, for he never so much as mumbled an answer. Then her eyes would fill with crocodile tears, she would sniff vigorously through her ferret's nose and turn her back disconsolately on him, on purpose. How's that for treatment? And from a freemason. Don't go much on their swearing of secret oaths to brotherhood and mankind when he can't so much as breathe a loving word to the wife who cares about him in his final hours. Ssh! I would whisper crossly. Didn't she ever know when to stop, the vituperative old wretch! Here she was, still criticising, while father's soul was caving in and his body crumbling to dust. They were tiring mornings those, by his bedside. He would plead pathetically with me every day to come again, Don't forget to come tomorrow, Else. His voice was thin and reedy. Please come and see me, As if I was the only person he had in the world. In fact I was. Emily meant nothing to him now that he couldn't stomach her Apple Pie, Nell had long been a thing of the past and of course, neither you nor Horace was there. His freemasonry might have been a friendly brotherhood, but none of them ever dropped in to see him and they knew he was dying because Roland told them at the meetings, yet they never had time to visit, always too busy with one thing or another.

Funny set up that freemasonry, muttered Lillian. Horace once told me about his initiation ceremony when he was only nineteen and father was Master of the Lodge. Said he had to roll up one trouser leg and bare his breast or something. I asked him why and he didn't even know the reason, so I don't think it did him much good.

Yes, but Horace never took it seriously, did he? He was always abroad. Roland used to go regularly to the meetings, and he took his secrecy oath very much to heart and never divulged a word of it. They never wanted women involved anyway. It was a bit of a macho set up if you ask me. As for doing good or whatever outside their own particular circle, all I can say is that some of those fellows who attended the meetings were a sour-looking lot. Smug they were, too. They'd come down to the bar for a drink afterwards, their faces smothered in secrecy, as though they possessed a knowledge the rest of us didn't have. To tell you the truth, I never had much time for them. Only put up with them because Roland wanted it. I just let him get on with it. But personally, I don't have any more time for sects of any description than I do for religion itself. Or for your Christian Science for that matter.

Look at you, she cruelly accused Lillian, spending months of your life coughing your heart out with bronchitis just because you believed the Lord wanted it that way. Damn stupid if you ask me!

I didn't ask you! Lillian fidgeted uncomfortably under the sheets of her borrowed bed.

Why do you think your Lord made men into doctors? Answer me that one! What's medical progress for? Your way is as good as crouching down to an early death. I would have thought we've an obligation to save and to savour life where possible, not just crumple up under a spluttering cough the way you do, refusing to call the doctor and hoping the Lord will reward you in some other life. You've got some funny ideas if you ask me.

I've told you already, I didn't ask you! Lillian felt the sheets almost pricking against her. The doctors didn't do father much good, did they, or Harold, or Roland for that matter.

Yes they did. They alleviated their final hours on earth. I mean, they weren't meant to last any longer, were they? When your count's up, it's up, as far as I'm concerned.

Well, there you are, caught in your own argument. That's just what I believe. It's all mapped out for us beforehand. Destiny they call it and no doctor can reverse Destiny.

I'm talking about alleviating pain, snapped Elsie feeling she was losing ground and frankly surprised that Lillian had made such a stand, dared to stand up for herself, particularly when she was sleeping in a *borrowed* bed. She ought to be grateful about that instead of laying into me. She turned her back on her sister with a determined shrug. and thought I must. Absolutely *must*. Get rid of that bed tomorrow.

IX

ALMERIAN RAINS

Elsie did get rid of the spare bed. A week later she sold the spare bed. Without a word to Lillian, she sold it, or rather gave it for a song, to a street hawker. Was she relieved! After concluding her deal, she hurried breathless with the excitement of a good thing accomplished, back into her bedroom. That would prevent Lillian from staying with her. There was nowhere she could possibly sleep now except sprawled on the floor of her lounge and Elsie considered that Lillian was hardly agile enough to camp on people's floors. After all, one had to preserve a certain dignity at eighty. If one didn't, then being eighty was positively degrading. She stared at her own bed and decided that her sleeping quarters looked somehow bereft, unbalanced, without the second bed. To remedy that, she pushed and pulled and panted at her own bed until it occupied a centre place in the small area off the lounge that served as her bedroom. She placed the two small bedside tables one on each side of her bedstead. On one of them there was a metal ashtray in yellow and black featuring a kangaroo and a boomerang, aboriginal art commercialised into a souvenir and purchased by Polly for her parting gift. For burnt cigarette butts to be stubbed out upon. On the other there was a small leather-cased travelling alarm ticking away beside a photo of the Young Roland, Roland complete with jaunty moustache and sleek black brylcreemed hair. Rather like a would-be Errol Flynn. He still accompanied Elsie in her solitary nights, from the photo that is. Some nights she would look at his paper face fondly, whisper an endearment before covering herself with the bed clothes, because Elsie, as we know, was compassionate despite her metallic nature. Other nights it might be a matter-of-fact peck on his glass cheek. Other nights she simply stared at him vacantly, without recognition, confused as to how to place him in her life, befuddled by the gin as to how much he really had meant to her, what her marriage signified to her now, had she ever been married, that is? Such a long time ago it was.

When Lillian turned up two days later, uninvited and unwelcome as usual, she didn't notice the missing piece of furniture at first and Elsie said nothing to her about it, let her discover it on her own. Which she eventually did, just after downing her fourth pre-lunch whisky. Fired by the liquid she exclaimed, she slurred,

Somebody's taken my bed away, did you realise?

Since *when* was it *your* bed? Gin made Elsie valiant.

Well, I used to use it.

I decided the room was too cluttered, couldn't get at my own properly to make it, pointless having two beds and anyway you only used it occasionally.

Lillian was Mortified. At long last, after all these years, her Mortification was complete, the ultimate in revenge had been accomplished, Elsie had got her own back for the taunting in the childhood bathtub. And although she didn't actually remember that infantile incident any longer, a peculiar sense of justice crept over her in pleasurable waves.

Where on earth will I sleep now?

In your own bed in your own flat.

Why is cruelty always meted out in the wrong doses at the wrong moments? Elsie had borne Lillian's company for years when they were younger and had then been too cowardly to spit out the awful truth that her sister was upsetting her marriage to Roland. That Lillian had even been part of the reason why Elsie had poked her tongue out at Roland. Yet, here she was now, lashing out at a decrepit and defenceless old woman. Defenceless?

Lillian still did have it in her to escape occasionally for, apart from her visits to Horace, she went abroad. And with the most disparate company. As she had once on a trip to Madrid, ostensibly to visit her niece, Mavis' Adolescent-now-older-and-wiser, as a matter of fact, yet the trip coinciding suspiciously with a Queen's Messenger. Dapper little fellow if ever there was one. Ideal he was for the job of accompanying the diplomatic valise in and out of England around the world. He was *fraightfelly* well spoken, excruciatingly timid and so it was as well that he had a Bag to travel with on the seat beside him instead of a fellow passenger, particularly on those long journeys, the *really* overseas journeys to places in Asia or Australia where HMG still deigned to maintain the odd outpost. If he'd had a real passenger beside him on one of those long journeys, he would have arrived at his destination smothered in confusion, would have forgotten the Bag and would have tumbled unwittingly into all sorts of dire trouble. No, it was preferable that he be accompanied by the Bag alone and in the spacious first class. He was in fact so self-conscious that he blushed to the roots of his sandy hair if anyone so much as addressed him. He would arrive at his destination, he preferred the *really* foreign places where people were black or yellow and spoke inaccessible languages, they were easier to hide behind. He would take HMG's car assigned to him at the airport, sit beside the Bag on the back seat at sufficient distance from the chauffeur so as not to have to bid him any more than a brusque time of day, be whisked to HM Embassy, be hosted up in the lift to the Top Floor by an ingratiating porter who bowed and scraped before the Messenger and his Bag. The Top Floor was reserved for Home-based officers only, for Those who had passed Civil Service examinations and reams of Red Tape, Those who worked with Top Secret files, Who nosed into Confidential papers, Those who had exclusive access over and above the locally-engaged staff to HMG's private bottle supply and the best of British titbits in the Embassy Shop. The dapper Queen's Messenger, Lillian's *friend,* would deposit the Bag on the reception counter of the Top Floor somewhere behind all the Red Tape, whisper a flummoxed good morning or afternoon to any Top Secret Secretary who happened to be present and retreat as rapidly and as surreptitiously as he had entered. Whenever humanly possible, he would catch the very next Homeward bound airplane thus evading any embarrassing invitation which any of the Top Secret officers might extend to him. With the exception, that is, of one invitation on that particular time in Madrid. An invitation extended not by any Top Secret officer but by Lillian herself who just *happened* to be staying with her niece-Mavis'-Adolescent and who offered him a rendezvous in a centrally-situated-hotel. Mavis' Adolescent-now-older-and-wiser experienced faint surprise at Lillian's goings on with a gentleman who appeared all meekness and who was almost two decades her junior. That was when Lillian said she had a rendezvous *just for a few hours*, although she really had come to Madrid to see her niece and family, and could Mavis' Adolescent pick her up at the centrally-situated-hotel just a little before midnight, she didn't fancy being whisked off into the Madrid night by any of those Spanish taxi drivers as she'd once been whisked off into the Egyptian desert by a camel guide. As fortune would have it, she'd had enough money in her voluminous bag to satisfy the Egyptian camel driver's greed, he was one at least who wasn't after the crepe cleavage, and he guided her back to the group of florid-faced tourists without further mishap. When Mavis' Adolescent arrived in the foyer of the centrally-situated-hotel at approximately a quarter to midnight, she saw Lillian engrossed in the most animated of conversations, all smiles and giggles and lid-flashing under her wispy grey brows, her short neck hunched comfortably into the luxurious backing of a red plush armchair. The dapper Queen's Messenger, almost two decades her junior and impeccable apart from a sandy quiff he had cultivated for the occasion into a sensual unruliness, was sitting on the generous arm of Lillian's chair, knees very close, actually colliding gently from time to time and in response to Lillian's smiles and giggles and lid-flashing-beneath-grey-brows, his face was glassy-eyed and a drop of unswallowed whisky decorated the corner of his lower lip. He was gazing at Lillian as if to say that she, and only she, could make him happy and forget the appalling shyness which was the bane of his life. Mavis' Adolescent, Lillian's niece that was, many, many years after her vomiting session in the toilet of the Sydney home, watched this interplay from a distance before deciding to approach the sentimentally entwined couple. She was both amused and aghast to contemplate these septuagenarian thrusts at love. Or infatuation. Because Lillian would easily be infatuated with a Queen's Messenger, more for his title and the important messages entrusted to his care, than for the dapper little gentleman himself.

Lillian was a daring tripper. Once she travelled from Paris to southern Spain by train, all on her very own when she was seventy five, almost as daring as Emily's first marriage to Father at seventy five. She'd awoken on that journey, jerked from her dreams-in-motion at four o'clock in the morning, to feel the whole railway carriage being hoisted into the air. They told her it had to do with the wheels of the train, they'd probably told her that it was to adapt the wheels to the gauge of the Spanish rails, but Lillian's French didn't run to that extreme and she spent the rest of the journey rattling through the Spanish hinterland in fear and dread of mechanical difficulties which might oblige her to spend a night in some unknown lodgings in the very heart of this utterly foreign land. For when Lillian went on her travels, she normally did so with others, tagging along in a group of British human noise, lapping up sights and sounds to the tune of shrill exclamations. Lillian made so many friends on her organised tours. *Friends*, all of them, who remained on the surface of life and its sensations. She still, incurably, frequented the bottom-pinchers and the back-slappers and the female gossips. With these she nourished her days. Yet this time she'd taken advantage of a *free* train journey and had decided to visit a *friend* who happened to be sunning herself in a southern region of the Iberian Peninsula, Almería as a matter of fact, just in front of Africa. At least, the *friend* had gone to Almería with the intention of sunning herself and of visiting mini-Hollywood, as indeed had Lillian. But alas, it was prevaricating spring weather and even in Almería it has been known to rain in that season. In fact it rained so hard, so absolutely torrentially, that Lillian and her *friend* who had been dining out one evening, were obliged to remove their shoes and stockings and wade barefoot back to the hotel. Lillian had never seen torrents like this one. The gutters overflowed and the water rushed murkily, swished noisily, gurgled succulently, pulled chaotically at her bare ankles. The night was dark in an ill-lit street and the two English ladies clutched at one another on their intrepid journey, shivering and dripping and whimpering at each other. From time to time they squealed as invisible objects wrapped around their toes, beat against their ankle bones, oozed pulpy under their metatarsals and all the time there was the frightening angry swirl of the overflowing drains. Cars swished by, spraying and flooding and their passengers gaped and gawked at the two drenched English ladies, for English alone could they be, their plaid skirts gripping their thighs, their jumpers their bosoms. Drenched and diminished in the half-lit street, perms bedraggled and handbags squelching liquid, they eventually found their way to the hotel. There they were the laughing stock of two novice receptionists who had never set eyes on anything quite as amusing as these two aged *señoras* soaked to the skin, all their artifices to beauty swept away in the deluge leaving only two pale faces, two blue noses, mascara running black rivulets from four eyes through white streaks of powder, hair straggling uncontrollably. Shivering, still clutching each other for support as if confronting an inquisition instead of a pair of amused receptionists, they stammered their room numbers in a Spanish which brought more mirth bubbling to the surface of the two novice receptionists. The two ladies, unladylike, stumbled towards the lift, decidedly uncomfortable both with their reception and because water was dripping and trickling ceaselessly, from the stringy perms, between their breasts, down their calves. It was a very damp Mortification for Lillian, that one. She wrote an energetic letter of complaint to the hotel manager. In English, of course. Advising him to fire the novice receptionists, a grumpy letter because the weather hadn't been as she and her *friend* had anticipated, Not that that was the hotel manager's fault but he had to admit that it had rather plastered gloom over their holiday. What would the Spanish hotel manager have made of the *plastered gloom?*

After that unfortunate incursion into Almerían Spain, the mini-Hollywood wasteland, Lillian decided to stick to her groups and always to take an umbrella wherever the sun was meant to be shining. She'd become *almost* wise in her old age. She struck Spain with a vehemence off her itinerary and she went to Cyprus, to Malta, even on safari to Kenya, where she broke her arm leaning over too far to watch a pregnant hippopotamus pawing the mud with its massive hooves. She'd never seen so enormous a living thing in her life. Not worth breaking your arm over Lillian. She had her arm attended to by a charming Kenyan doctor to whom she later referred back Home as a witchdoctor, quite surprisingly as he had graduated from London university with honours. Lillian had difficulty with her prerogatives at times. She muddled concepts. She muddled places and names and events and Elsie used to tell her it was time she put an end to her cavorting abroad, hadn't she seen enough of the World? Elsie thought that the World had probably seen enough of Lillian. After all, her visits had been frequent but her penetration into foreign lands limited. She'd visited. But she had not penetrated. And so for once in her life, Lillian took heed of Elsie and decided that perhaps she was right. The World could get along without her visits and, besides, she was cosy and warm at Elsie's flat. Before she'd rid herself of the spare bed, that was. Where was she to sleep then?

Elsie's flat was forlorn and more mundane than ever without a spare bed. There'd been spite and resentment in Elsie's action. A spite and resentment which it was too hard for Lillian, after four glasses of pre-lunch whisky, to analyse. It was a spite which needled deep into her conscience, a resentment which hung over her like a stifling pall. She wanted to extricate herself. She was feeling victimised by Elsie. But she didn't know how to get away. The path was long and the road rough. It was cold outside. And Lillian was very, very tired. Where would she sleep then that night? She brushed the problem away into oblivion over lunch as she masticated tough roast beef and starchy lumps of potato and stared glumly at the yellowing blue of Elsie's latest rinse. Her hair looked hollow, empty, with the light filtering through it, Lillian thought. Sparse and frankly ridiculous, that scalp rinsed with blue. Her own hair was still thick, covered her scalp it did, even if it could no longer be called lush, but it was better quality hair than that of her sister-who-had-sold-her-spare-bed, Emily had always praised her for her hair when she was a child. A cold sweat of anguish interrupted Lillian in the middle of her caramel cream. After the cold sweat, a lump of junket slithered down the wrong way nearly choking her and her protruding eyes streamed with nausea and with tears of feeling rejected. Elsie didn't even pat her on the back. She let her get on with the coughing and the streaming. Her heart was not to be turned. And it was too late now to summons the spare bed back anyway. She knew that the junket had little to do with Lillian's choking. She, Elsie, had not been born yesterday.

The afternoon passed with its customary dozing. At eighty odd and with four whiskies and a solid helping of starchy potatoes inside one's body, there was little which enticed one away from the home fires, even though they were the fires - or radiators - of someone else's home and the spare bed had been taken away. For many years now, since the retirement from their respective jobs of work, both sisters had regarded their afternoon doss as a hallowed thing and if, when they awoke, the winter's afternoon had yielded its still grey to the dark of early evening, No matter, for it was time for a cuppa to be followed smartly by the first whisky, or gin, of the evening. When spirits rose. This habit of alcohol, it bound them relentlessly to unflinching routine. Everything else in their lives bowed down to the dictates of alcohol. Elsie and Lillian themselves bowed down to the dictates of alcohol. It ruled them for two or three hours before the lunches which they often forgot to eat, and again, it ruled their evenings almost entirely, something like six hours of drinking, when it was difficult to calculate whether it had been six whiskies or eight. The drinking, the spasmodic conversation, mere utterances really, the dozing in and out of television programmes, the preparing of a sandwich too often left to turn stale by the morning, cigarette after cigarette and the repetitive reading of books, these last being exclusive to Elsie. Lillian hadn't smoked for years and she didn't read books. We know that. Whatever else, always, the drinking. A day wasn't worth living without a drink.

This then was the shape and content of their evenings, whether alone or together. The alcohol was nibbling at their brains, like a grub at a cabbage leaf, not the voracious devouring of the caterpillar, rather the slow yet inexorable consuming of the unhurried slug, a lazy chewing in spurts and starts, which advances with cautious inroads to gnaw at the very marrow of the mind. Old age is sore and laborious in its unadulterated state. With alcohol, it is aggravated to a precocious senility.

Against her will, Lillian needed Elsie and her spare bed. Because she needed her, she thought she desired to be with her. All she really needed and desired was to pamper her Self. She would happily have seen Elsie far distant. At least if she'd been far distant then she, Lillian, could have used Elsie's bed in the absence of the spare bed. Where was she going to sleep that night? Deep-rooted routine prevented her from so much as considering returning to her own flat after a whole afternoon with Elsie. She looked about her through a fogged brain, her glazed eyes rested unseeingly on the objects in Elsie's room. She was hunched into her solitude when Elsie stated abruptly that she was Off. To bed. You'd best be Off too. Home to your place. Lillian cringed on hearing the verdict she'd been dreading to hear all afternoon. Home to your place. It rang out with the cruel clarity of an icy morning. There was a long silence. After which. Elsie rose, knocking her ashtray, as she habitually did, butts and ash cascading to the carpet, and wended her way, as she habitually did, to the toilet to empty her bladder.

Meanwhile, Lillian had had a brainwave. She had no intention of being ousted from Elsie's flat, particularly as she had no desire to return to Horace for the time being. She was in a sense even grateful to Elsie, whatever she'd done with the spare bed, to be able to be with her because nights with Horace were becoming increasingly disagreeable. Many a time she was called upon to guide Horace to bed, he in his cups, she in hers. She would offer him her worn bowed shoulders as support for his sodden weight, his hefty body, beleaguered by whisky and, clinging to his hands, drag him along the corridor from the lounge to his bedroom, Horace in turn dragging his gammy foot as best he could behind him. Lillian was like St Christopher guiding the weary traveller, although she couldn't always manage to get him safely to his destination. If she was full of whisky, she would trip on a piece of rucked carpet and down they would go, both of them, crashing to the floor, a flaying mass of ancient inebriated limbs, a casting of oaths to right and left, it was *always* Lillian's fault, this business of crashing to the floor at night, it was smothering Horace with bruises, it was the degradation of the eighty year old sprawler. Then of course, she could never haul him up, not for want of trying, the puffing efforts which made her almost sober, were useless, Horace weighed a ton. Invariably, he would have to spend the hours until he sobered sufficiently to pull himself up, prostrate on the hall floor, bruised and befuddled beneath a blanket, which Lillian would pull haphazardly from a wardrobe to cover him with chaotic folds. Sometimes he knocked his hand or his head, gashing and gouging at his own body and limbs and extremities as he crashed downwards, as if to leave a reminder which he might heed the next morning to moderate his habits. Sometimes he knocked pieces out of his teeth. Mostly, the following day he remembered nothing of his misdemeanours and wondered, in a passing moment of reflection, how he had so many wounds, the war had finished long ago, not that he'd ever been gravely wounded during the war, as a sea-farer the worst which had happened to him had been a leap through his porthole onto the deck outside to avoid a jagged piece of shrapnel which had shot through the open door of his cabin after a mild explosion on board the ship. After Lillian had ascertained that Horace was warm and out for the count, after she had done the appropriate amount of fussing, she would search for the comfort of her own little bed in the primrose room and flake herself out, exhausted after her efforts and swearing to leave Horace the very next day. Lillian hadn't been enjoying her visits to Horace of late. So she was determined to cling onto the modicum of comfort and company which Elsie and her flat afforded her.

Thus. Whilst Elsie was evacuating her water, and her gin, Lillian rose to her feet and began grappling with the cushions, the heavy sofa cushions first, she cast them to the ground and kicked them stumblingly, one, two, three, into a line, then two of the softer decorative cushions with bedraggled edges, she threw down as a pillow, then she looked around her for something to cover herself with. For Lillian was making up her own bed. Out of the way, under the lounge window concealed from Elsie's view, behind the lounge sofa. In her own bland and unintelligent way, she was not to be beaten by the sale of a spare bed. Her eyes alighted on her overcoat. It would make an ideal blanket. Without so much as a goodnight to her sister, without undressing or going to evacuate her water, and her whisky, she crumpled down into the grubby cushions smelling of tobacco smoke and London grit and fell like a child into a deep sleep, wound about within her rumpled clothes. Elsie's first thought as she emerged, lighter, from the bathroom, was that Lillian, her sister that is, had died. Behind the lounge sofa she saw two of Lillian's ankles protruding. Oh Lord God, she muttered in apprehension, She's died on me. Quick to react despite her gin-gnawed brain, she was on the point of lifting the telephone to ring an ambulance when one of Lillian's two ankles suddenly twitched. Elsie ran her fingers nervously across her moustache. Had she fallen? Had she harmed herself? Better look! By the time she'd hoisted herself onto the sofa to peep at Lillian over the back of it, the snoring had commenced and Elsie couldn't believe her eyes. Lillian! Bedded down for the night. Sprawled on the floor of her lounge, just as she had thought it would be impossible for her to do. She wasn't agile enough to camp on people's floors. Lillian had disavowed that forecast. What had she done with her dignity then? She certainly hadn't preserved it. Oh, Lillian! Degraded at eighty-three! This was preposterous. But what could Elsie do, save go to her own bed now? She couldn't possibly wake her, send her out in the cold, she might die. Elsie's compassion moved within her. Well, she would have to sort it out in the morning.

But as she pulled at her zips, fumbled with her buttons and nestled into the hollow she'd made over the years in her own mattress, she knew that she could never oust Lillian. Lillian had found her own new piece of space. She had rallied her wits and her old body in the face of sisterly spite, she had swiped adversity in the face and for once, just for once, Elsie had to admit that she recognised a certain courage in her elder sister's reaction. Perhaps, after all, Lillian was to be reckoned with.

X

HORACE'S DECLINE

Horace, meanwhile, was ageing rapidly, a downward crescendo, a *decrescendo* of giddy velocity, for since Mavis, his sweet, caring, subservient wife, had departed this world, Horace's decline had been vertiginous. From a meticulous, competent, hygienic gentleman, he had hurtled towards unkempt, incompetent grubbiness. He had willed himself into precocious senility, desiring to be rid of the time left to him as quickly as possible.

He's not himself any longer, Lillian would bemoan. He's caved in, given up, Elsie would state. Although younger than both his sisters, his ageing process had taken on a more definitive pace. There was an inexorable quality to Horace's ageing. After his bereavement, it had begun with the dragged foot, a physical disability which was actually little more than a slight discomfort and which, with willpower, he could have overcome. But the desire to overcome was lacking. He maintained certain of his foibles, but he no longer cared about the running of his home, about the position of his ornaments, about the surplus drops of water on his aluminium draining board, For the simple reason that Horace no longer ventured into his kitchen. That was because of his agoraphobia. He suffered from something which was ostensibly dislike, but inwardly panic, of people and anything public. He suffered from a fundamental insecurity and his lounge chair and bed were the only secure things with which he could identify. Both his sisters, for all their quaint and not so quaint quirks, were more alive than their brother, their ageing was less *inexorable*. Horace didn't suffer from lightness in the head, which was Lillian's problem. Horace really didn't suffer from anything at all. He had no ailment which medicine could or could not cure. He had simply given up. Lillian, on the other hand, suffered from osteoporosis and a feeble brain, but she *wanted* to go on. Elsie, on another hand, was going blind from hours and hours of repetitive reading and she suffered into the bargain from clogged arteries and even though she didn't particularly *want* to go on, she certainly wasn't going to give up. And so it was the *giving up* which put Horace into the fast lane ahead of his sisters towards the end of the journey.

Normally unconcerned about whether or not one or other of his sisters visited him – preferring that it be, of the two, Lillian because he could monopolise her, Elsie constituted a greater obstacle with that metallic nature of hers – Horace was now starting to complain, *almost* cantankerously, that both his sisters seemed to have forgotten about him. I don't know, he would comment, *almost* forlorn, to his daughter Harriet over the telephone, Harriet who lived only a forty minute car-drive away from Horace and his mute village. They haven't been down here for ages. It's weeks since they telephoned me. True it is that time drags for the very old. The concept of time alters its hues and the old calculate time badly, to the point of miscalculating it, and that is why they impose with ease on the lives of younger generations. With the aid of failing memory, they forget whole portions of days just gone by, they forget and mingle events and people. This is why Horace imagined that it was months since he'd seen his sisters. This is why Elsie imagined that she'd only been to see him a week or so ago. This is why Lillian said that she would go and see him tomorrow and tomorrow never came, every day that passed she would go tomorrow. There were entire days when even Lillian would forget about Horace. On those days, there was no tomorrow at all. Sometimes they even seemed to forget completely that Horace existed. He floated nebulously out of their London lives. But just as nebulously would float back again. Because of this floating away at sporadic intervals, Horace was known to get on the phone to Harriet, the only one of his offspring who lived relatively close by, and say that Lillian was missing, perhaps they should get the police after her, for days he'd actually been trying to phone her and there was no reply. Harriet suggested he contact Elsie which he had not considered doing himself but which he did and Elsie, although not quite sure, swore that Lillian had been over to her place *quite recently*, then Why hadn't she phoned Horace? A couple of days later which to Horace seemed well over a week, he tried Lillian's phone yet again to discover that it had been cut off. Now this was wont to happen because Lillian would forget to pay her telephone bills. Someone had better go up to London, she might be lying dead in her flat, but Harriet assured Horace that Elsie had the key to Lillian's flat and would know if that had occurred. Elsie's keeping the worst from me, complained Horace. Who would have imagined that Lillian meant so much to him? Utterly tetchy by now, he was. Why didn't Lillian arrange to have her phone put back on again? Once before when that had happened, Harriet had beguiled Lillian into signing a check and sending it to the telephone company. Getting Lillian to sign a check for anything at all was always a matter of haggling and beguiling. But Lillian was adamant, she would not sign any check and she calmly averred that she had been *in person* to pay her bill, the Director General of British Telecom had invited her *personally*, singled her out from all the telephone users, into his office to pay her bill, her months' and months' outstanding bill, What a charming man and What a beautiful office on the top of London, he invited me to tea to pay my bill, Lillian always believed in going to the Top to resolve her problems. It had been an honour to pay her bill sitting in that luxurious birds' nest, sipping tea made for a Director General. Harriet didn't believe her, Then why have they cut off your phone, you obviously haven't paid your bill. Oh, it's their mistake. British Telecom often make mistakes with their billing, the Director General told me that over the cup of tea he gave me. He was most apologetic to me, Such a nice man. Lillian still lived cocooned in her world of imaginary celebrities. But that had been the time before last when they'd cut off her telephone. This time Horace was convinced that Lillian had disappeared for good. The police must be brought in to track her down. Where could she have got to? Oh, here she is, exclaimed Elsie to Horace down the telephone.

Lillian had just shown up, walked into Elsie's flat without so much as a knock on her door, using the duplicate key she'd had made herself from her sister's key. Where had she been? They'd all been worried, about to call the police, Horace on tenterhooks. Elsie herself hadn't really been in the slightest concerned, with her sixth sisterly sense she knew that Lillian had come to no harm, yet all the phone calls from Horace had made her edgy. Lillian registered surprise at all the fuss as to her whereabouts. She didn't realise that her phone had been cut off, that British Telecom had done the dirty on her yet again and she'd been wandering in London, doing her dithering and ambling through the streets, loitering around shop windows in icy winds for, no matter the weather, Lillian apparently oblivious, would spend whole minutes, round minutes full of substance, peering at the colourful posies of artificial flowers, the tiny delicate ones with gauze petals, staring hard at them until her big old eyes watered with the strain of her staring. Every morning she would wander down the same lanes, dawdle past the same shops, dither across the same level crossings, amble around the same corners, loitering, envying the buyers, milling with the crowds. A part of London. Being a part of it all. Belonging. As Lillian had never properly belonged to a family of her own, she had adopted London and the Londoners, clasped them she had, to an imaginary and magnanimous bosom which was hers, at least when she wasn't off gallivanting elsewhere. On her wandering days, she was so taken with London and its passers-by, her adopted family, she barely cast a fleeting thought in the direction of Elsie or of Horace, both equally her saviours and solace in times of solitude. She beat her ancient way through the crowds feeling her senses titillated by an exuberance, a strange sort of freedom, that of not being hassled or *possessed* by either her sister or her brother, here in the streets of London she could be her anonymous wavering self and not be accused of being so.

During Horace's perturbations about her, however, she had not lost herself, but she had lost her handbag. She'd become obsessed about the loss of her handbag and quite positive, after giving the matter much erratic thought, that she'd left it on a bench at Waterloo Station. She would go and retrieve it. She battled, this time with seemingly more hostile crowds, jammed together on escalators, crowds, Londoners who really didn't appear to be like those more amiable people she had earlier clasped to a magnanimous bosom, she was concerned at the loss of her bag and her mood therefore was far from magnanimous. She spent a whole morning struggling to Waterloo Station in pursuit of her bag. She wouldn't take a red double-decker because they reminded her of Elsie, she'd been *put off* buses panting up those steps behind, always behind, her sister. Instead, she plunged down into the underground, clutching her old age pensioner's travel pass which she had fortuitously left in the pocket of her trench coat and not in the mislaid handbag. Now Lillian was in pursuit of her bag and she was convinced it would be on the bench at Waterloo Station, yet she had no inkling whatsoever of why it should be there, given that she only went to Waterloo when she went to Horace's and she hadn't been to Horace's for quite some time. Strange that conviction about Waterloo. But she struggled onto the Central Line and thence to the Bakerloo Line, peering laboriously up at the publicity spots as the train rattled and rumbled through black tunnels. At Waterloo, she alighted and fought her way, somehow or other old and frail and tiny as she was, out into the big mainline station. She wandered aimlessly, her mislaid bag forgotten, towards the departures board and saw that the next train for Exeter was not due to leave for another two hours. She had got there early and what on earth was she doing here on the station without her bag, she couldn't possibly go to Horace's without her bag, she must have left it back at her flat, would there be time to fetch it before the train left for Exeter. Without more ado, she descended once again into the uninviting holes of the underground, onto the Bakerloo Line, thence to the Central Line, staring laboriously up at the publicity spots as the train rattled and rumbled, backwards this time, through its black tunnels. As she looked at the men about her she decided, with a bizarre sensation in the pit of her stomach, a sensation which was less and less familiar to her nowadays, that any one of them could easily follow her down those long passageways, rape her in a flash in a concealed corner, leave her raped for dead, it didn't cross her mind that at her years and without a handbag, she was hardly a catch for any potential rapist or robber. Lillian regained her flat, but she couldn't open the door because she had forgotten her key, left it in the lost handbag. Damn! was her first reaction. Elsie had a key to her flat and the one she had in her pocket was the key to Elsie's flat. That way they could more easily violate each other's privacy. Sisterly prerogative. But when Lillian arrived at Elsie's flat to find her sister on the telephone allaying Horace's fears as to her, Lillian's, whereabouts, she just thought she'd come to spend the night with her sister. It wasn't actually until a few days' later, when she returned to her own flat, couldn't get inside, had gone around to Elsie's flat again for the spare key, re-returned to her own flat, that she sat down, exhausted, with a glass of whisky and Saw her handbag sitting in the chair opposite her. She knew something had happened to her handbag, but couldn't recall what it was. Something she had dreamt about more than likely.

Horace, needless to say, was relieved that Lillian was safe and sound. Yet he was beginning to feel the cold of his lonely days and nights, beginning to tire of his own breathing as the only proof of human life in his house, beginning to admit to himself, if begrudgingly, that life was easier and frankly more amenable with a woman around, even if only a sister. And as he dozed in his bed in the early grey dawns, he missed the gentle scraping of slippered soles on his carpeted hallway, the padding of a Lillian, or even an Elsie, to and fro in and out of bedroom and toilet, the painstaking crinkling and pulling at the paper around a new toilet roll, opening a new toilet roll can be an amazing trial for old arthritic fingers. Often the crinkling and crackling, the whispered female oaths over the inaccessible toilet paper, would awaken Horace and he would bark virulently from his crumpled sheets and the four dented pillows against which he was propped, and frighten the wits out of Lillian who had forgotten that there was anybody else in the house. When Horace was alone, his thoughts would wander subversively, particularly in the stealthy creeping of early morning hours, to his daughter Harriet. Many was the time when he felt the old fire creeping around in his emaciated loins and he would pinpoint Harriet as the idol of his desire, his ancient grappling with things sensual, and convinced that Harriet was in fact Mavis, he would imagine her lifting her long skirts up to knee length so that he might feast his eyes on the velvet curve of her calves, such an incestuous thought might caress any father's weakening mind, a tingling in the tips of his fingers betrayed his fumbling old passion and the faintest tweaking at the tip of his atrophied organ, a feeble attempt to stiffen what was already past stiffening..... That was in the earliest hours of dawn, before the true declaration of day, when life with its time and events has a hesitant quality. Horace's thoughts about Harriet/Mavis had a hesitant quality, robed in dawn mist, let it never be thought that Horace ever became obstreperous or immersed in an irrevocable sensuality about his daughter/wife. He fantasised a little. That was all. It was within his right to fantasise.

Perhaps he wouldn't have fantasised so if he'd still kept up his diaries. Writing his diary would have kept his thoughts from their mischievous travels. Now Horace had twenty diaries stacked one upon the other on a shelf of his desk, one hard back against another, exquisite leather-bound diaries dating back twenty years, the date printed in elaborate gold figuring on the outside of each one. Each tome had three hundred and sixty-five pages, one whole page and its reverse side for each day of the year and three hundred and sixty-six in the leap years. Writing space worthy to be filled with the noblest of thoughts, the most acute of observations, the most intricate of ideas, the most occult of desires. But alas. Horace's twenty diaries, twenty years of Diary, were as pristine and almost as naked as they had been on twenty January the Firsts. Horace had kept his diary. Let it never be imagined that he hadn't. He had kept his diary with extraordinary meticulousness, a meticulousness which even Samuel Pepys might have envied. Having served the war years in the Navy, Horace was accustomed to keeping a logbook. Not that he had ever been captain or first mate of a ship, but he had been proud in his day to maintain detailed entries in his own private log of the time and wave movement crossing equator and date line, details of the ship's stores taken on at such and such a port, sighting of whales, porpoises or other inhabitants of the deep, even of submarines whether enemy or otherwise. Horace's log was of veritable assistance to the lackadaisical first mate who was something of a shirker and something of a boozer and who had trouble keeping his log accurately. Horace had a life-time of log-keeping behind him, thus, on the day he retired from his insurance company where, it must also be said, his agenda had been the admiration of all the members of his department, it was logical that he purchase his own very specially bound diaries in which to record the ephemera of his retirement years. Horace's diaries were quite an outlay, but he considered that this life-long custom merited a respectable sum of money and he had therefore no qualms about choosing a diary of the most luxurious leather. Form was, for Horace, of more importance than content. For the content unfortunately in no way matched the form - none of the impulsive scribbling of poems or thoughts on serviettes in restaurants, as some of the world's best writers have been wont to do - the exquisite leather binding and gold figures stood out in vulgar ostentation beside the poverty of the content. Like the finest porcelain dish which contained but the most meagre of fare. Perhaps it was the poverty in Horace's mind, for in his retirement he sighted no whales or porpoises or submarines, or insurance contracts for that matter. In reality, there was little to recount. Day followed after similar day and the only annotations which occurred to Horace to record were The day, for example, when he had his Vauxhall car serviced - it had been Elsie who'd convinced him of the value of a Vauxhall, remembering fondly the one that Roland had bought years earlier - The time Lillian's train was due from London, The date he planted hyacinth bulbs and the anticipated date of their flowering, The weekly appointment which Mavis had kept at the hairdresser during her lifetime, every Thursday for twenty years Horace had noted down Mavis' hair appointment, The visits Harriet made which were invariably Mondays and Thursdays, for twenty years he had noted Harriet's visits down every Monday and every Thursday. Occasionally he remembered to write in somebody's birthday and the time Elsie's train left for London. Little else. These insubstantial remarks were lost on the crisp white of the pages, the pages cried out for a substance which Horace was incapable of giving them, they cried out to be smothered, their virgin whiteness to be desecrated with a veritable entanglement of thoughts and ideas, with septuagenarian confessions, with memories of better and worse times. Had Horace's life really been as dry and virgin as the pages of his luxurious diaries? Strange too that he hadn't plastered their glaring virginity with some sort of lurid comment or even vulgarity of which there'd been plenty amongst the past events and acquaintances of his days. It all seemed to have gone. Dried up. Withered away in the retirement of his mind. What was worse, however, was that after two years when Horace could see for himself that he wasn't filling the pages of his diaries, he still insisted on purchasing the elaborate version during the subsequent eighteen years, which meant that some seven thousand three hundred near-empty pages lay on the shelf of his desk. Gathering dust now.

When Horace was alone, the one relief to his solitude was a weekly visit from the cleaning lady. Rose would arrive, let herself in in the early hours, in those hours when the tip of Horace's atrophied organ was very slightly damp, the tiniest dribble of unquenched desire, drying in oblivion. And Horace's eyes would mist with sentiment at the apparition of his faithful visitor. Old men easily confuse kindness, or mere presence, for attachment. For Rose had been *doing* for him for three years now, she was part of his week, almost part of the furniture she dusted. And Horace felt a tenderness for her, a tenderness in his old soul, nothing like the mysterious tugging he experienced for his daughter Harriet. His sentiment for Rose was of a less complex nature. It was a diaphanous tenderness, something more easily accessible than those underworld feelings he had for Harriet. He would open his eyes and there she would be, the click of the front door and Rose, freshly dismounted from her bicycle, standing in the hallway at a respectable distance from Horace and his dribbling organ, not that Rose remotely imagined what was happening beneath his rumpled sheets, not even Horace himself imagined that. She was a paradigm of respectability, her comportment at all times being of the utmost transparency, so transparent that even Lillian could see right through her. Rose was softly rotund, her plump cheeks flushed pink from her bicycling, her eyes twinkling out of the fleshy folds of her countenance. She appeared *almost* contented, had it not been for the incongruously disgruntled mouth, harshly pursed lips which barely moved when she spoke, as if she were loath to let the words escape from her buccal cavity. Rose spoke very little. And when she did her voice was breathy, lightly rasping. She bid Horace the time of day, twinkled her eyes, pursed her lips. It was confusing this twinkling and pursing. Horace could never decide if she was in good or evil humour. If he looked at her eyes, she was in a good humour, if he looked at her lips, she was in a bad humour. Rose had immovable hair. Stolid greying waves which clung to her scalp as if stuck down with glue in the curve of the wave, the crests following on, one behind the other, all exactly the same size. Her hairstyle was harsh and immovable, rather like her pursed lips. And when she walked, her plump arms hung on either side of her ample bosom, also immovable. Or so it seemed, for as she walked, her arms stayed. They did not swing. After bidding Horace the time of day, Rose made for her dusters and for Horace's hoover. She busied herself with dexterity, flashing in and out of Horace's vision as she flipped and dusted tables and chairs and ornaments and hoovered the wall-to-wall carpets. For all her portliness, she moved rapidly. She was a jewel. She made Horace's house gleam. In only two hours a week too. When she had finished her work and if Horace had had a *stiff night* and didn't feel like rising from his bed, he would try to inveigle her into coming inside his bedroom, just that bit closer, to chat for a while before she went on her way. Now Rose had never married. Sentimentally jilted when still a schoolgirl, she had then, at the tender age of fourteen, pledged to herself and to her prematurely widowed mother that she would never betroth herself to a man, that she would never allow another of them so much as to touch her. Rose stuck to her pledge, weathering the *passionate years* with stoic self-containment. It all came out in her own bed on her own pillow, the fury and the tears, the resentment of a pledge which her obstinate heart would not allow her to break, for Rose would never retract a promise, either a silent one made to herself in a paroxysm of adolescent anger, or one voiced to another. Rose was honest. She kept her word. Her honesty gleamed through at Horace like her dusted furniture. This is why he reserved so tender a spot in his heart for her, at least when he was alone. If he'd had to hire Rose for her beauty, she wouldn't have been in the running, it was her honesty that attracted him. So honest was she that she would pay herself with Horace's permission from his wallet which he kept beside him perpetually. If he was in his lounge chair, the wallet would be beside him on his little Indian table, if he was in his bed, the wallet would be beside him on his bedside table. Horace was sufficiently mercenary and, lately, wary of thieves so as never to be separated from his wallet. Rose was honest and never extracted more than the seven pounds she earned, but the problem of extracting the money herself was of vast dimension to her, For if Horace was in bed it meant she would have to sidle up between the wall and his bed, *almost* touching his sheets, oh Lord, so close to that great male body, still unwashed into the bargain and revealing soft grey curls on his chest, Why didn't he do up the top button of his pyjamas? In her embarrassment Rose *almost* hit the wall with her snub nose attempting to avert her gaze from unwashed body curls. Her heart beating heavy thuds, she would extract seven crisp, as yet unused, bank notes from the wallet and because her portly frame would not permit that she turn around in the narrow space between wall and bed, she would be obliged to back away from Horace, flustered, positively heated around the temples, at having been so *accessible* to a man at her age and after having sworn that famous pledge, that life-long pledge. To retrieve her pay was the only time she allowed herself to cross the threshold of Horace's bedroom, in spite of his pleas for her to chat for a while, keep him company. The company he'd always spurned in his later years, he craved for now from his faithful cleaning lady.

Horace thought that Rose was a simple soul. Honest and simple. Honest she was. Perhaps not quite so simple. For she had Horace weighed up, and Lillian also, for that matter. Rose was honest, but she was not above gossiping to the local shop-keeper about the *goings-on* at Horace's house. She referred to Lillian as a Trick and to Horace as a One. Lillian was a Trick because of her imaginary tea parties, for many were the times when Rose would arrive to find the large mahogany dining table set up for at least ten people, laid with the most exquisite pieces of Mavis' dowry, silver and porcelain pieces, the best she could find, if somewhat depleted and cracked with Time. Lillian would confide in Rose and Rose in turn would confide in the local shop-keeper whose name was Hannah, that the most important people, celebrities in fact, were on their way down to Horace's country home for tea that afternoon, *theatrical* celebrities some of them, Rose said Ooh to Lillian and What a Trick to Hannah. Celebrities travelled with amazing frequency in and out of Lillian's mind. Not only had she laid up the dining table with Mavis' best china and cutlery, but she had cut up tiny squares of cheddar cheese and a mass of dainty marmalade sandwiches, all of which Rose had discovered sitting on a plate in the cupboard where she kept her dusters. She asked Lillian what the cheese and marmalade sandwiches were in aid of and Lillian told her that all the food was destined for her guests, they would be hungry after their journey. At other times she'd discovered rolls of toilet paper in the fridge and a plate of crumbs for the birds in the freezer complete with knife and fork. Lillian was a Trick, but she definitely wasn't *all there.*

Before Rose would depart on her bicycle, she used sometimes to offer to make Horace and Lillian a cuppa. If Horace was alone, there would be no problem attached to this But, she confided to Hannah in low tones so as not to be overheard in the local store, if Lillian was staying there, she'd invariably find the electric kettle with its spout clogged with tea leaves and its elements stained beyond repair from the large quantities of tea leaves which Lillian had spooned into it. A waste, said Rose spluttering her confidences with breathy rasping, a Waste of an expensive kettle, Lillian was a Trick but she did need controlling, Horace was a One because he was rude to his old sister, yet he couldn't seem to control her. Listen to this will you, this time lowering her voice to a near whisper, Completely naked she was, Not a stitch to her name and There for all to see in Horace's porch, nearly fell off my bicycle I did as I approached the house and saw Lillian there fetching the milk and the newspaper with her withered old bosoms swinging in the fresh air, No, I'm lying, She was wearing something: her slippers. And Rose tittered and chuckled, spluttered and whispered and Hannah, rather graver, nodded, *almost* impassive, she was a rustic, wondering whether it was prudent to laugh aloud, *wanting* to laugh, but on her guard against customers with ears longer than was good for them. Yes, Rose gossiped. But she was a good scout. And who wouldn't gossip with such juicy morsels to tell the world? When

Horace was alone, he was grateful for Rose. When he had company, he relegated her, Rose, who was beginning to believe that she was an indispensable cog in Horace's wheel, to the category of *That old tart, she's only the cleaner*. Horace could be lethally disparaging at times.

Not only could he be disparaging, but he also filled his slippers daily with urine. Harriet became thoroughly sick of buying the paternal slippers which had to be Clarks with fine leather soles that slid softly over the carpet. Slippers with rubber soles would have prevented Horace from being mobile at all, the rubber would have caught on the carpet pile sending him flying, he could never have been expected to have dragged his gammy foot along with a rubber sole attached to it. For Horace was shuffling more and more like a snail these days, depending almost completely on a metal frame which the hospital had loaned him. Mavis had had a metal frame too, Was Horace trying to reproduce Mavis' suffering in himself so that others would be obliged to wait on him hand and foot as he had done on Mavis? If this was so, there was a tinge of natural justice in his motives. A tinge of cynicism too. The *picaresque* of old age. Horace had always had a bit of the Rogue in him, honourably so, but the Rogue all the same. Because he walked so painfully slowly now, because he consumed large amounts of alcohol, because old age had settled upon him, silently, inexorably, as mildew settles upon wood after the rains, because the enthusiasm for all form of mobility had drained from him and because his bladder had weakened and lost its youthful elasticity, he would fill his Clarks slippers daily with urine and Harriet, or Rose, or Lillian, or Elsie, would have to empty the remains of it down the toilet and put the slippers to dry perfuming them with strong disinfectant powders. Horace had four pairs of number forty-three Clarks slippers which he used in rotation. Hannah also got to hear about that.

*   *   *

It is not surprising that the young find old age repulsive and smelling of urine. The sadness of the journey's end is too distant for them to be affected with the sentimental pain of a state they cannot possibly imagine, let alone feel. The young are impatient with the foibles and pleas for attention of the aged. Life patterns mould into one another, but the moulding and weaving is gradual. From youth to old age, from the beginning to the end, from alpha to omega, the process of weaving is slow. And the youngster throws up his arms in horror at the yellowing photograph of the twenty-year-old girl in the frame beside the grandmother's bed, Could they really be one and the same, this celluloid glamour girl and this wrinkled body living out its final hours?

And the loneliness of age is born in part from the great distance it has run, Ahead of all that hums and buzzes around it, willing it to continue with enthusiasm, when all it really wants is to lie down in peace and sleep for ever. And in those brief moments when it is not longing for rest and for oblivion, it returns, swiftly picaresque, to roguish infancy, tantalising and frustrating the impatience of Youth.

XI

ELSIE AND HORACE

It's freezing! Bloody freezing! Elsie never minded her language. Particularly in Horace's company.

Oh, you always say that. Don't know why you bother to come down here if you're always so cold.

I'd come more often if it wasn't so damned icy. Look at that frost on the window. Enough to freeze the cockles of your heart.

Didn't know you had a heart. Horace watched his sister poking at the windowpane with the tips of her fingers and thought she looked frankly ridiculous. You're just fanatical about the cold. Nothing cold about my house!

No. Only the windows.

Well come away from them! Stand in the middle of the room. Horace was irritable.

If you'd draw your curtains at night, it wouldn't feel so cold.

Don't talk rubbish!

I'm not. It's like putting clothes on a naked body.

Horace was fanatical about never drawing his curtains at night. Said he didn't care who was looking in at him from the outside and who anyway would be roaming around a little village in the middle of the night. Nothing worth stealing here, only the odd bits and pieces of Mavis' dowry, chipped into the bargain. He had his sisters and Harriet, the three of them, frenetic about the imaginary faces they saw leering in at them from the black night outside. But he would not close his curtains. Obstinate.

What's there to see in here, anyway?

The bottles of drink on the floor around your chair to start with, spat Elsie.

Bored with a conversation which was leading nowhere, she picked up her book and began to read page ninety-seven for the fifth time. Horace remained in irritable silence until he saw her turn the page, to page ninety-eight. And could no longer contain himself.

Always reading aren't you, he blurted critically.

What's that to you?

Haven't you got anything to talk about?

Why don't you read something for a change? You can't keep talking about nothing all the time.

I don't talk about Nothing. I talk about Something.

Well, it doesn't interest me!

Why do you come and visit me then?

Don't know. Often ask myself the same question.

Fits and starts of acrid communication. It was always the same when Elsie was with her brother. Perpetual retaliation. On the defensive. Criticism. She wanted to leave after she'd been with him only an hour. She never stayed long. They might have killed each other if she had. He hated her reading, he was jealous of her books, and he hated her smoking, Burning holes all over the house, Dropping ash everywhere, he'd complain, Ash in the food she serves me, trails of it on the carpet after her, smouldering fags in the toilet, singed paintwork on the windowsills where she puts them down and waylays herself over something else, she almost set fire to the booze cupboard once, to say nothing of the hot fat sizzling on the stove, she forgot about that too and it all went up in flames, made a right mess of my kitchen ceiling, it all had to be re-painted and she didn't offer to pay a penny of it.

Elsie, in turn, hated Horace's sedentary existence, his grumpy nature-too-like-her-own-for-comfort, like Lillian she wanted to watch her favourite television programmes but with Horace glued to his lounge chair, that was never possible, she hated the silence of his house and the mute village. The only time she very slightly enjoyed being with him was on the days she could get away from him and go into town. That was *almost* stimulating, the long ride on the country bus owned by John the Driver who was a country bumpkin according to Lillian but who only charged ten shillings, well fifty new pence they call it now, to go all that way into town. He used to drive around all those quaint little villages, picking up passengers from the thatched cottages, old biddies who yapped incessantly, thought Elsie, although she smiled politely at them when they clambered onto the bus behind their shopping baskets and plastic bags. She really thought they looked awful in their army green quilted jackets and hair grips holding back dirty grey locks. To her urban mind they looked not only awful but a bit like gardening utensils, their gnarled knuckles like the handle of a spade, their teeth like the jagged prongs of a rake, their stumpy legs like tree trunks and their voices sounded like the whine of a lawnmower or hedge-cutter. Not that Elsie herself was good-looking. She knew she wasn't, but she did credit herself with having a *city allure,* something these country folk could never boast of, born as they were, she considered, in the backwaters of Britain. But it was useful that little bus, if you could put up with the biddies who sometimes, Elsie thought, smelt suspiciously of horse manure, good lord, her own charlady's fingers looked refined beside their massive rustic appendages. It was useful because it stopped right bang in the centre of the town, when you got off you were face to face with Boots the Chemist and Woolworths and Marks, and Laura Ashley and Barclays were only just down the road, Very handy little bus and John the Driver would park for three hours, giving you time to do all your shopping, what's more you could leave your heavy bags on the bus seat while you went window-shopping or for a quick one in The Red Lion, John would take care of them. A handy little bus it was. It made a day out, a relief from Horace's bossing, Don't know what's got into him, Elsie would muse to herself as the bus wound its way homeward, He was never like this when Roland was alive, when Mavis was alive.

If Elsie and Horace had been attacking the bottle, which was every lunchtime and every evening, their voices thickly mulled would rise in unison at those moments when they were *almost* united and they would vociferate their utter lack of farsightedness, for In their Cups the United Kingdom became the unflinching yardstick for every possible standard in the world and Elsie would raise her hackles and champ at the bit about Polly who flaunted praise for Australia and called the English, of whom she herself had once been one, The Brits. Now that was plain Derogatory, Elsie couldn't stand that. In his Cups, Horace would declare in belligerent blurbs that the United Kingdom was the only, Only I'm saying, place to live in the world. In her Cups, Elsie would reply, Well you don't need to convince *me* of that, That fellow got locked in the pub toilet that time, don't you remember?

What *are* you on about?

In their Cups, they never stopped their talking about nothing, round and round the same stupidities. That was In their Cups. And Out of Them sometimes too. And if they were normally at loggerheads, it was their parallel esteem for the United Kingdom and the Queen which brought them *almost* together, and their adulation of all that was mediocre and their mirth at seamy jokes. Yet such moments of unison were brief, the metal edge of both their natures would come to the fore to nip the unison in the bud. Horace and Elsie were of a kind. It was bickering they were best at.

That's why her visits to Horace were brief.

XII

THOSE SENESCENT YEARS

If Horace was in his *decrescendo*, Lillian was careering towards an amiable senility. She lived, as we already know, in and out of the primrose room in a flurry of tissues. It was well over a year since she had been away from London, London was there tucked away somewhere in a cobwebby recess of her mind, but she was no longer in any condition to stroll the streets of her London alone, particularly now that her sister, Elsie that is, had left for Australia. Some soldiers came and took her away Lillian used to tell people. They had *deprived* her of her sister. And when she remembered Elsie there was a pain in her heart, a sore and suffocating lump which was Elsie's presence in Lillian's mind. She wanted to scream and pummel the lump away, extirpate it, exhort it into the true live Elsie she had always known, the bitter metallic Elsie she loved and never wanted to be with and the Elsie she hated and wanted to be with. Sometimes the pain of the lump was so intense, it was as though she and Elsie were identical twins, in the absence of one of them they had become kindred spirits and to Lillian now, when she recalled that soldiers had taken Elsie away on a plane to Australia, Just for a holiday Elsie had said, I'm coming back you know, when she recalled that Elsie had flown up and off and away from her, everything about Elsie had become miraculously beautiful and bountiful. Elsie had been her one and only trustworthy companion, Elsie had been a faithful counsellor, Elsie had been an efficient help with everything, Elsie had even been tolerant and *sweet*. And good-looking. Eighty-seven years of Lillian's life had had to pass before she was aware of the value, the solid shining metallic value of her sister Elsie. She couldn't understand why they'd taken Elsie away. It was cruel, that. They'd mumbled something about her ailing. That was a lie. Elsie had been perfectly well the last time Lillian had seen her. They'd lied to her. It wasn't fair, this separation, this *terrible* thing that had befallen her, They've ruined my life, taking her away. She blamed the young people in the family, Horace's children had something to do with it, Mavis' Adolescent from Spain and Harriet and the Other One, what was his name, the One in Australia, who often came to England to stay with Horace, his father, short visits admittedly, but he was there long enough to come to blows with Lillian. It was their fault. They had made the soldiers come for Elsie. Lillian was delirious, muttering in bed at night, whispering about it all in the toilet. And you wouldn't credit it, the only thing that Elsie had thought to leave her as a momentum was a pair of her underpants, underpants which Lillian had actually taken herself from Elsie's cupboard, unwittingly of course and without her sister's knowledge. She didn't even leave me anything else. Just like her! Sometimes Horace would let her speak on the telephone to Elsie and she would ask her how she was in a tone of voice which seemed to indicate that she had only seen her a week or so ago, then she would ask her where she was, Where is it you are? she would say, In Australia, *are* you? Ooh, I didn't know that, Nobody told me that. And she would turn to Horace, still clutching the receiver, Who is this on the other end of the line, I can't make out a word. And when the communication cut out and Elsie well and truly gone, on the other side of the World, Lillian would deny that she'd spoken to her at all. She never told me that, she would say in answer to Horace, Yes she did, you've just been speaking to her.

Lillian was really very confused and here she was, Stuck down in the country beside her brother Horace and she couldn't get away. Retained there. They wouldn't let her get away, I must go back to London, I must find out what's happened to my sister, I must go back to the office, I haven't been to work for such a long time, They'll be wondering where I am. Those memory slips were fortunate. In fact they were her saving grace, because her tragedy would have been all the more acute had she been as perpetually lucid as she was on the day they sold Horace's car. The lumbering old model of a Vauxhall which had been his faithful companion for over twenty years, every Thursday it had assisted him with his shopping in town for over twenty years, yet now it had lain fallow in the garage, dripping oil from its innards, for month upon freezing month. He would never drive it again. On the day he sold it, tears came into his eyes and into Lillian's too. She wept crocodile tears of whisky over the kitchen stove, dropping her water in salty blobs onto the dinners she was dishing up. The sale of Horace's car was her final rupture with the Outside World. Or so she felt. Harriet, or Mavis' Adolescent when she was there from the Continent, or the Other One from Australia, used to take her out for drives in Horace's over-twenty-year-old Vauxhall. Even though Horace himself refused to budge from his lounge chair, he preferred anyway not to have to witness anyone else manipulating the old vehicle of which he'd been lord and master for so many years, Lillian would put on her best scarf, her raincoat and her old gardening shoes which were the only comfy pair of shoes she had since her nails had begun to grow over and under and back into the skin of her toes. She would be the first out into the porch. She loved that old car, No matter if it was like an old shunting bus, No matter if it didn't have power steering, No matter if it stank of exhaust, No matter if it refused to go at more than forty miles an hour. All that was like water off a duck's back to Lillian. Sometimes in the old Vauxhall they would take her to a nearby shopping centre to have her hair cut, although I must get it done in London, I made an appointment with my hairdresser there, Or to buy a pair of slippers, or a warmer dress.

Like her sister Elsie had been, Lillian was always cold in Horace's house. She assured Mavis' Adolescent that she liked the dress, that it was comfortable, a good fit, a pretty blue she agreed, but several months later she complained bitterly to Mavis' very Adolescent who was sifting through the clothes in Lillian's wardrobe to help her to dress, that that was a horrible, uncomfortable dress which *someone* had forced her into buying. Deep down, Lillian experienced an occult need to let people know that she didn't enjoy being pushed around, patronized. She was hitting back, wanting to hurt where she herself had been hurt. In her pride. In the Vauxhall, however, all that mattered to Lillian was an hour or so of freedom from the unutterable silence of Horace's house, from the unutterable loneliness of being just a sister to a brother, from the humiliation of being trampled upon by an irascible old man who, despite his grousing, needed her and Whom she in turn needed. Many were the evenings when she would let slide her whisky tears of self-pity into the washing up water.

Such was the displeasure of Lillian's days at Horace's that she would demonstrate her frustration by locking Harriet out of the house, and the Other One too when he came to stay. As for Mavis' Adolescent, she only had to spend five minutes in the garden to find herself locked out. There was a spite and a vengeance in Lillian's pushing of the catch on the doors, that latch-key click of rejection, sudden and surreptitious, yet sure and metallic-as-Elsie. She normally *ran* Horace's house now in her own haphazard way and all these youngsters of his were an intrusion, she couldn't keep up with them, they made her feel inferior with their supercilious efficient youth, they were detestable, martialling her around as though they were soldiers, like the soldiers who'd taken Elsie away, and if they all coincided at Horace's house together, Lillian felt excluded from their conversations, she couldn't keep up, she couldn't hear, so she would sit in a chair shooting them black, whisky-sodden looks, an obnoxious defeated hump with a sagging cleavage and a dowager's hump on her neck. When they made phone-calls to the Outside World, Lillian was jealous. She would hover. Busy herself unnecessarily near the telephone. Pretend to be searching for a tissue, Don't mind me, You go on talking, or hide behind the wall, listening, flapping, straining her ears, Pining for contact herself with someone, with something Outside Horace and his mute village.

The village was mute, or *almost,* but Lillian was always ready to be taken for a walk, ready with the cunning of a child who knows she might be excluded from an excursion. Canny old age. Harriet would only have to *whisper* to Horace that she was just going to pop down to Hannah's shop and there was Lillian waiting, like an excited puppy, at the front door, her raincoat on skewwhiff over her petticoat, a slipper on one foot, the old gardening shoe which was comfy on the other, her countenance a mixture of pleading and guilt for having overheard what she was not meant to hear, that Harriet was just going to *pop down* to Hannah's which meant that Harriet was in a hurry and didn't want to be waylaid, beleaguered by the encumbrance of Lillian's faltering step. When she was fortunate enough to be invited to beleaguer and falter her step, Slow the progress, Slow, she would remark on exactly the same things at exactly the same point with exactly the same words. She made the same comment each time about every cottage or about the inhabitants of every cottage she passed and Harriet would dread meeting up with anyone because Lillian invariably repeated Horace's curt comments pertaining to whoever it was before they were out of hearing. In particular the Reverend, that *insolent bible-bashing fool*. There was a morbid pleasure in Lillian's repeating of Horace's comments, a mischief, as though she wanted others to know what a cantankerous old B..... she had to live with.

Lillian seemed to have turned, with a vituperative sense of purpose, against all those who were doing their best, which was perhaps not everybody's best but was a Best just the same, against all of them in Horace's family who had taken her, in some measure, under their wing and who were trying to shelter her in her dying days. She resented them. She resented them interfering with her clothes, telling her what she had to put on, Hadn't she dressed herself for the last eighty years and here they all were poking their noses into her wardrobe, her papers, her money, forcing her to sign cheques and to pay for things she'd already paid for, it was intolerable. It was as though they wanted to rob her of the little money she'd saved up for her old age, living off Horace and Elsie most of the time it had been easy for her to save, but now they were talking of her relinquishing her flat in London. Intolerable it was, she would need that flat when she returned to her job, I can't be on holiday for evermore, she would say. And here they are, all *at me,* Harriet, Mavis' Adolescent, even the Other One from Australia, she'd actually flung the proxy form to cancel her flat back in the Other One's face, Rampant cruelty she said it was, trying to steal the only place I have to live in, But you haven't been near it for more than a year, exclaimed the Other One. Lillian was irate, puffed and red in the face, How would you know, you're never here, she retorted rudely. The Other One drew himself up, Well if that's the way you want it my dear, that's the way you'll have it. And Lillian clung, clung ever harder, to her London flat, wasting money, paying her savings out religiously every month to her landlords, preferring it that way to the idea that any one of Horace's hoard might benefit from the extra money she'd have if she didn't have to pay rental. Anyway, she thought in her lonely hours, Any of my money left over I shall leave to the dogs' home. As for the flat, it was not until the very end, until the final weeks of her life, that she allowed Harriet and the doctor to tie up her ends for her, close down the flat, those final weeks when she forgot that London existed, forgot about her sister Elsie and Australia, when it all gradually faded into one large spot, rather like the spilt ink which seeps into a formless blob on blotting paper, This was how Lillian saw her life during those final weeks.

But in the months prior to the final weeks, Lillian was constantly taking umbrage. She regarded anything that anyone did for her as an assault on her privacy. She took particular umbrage at Mavis' Adolescent who would go into the primrose room, which was looking daily more and more like a rubbish tip, and remove her soiled underwear which she'd placed to dry over the heater. For Lillian, like Horace and his Clarks slippers, had many an accident. It was the booze. But she wasn't going to tell Mavis' Adolescent about those accidents, the knickers and petticoats would dry out by themselves, but when Mavis' Adolescent helped her to bed the odour in the primrose room was so pungent that she would immediately gather up all the soiled garments and Lillian would sink, ruffled and defeated like a guilty child into her pillow, an unfinished glass of whisky on her bedside table. And on those nights when Lillian went to bed with a perturbed spirit, she would awaken during the night, go out to the kitchen and begin to make tea inside the tea caddy. A hotchpotch in the tea caddy it was. An undrinkable hotchpotch. She would hover in the night gloom of Horace's house, peering at his ornaments, opening and shutting wardrobes and drawers and the moonlight would illuminate her veined hands as they fumbled from one object to another. Lillian would tire herself out with her night walking and be obliged to return to her bed before lunch the next day. When she'd been up half the night making sandwiches for all the *friends* she hadn't seen for years, it was natural that sleep nagged at her the following morning. And so her life became anarchic. And Horace followed suit casting his lifetime methods to the winds of old age. It was the downfall of Horace when Lillian went to live with him on a permanent basis. They both became unmanageable because as Lillian made hotchpotch in the tea caddy, so did she mix her whiskies, and Horace's, with gin or martini or with anything going really. They were drinking the most exotic mixtures and not realising why it all tasted strange. Harriet, particularly, was strongly disappointed in Horace towards the end, with his incapacity for trying, with his capacity for swallowing alcohol. Their days and nights became chaotic and if Rose had caught Lillian naked swinging her bosoms to the winter dawn in the porch, that was Nothing, Because one night Horace had fallen, his massive frame stuck between toilet and wall, leg doubled under him and he couldn't budge. He was in agony. He shrieked at Lillian to call for help from a neighbour and horrified by Horace's predicament, the entire event magnified in her brain because she was drunk, Lillian lanced herself stark naked out into the night, the alcohol allayed her fears of the dark and evidently kept her warm for she suffered no dire consequences. There she was discovered by some neighbours who fortuitously happened to be walking their dog, Lillian groping on the grass verge, grappling with twigs and damp leaves, her bosoms swinging this time to touch the dew-kissed blades, and wondering why she was where she was. It was Horace who eventually told them why she had been out into the night.

Now if Horace had difficulty walking because of his gammy foot, Lillian had difficulty putting on any of her good shoes because her nails were growing, curling, embedding themselves into the skin of her toes. When she remembered that they were painful, she could only wear her slippers and the comfortable old gardening shoes. Mavis' Adolescent took one look at Lillian's feet and decided she was not the one to tug at those horny appendages and she duly called the Chiropodist. Lillian was offended to say the least because she said that she had an appointment with her London chiropodist, But this one is an especially nice Chiropodist. A man. And Lillian took that information away with her into the primrose room to think about. For three days Mavis' Adolescent reminded Lillian that the Chiropodist was due in three, two, one day's time and for three days Lillian said she knew nothing about a chiropodist and had made an appointment in London for her feet. On the day of her appointment, Mavis' Adolescent said nothing to Lillian about it, she didn't have to because something in Lillian's mind had clicked and she appeared in the lounge as fresh as a rose, wearing her most becoming summer dress in the middle of winter. She looked fresh, and new, and excited, and when the Chiropodist arrived, Such a Pleasant Fellow, she followed him meekly into Horace's study, enchanted at the prospect of spending some time alone with Such a Pleasant Fellow, of having her horny nails clipped, of having the withered chafed skin of her feet caressed by Such a Pleasant Fellow. Mavis' Adolescent left them to it, the gentleman with his wide smile and scalpel, Lillian with her flimsy dress and scaly toes, with her old woman's teenage laugh, she giggled incessantly at the Chiropodist's chit chat behind the door of Horace's study. She had risen to the occasion, burst forth from her greying nights and anarchic days to impress the Pleasant Fellow with her octogenarian It, a little the worse for wear now, but her It all the same. Lillian spoke for days about the Chiropodist's visit. It had given her a new lease of life. Horace couldn't understand it, What's he got that I haven't? Well for a start, he's not my brother, is he!

Lillian had difficulty deciding where exactly her affections lay. It was a time of visits from the Outside World. There'd been the Chiropodist and there'd been, of all unlikely visitors to Horace's house, the Guitarist. Now the Guitarist belonged to Mavis' Adolescent. He was her son, which meant that Lillian was his Great Aunt, What was he to Lillian? She had no idea. He'd just come for a couple of days, He'd just appeared one night in the kitchen and serenaded her with old Spanish airs over the greasy oven dishes and Horace's aluminium sink, He played her tunes which brought tears to her eyes, memories of the Spanish hinterland, the Almerían rains, the golden sands of Murcia, the almond blossom of Mallorca, of Martinez's restaurant at Piccadilly where another Spanish guitarist had serenaded her with *una paloma blanca,* she'd only been in her early seventies then, and Lillian's heart thudded energetically in time with his strumming, she forgot the greasy oven dishes and sat on a kitchen stool beside the Guitarist swaying and remembering and weeping nostalgia and wishing it could all start over again, Such a pleasant fellow the Chiropodist, Such a nice fellow the Guitarist she said to Mavis' Adolescent the following morning, Do you know him? When he appeared in the kitchen, not to serenade her again in her pink quilted dressing gown, but for his breakfast, she asked him four times if he wanted a piece of toast and four times he refused. He wanted cereal.

She often spent hours and hours of the day in her pink quilted dressing gown, unless she sensed with the canny sense of the old that Harriet was coming to visit and might take her out into the mute village to see Hannah. For dressing had become a major problem in her life, it was so time-consuming. She'd never been talented as a decision-maker, Lillian, but choosing something to wear really did need a great deal of thought. Each day she would pull all her clothes out of her wardrobe, wander apparently aimlessly into Horace's bedroom and ask him what he thought she should put on. Now Horace had no eye for colour and no particular interest in Lillian and her skirts, nowadays we know that his interest was limited to Harriet's/Mavis' skirts, and his replies to Lillian were brusque, cruel and bitter, perhaps because Lillian was not Harriet/Mavis, he was always asking Harriet to stay and she wouldn't. His replies brought the tears flooding to Lillian's big tired eyes and, destitute, she would return to the primrose room and sometimes to her bed again, heaping herself sorrowfully on top of her crumpled jumpers and dresses. But there were days when she didn't ask Horace's opinion on what to wear, Why should I, he's nothing to me, only a brother. Yet neither on those days was she any the quicker with her dressing, she would spend long moments standing in her petticoat trying to fathom out whether her petticoat was the dress she wanted to wear or not. If she felt cold she would put a jumper over her petticoat and then turn to making her bed, Time, so much Time to collect up all the dresses and put them over her chair, how Long it took to straighten the sheets, her back ached as she pulled up the blankets, her mind wandered, to the Chiropodist, to the Guitarist, to the Queen's Messenger, now who was he? as she stretched the quilt in a crooked diagonal from one end of her bed to another, how tiresome a task this bed-making had become, Why bother and she would pull the quilt back again and her back still aching but driven on by a maniacal sense of reversing life, the day and her fortune, she would re-rumple the sheets, Now I've just got up. Some days, she would start all over again. When she was satisfied that she was presentably dressed, she would approach the mirror on the primrose wall above her dressing table and peer at the old face reflected in it, sometimes wondering who she was looking at. When she remembered, she would smear her lips with vermillion lipstick, flap some white powder in blotches over her nose and long gaunt cheeks and shapeless chin, *chinless* Elsie had called her once, then turn her laborious attentions to her hair, now long and wavy, a perm which had become chaotic, which floated in the wind on the days she was taken to Hannah's, not today because there was no sign of Harriet anywhere, she plucked a little, tugged a very little at the grey locks and became waylaid by a Christmas gift card sitting on the dressing table, dating five Christmases earlier, Love from Rachel and Marcus Ludbury, something about the compliments of the season, she wondered who Rachel and Marcus Ludbury were, decided she didn't know, thought the card was pretty with its Christmas tree laden with gifts, Was there anything inside those parcels? In an old suitcase inside her wardrobe Lillian had three large paper bags full of birthday cards, Christmas cards, season's greetings, gift cards, pink, red, white bows and coloured wrappings, she kept all this paraphernalia. Now it was virtually her only contact with the Outside World, particularly since Horace had sold his car. Each day she would open one of the bags and peer forlornly at its contents, forgetting to finish her dressing, forgetting to remake her bed, forgetting that Horace was waiting for her, forgetting ..... forgetting .....

XIII

THE LAND OF OPPORTUNITY ... AT LAST

If Horace was in his *decrescendo* and Lillian careering towards her *amiable senility* and forgetting ..... forgetting ..... Elsie found herself back in Australia, an abrupt and swift transfer, rather like a kidnapping, had taken place. It was not the soldiers, not Lillian's soldiers, No, She had been declared by the doctor, by various members of the medical profession in fact, not only unfit to live alone but quite incapable of fending for herself. She had been threatened with being moved to a Home. Something very drastic had occurred in Elsie's normally competent life, the life where she had fended for herself all through the long years of her widowhood. This undignified end, being informed that she could no longer manage and had to be cared for, was an incongruous end and would have been an insult to her had she indeed been either fully aware of or responsible for her actions.

Alas! It was the re-wiring of her flat which sparked off Elsie's folly.   Her friend Kathleen had warned her that the Council intended to re-wire and renew all the electrical points in the entire block of flats, she Kathleen had already had hers done and You wouldn't *believe* my dear the mess those people leave behind them, odds and ends of wiring dropped all over the flat, in the grooves between carpet and wall, bits and pieces of the stuff clinging around the legs of chairs, poking out from beneath your sofa. *Dreadfully* dirty people, they are. But Elsie very rapidly put Kathleen's words behind her, that is, she entirely forgot about her *friend's* warning, like her sister Lillian, she'd been doing a lot of forgetting .....

forgetting ..... recently, and she'd become very involved with visits to a psychologist who was assessing her mental capacities, deciding on her decrepitude, pausing over her mental pulsations. Indeed, much of Elsie's time was occupied with visits to one department or another of the hospital. She'd become a *regular* both in the psychology wing and in the optometrist unit, as well as in the general medicine department. She spent, in fact, far more of her time in medical waiting rooms than she did in specialists' consultancies. She was a *regular* in those waiting rooms together with many other *regulars*. The *regulars* were quite well acquainted with each other, some were blinder than others, some mentally less competent than others, most of them were old and lonely without a friend in the world, in that respect Elsie was fortunate, she had Kathleen. Doctors' waiting rooms can be utterly depressing, all the more so because the patients develop a decided taste for elaborating on their ailments, they have not the slightest interest in the ailments of other patients, there they become grossly obsessed with their self-ailment and even though no other patient is interested, the waiting room is a place where the respective ailments come out for airing, which is of far greater benefit to the patient than all the medical prescriptions and all the doctors' advice and prodding and peremptory probing. Airing an ailment is like applying a soothing liniment to it. This is why most of the patients come away feeling more robust than when they enter. A waiting room is only really depressing for those who suffer temporary illness, it is the long-term sufferers who actually benefit from their hours in waiting rooms. In the psychology wing none of them knew why they were there; they were there because their general practitioners had recommended that they visit the psychologist. Without exception they all, including Elsie, actually enjoyed their visit to the psychologist, he never hurt them or jabbed needles into their bodies, he just sat calmly talking to them, friendly, scribbling annotations on his pad, asking them questions which they enjoyed answering, occasionally inviting them to draw pictures of trees, to fill in missing words, like games really. It was fun visiting the psychologist. Elsie thought so anyway, fun while it lasted, because by the time she had got herself home, picking her way amidst the obstacles on the pavements of Farringdon Road with the uncertainty of the *almost* blind, she'd forgotten she had seen the psychologist.

So it was not surprising after her flat had been re-wired and re-pointed and she couldn't find any of the switches in the places they used to be, that she did not know where she was, Strange, some of the things looked familiar, *her* things, her sofa, Lillian's bed cushions with the bedraggled tassels, not that she'd seen Lillian for a long time, for months in fact, although to Elsie it only seemed like a week because she was always relieved as we know to be rid of her sister. Yes, she recognised some of her ornaments and pieces of furniture, but when she pressed switches, lights didn't come on in the right lamps, she couldn't make her oven work or her electric kettle, she was missing out on her cuppas. Fortunately Kathleen came to the rescue, she made Elsie a cup of tea and one for herself and then she explained in her theatrical wheeze just which switches Elsie must turn on for what, twice she went around the flat with her explaining, repeating, emphasising, making the muddle in Elsie's head thicker and thicker. Then Kathleen went away and Elsie promptly forgot all her instructions. It was days before Kathleen came again, days when Elsie went without her cuppas or anything warm to eat, when she lost weight, so thin and frail her little frame, she was alienated in her own home, alienated from her own self, she sat bewildered on her chair in the dim light which the television screen afforded her, true it was *on the blink* but the spurts of light which shot from it were better than nothing, she couldn't understand it, they'd taken her switches away, they'd taken the light out of her life, she was cold and hungry and miserable and for perhaps the first time in her life, she missed her sister's company.

Elsie dissolved into tears, chesty sobs, crying and crying, remembering those who had populated her past, Where were they now, Roland and Mavis and Nell and Father, Mavis had been sweet and kind and understanding. Elsie sobbed her heart out for Mavis. It was as though all the softness which had lain encrusted behind her metallic shield for eighty years was welling up and pushing to the fore, all that softness, Elsie's *essence*, tucked away to the back. And she missed Mavis now, Mavis with her sweetness. Where were they all, Mavis and Roland, what had happened to Horace and Lillian? Everything was confusion, blur and confusion, memories fading fast into persistent rumours and whispers in her brain. She drank herself to sleep in the lounge chair. Even her gin supply was running low, her cigarettes, she would have to go out for more. She was too weak to go out for more. Too scared of the traffic, the noise, the bustle of Farringdon Road, she was scared of falling because she could no longer see properly.

Frail and alone and slumped to sleep in her chair. She woke with a start in the middle of the night and felt the need to empty her bladder. Aided by the red white and green neon-clicking flashes from the Italian restaurant across the road, she groped her way to the bathroom, she sat down on what she thought was the toilet. It was the bath. She fell backwards and cracked her head hard against the protruding taps, Such a hard clinical crack, her skull against the tap ..... It was the doctor who found her the next morning, the doctor who had asked the porter to let him into Elsie's flat when she hadn't answered the door bell, and there he found her, slumped in her bath tub, barely conscious, bitterly cold and not at all sure where she was. He took a cursory look At the grime in the bathtub, At the mass of loose coins and bank books and medley of other personal effects strewn all over her dining table, At the bottles of pills he had prescribed weeks ago and which she'd not yet opened, At the bottle of gin overturned by her chair, its remnants still seeping into a grotty sodden patch on the carpet, At an ashtray overflowing with cigarette butts and he telephoned her daughter Polly in Australia whose number was in Elsie's agenda beside the telephone.

It was Polly who came to take her away to Australia, not soldiers sent, as Lillian had imagined, by Harriet and the Other One and Mavis' Adolescent. It was Polly, pouring forth remorse for having abandoned her old mother for so long and now it was too late, Polly who surged across the world in an aeroplane to take belated possession of Elsie, take her back to the Promised Land, to her Land of Opportunity which had *not* been Lillian's Land of Opportunity. There was a day of adieus in Horace's house. Neither Lillian nor Elsie quite knew what it was about, that day. But Horace knew. Even in his decline, in his *decrescendo*, he knew and He knew that he wanted Elsie back again before she'd even left. He too was forgetting ..... forgetting ..... how he'd loathed her visits and her complaints about his cold windows. Nothing would be the same again after Elsie had left. An era had ended. So Elsie left her beloved London, she left the United Kingdom, her Queen and country, she left the Brits. All that behind her. Her diary behind her too, for in her *old* old age, Elsie had forgotten ..... forgotten ..... to write her diary, it had become little more than sporadic and wavering jottings in a small agenda. Similar to Horace. Officious council cleaners cleared away the cushions of Lillian's makeshift bed, the stale food in her fridge and the empty bottles in the old cocktail cabinet. All Elsie's belongings went to the poor or to the compost heap. All the bits and pieces of her English life.

She was to *start again* at eighty-five in the Land of Opportunity.

*   *   *

That complex relationship between sisters mingles such conflicting sentiments. It is a love that we accept despite ourselves. It is an un-chosen love. As it is not chosen freely, we rebel against it by actions, words and thoughts that are often petty and even cruel. That is how we seek to disentangle ourselves from the *condition of sisterhood.*

Elsie and Lillian couldn't escape from the dependence of their sisterly love. Perhaps they even began to thrive on nurturing their emotions of antagonism and irritation. Lillian so often dreamed of freeing herself from the mesh. Elsie was forever infuriated by her feelings of dependence and responsibility. But they were a magnet to each other. Life occasionally separated them, but they returned again and again as if drawn towards each other, like a moth to a flame, towards the other sisterly half. Before each of them will be able to surrender her soul to her god, or to her Christian Science, or to her nothingness, will she reconcile herself to her imposed condition, discover a friendship which is thickened by blood, the beneficial side of sisterhood?

XIV

INCONGRUOUS ENDINGS

Aside from that complex mesh of sisterly sentiment, Elsie's and Lillian's drinking habits had cast a heavy shadow over their relationship. A habit which in the early days was, for Lillian, no more than an innocent threshold to the exuberant social life she craved, but turned with time and assiduous practice into a lifestyle bound to the bottle. Not a day passed without a few drinks. By the time they reached their later years it had become such a habit for both of them, and for Horace too, that life lost its colour without a considerable daily intake of whisky or gin. Yes, they had their merry moments, but they were rarely drunk. They were certainly not drunkards, but saw themselves as civilized drinkers, maintaining a certain balance, thanks to a hardy tolerance for alcohol. And they never lost their self-esteem. That only began to fade towards the very end. So for Elsie and Lillian, alcohol played a considerable part in undermining any joy or comfort their sisterhood could bring. It *affected* the relationship, perhaps repressing a generosity and acceptance that might otherwise have existed. Instead, both looked backwards, recalling the resentments and perceived injustices still felt from when they were young siblings surrounded by peasoupers, chafed knees, rough bath-towels and aunt Emily's ferret's nose.

* * *

They were feeding Horace on soups now, on cartons of vitaminized liquids. Indifference had stretched even to his food, Or to the lack of it, because he simply refused to eat anything solid at all. Mastication was a trial, the lumps stuck in his throat, Go on, eat up, it's doing you the world of good, Harriet or Rose or Lillian would coax and Horace would look at them through faded blue eyes, sunk way back in time, hollow sockets of calm rebellion, manoeuvre the lump until it was firmly lodged under his tongue, for he had no intention of choking, shake his head feebly and protest through sighs that he could eat no more. His gaze was a mixture of sheepishness and obstinacy. It's doing you the world of good. Did he want this world of good? Not much point in getting the lumps down you when all they did was to come out, embarrassingly, at the other end. No. He wanted no more lumps. Unpalatable stuff prolonging all this stupidity around him, all this fussing. Horace knew he had finished with life. He intended just to sit, sit it out in his chair and be as pointless as possible. Nothing was worth anything anymore, he would reflect in the long moments of silence or in the tutting and flitting of life around him. He was withdrawing far away, into a remote place of his own, he was taking refuge inside a shell, let it all happen on the outside, he would be pointless and useless on the inside, make himself as invisible as possible. He had even forgotten to dominate and manipulate, the occasional throaty bark in Lillian's direction being as much as he could manage. He let them get on with it around him, if that was what they wanted, doctors, nurses, home helps, Harriet, Lillian. Not Elsie because they'd taken her away to Australia.

In Australia, they said, she had turned bronze in the sun, the golden colour of health, health at skin level anyway, for the bronze tan was the face Elsie turned to the world. Within, she was anguished and blistered.

She loved Polly with the love of mother-to-daughter, she even accepted the Australian husband and the offspring the couple had born to the world, with reservations it is true, but she accepted them.

In Elsie's eyes, Polly had her limits, Polly was a *limited* human being – like all human beings – but Elsie being Polly's mother was especially aware of her daughter's limitations. Polly forced her, literally launched her, at eighty-five, out into the Australian Way in the Promised Land. On no account was Elsie to be bored. Never must she remember that life had been of a different hue in London. Let her not recall that long and distasteful era of her existence, only eighty-five years, they could be obliterated, her folly, her psychological disruption, her semi-blindness, her clogged arteries, all could be obliterated with optimism in her new life. They must not allow her to pine for a sister and brother across the seas, they were best forgotten for what they were worth. Polly had it all very clear. Activity. That was the remedy for her mother's nostalgias. Plenty of activity. She *farmed* Elsie *out* during the mornings to a Centre which organised excursions-for-geriatrics. Elsie saw the sights of Sydney that way. She saw them, and remembered London. She made friends. Even better friends than Kathleen. It's easy to make friends at eighty-five. Who said life begins at forty? She tried very hard to forget Kathleen and Horace and her sister Lillian. She tried hard because although she'd sworn to herself that she would return to them, her sixth sisterly sense told her that she would never, that is Never Ever, see them again. Often, she really did forget them. They floated out of her mind's eye as if they'd never been a part of her, Horace raising his glass to his lips, Lillian with her giggles, her knee-slapping, her ridiculous statements, Thirteen thousand miles is enough to obliterate anybody's memories. Yet the mind is stronger. It travels thirteen thousand miles in less than a second, it travels in youth and can still travel in old age, more slowly perhaps, hesitating a little *en route*. Elsie travelled frequently. As she lay in her Sydney bed in the early mornings, when the kookaburra calls to its mate across eucalyptus trees and the ripples of a blue harbour, Elsie travelled, always backwards, never forwards. Her world was at the back of her. In front of her there was nothing, nothing but this blue and green asylum. They had separated her from her very life's blood. She'd become, at eighty-five, an unidentified person, a *persona non grata*. Her life in the Land of Opportunity had become as much of a nebulous ink blotch as that of her sister, way back in the Old Country. Elsie lived with her memories, through from her early-morning-bed until the quiet of the night, the velvet Sydney night. She eyed the life around her during the daytime and knew it wasn't her life. A lack of belonging dampened her soul and despite Polly's efforts, she pined. Elsie pined for her Queen robed in splendorous pageantry, the Queen who'd *almost* smiled and waved at her. She pined for Kathleen and her wheezing gossip. She pined for the icicles on Horace's windows. She even pined for Horace himself. But at the centre of her pining was always her sister Lillian. They'd taken her away from Lillian when Lillian needed her. What would her sister do without her? Lillian depended on her. They'd quarrelled and argued. Of course they had. All sisters do that and she and Lillian were no exception. How she missed her now. She had forgotten ..... forgotten ..... how much Lillian had irritated her and the relief she'd experienced when Lillian was away at Horace's. All she felt now was the cruel wrench of enforced separation, the same blood flowing in different directions and she nursed her wound munching her food in silence as Polly chatted gaily at her like a parakeet. Two separate rivulets of vital blood which should have flowed together in one and the same stream. And Elsie knew pain, short sharp metallic bursts of pain which glinted against the raw red of her heart.

She rose one morning, as she rose every morning, she dressed and ate her breakfast. She should have been off on a geriatric excursion but she'd decided not to go, she was thoroughly tired of all this regimentation. She would wander instead, at will, muse about the sister from whom she'd been separated. She set out along the path leading to the geriatrics Centre. From habit. But with a sniggering sense of purpose and desire to flaw *the regimenters*, she took a small lane off to the right before arriving at the Centre. Elsie walked along, at a smart pace considering her years and her poor sight, drinking in the buzzing sounds of contented insects, sniffing the early smells of spring and feeling wickedly, deliciously, independent. She'd confided in nobody about this premeditated act of truancy. As she walked, she imagined that Lillian was at her side, she held conversation with her, a routine conversation more docile than the real ones they had had, a conversation which simply carried on from where they'd left off, as though they had never been separated. Elsie was tender, sweetly gentle with her older sister, the distance between them had mopped up the bitter astringent of her scornful tongue and Lillian answered, soft and complacent. They were wrapped both of them, in a limbo of sisterly love, there was sweetness in the air and in their voices, they moved in unison, twins of sisterly blood, old sisters, old blood. They spoke in tune to the cracking twigs, to the humming insects, honeyed words of forgiveness, they spoke too as friends, real friends. Something more than sisters.

Nobody had followed Elsie down that lane or they would have considered her mad, conversing with the imaginary figure at her side. The twigs cracked sharper under foot. Unbeknown to herself and to her invisible companion, for Lillian had moved up a rung from Only-a-sister to a Companion, Elsie had strayed from the cement slabs and was wending her way down a bush path which led to the water, rippled blue in the early spring. Amidst hornets and inquisitive baby lizards and eucalyptus, Elsie placed Lillian on a pedestal, she wreathed her brow with garlands of wattle, Lillian her Companion and demi-goddess, she forgave her foibles and beseeched forgiveness for her own misdemeanours. Unbeknown to herself, she was making her peace before it was too late. She thought it was the pleasantest thing in the world to be here on this slope above the blue water, here in the warm with Lillian her Companion beside her. She was swooning with positive sisterly sentiment. Love and compassion seeped from her heart. And she knew that Lillian would never leave her again.

Elsie did not return from her bush-walking. She had roamed on and on, lured by the water down to its edge, old and carefree cracking the twigs beneath her. At peace with herself and with Lillian. Accompanied. They discovered her body two days' later, frail and peaceful, nothing metallic there, nestling timidly in her reserved English way, into twigs, sheaths of eucalyptus penetrating her perm.

When Lillian heard that her sister had died, her soul cracked open. It bled profusely. She howled her way into madness. That was one night. The next morning she'd forgotten ..... forgotten ..... But a thread had snapped, the fine silver thread which had fastened her to sanity. With Elsie away, out of her mind for good, Lillian could wander unobserved, un-criticised, unafraid of putting her foot in it. Wander. Only in her mind though, because she was still a prisoner in Horace's house. She sat for long hours on the side of her bed in the primrose room tying tiny knots in a ball of wool she'd found. She wandered so far from Horace in her mind that when she eventually emerged from the primrose room and caught sight of him in the lounge, she had no idea who he was. She emptied the remains of her food inside the washing machine. She tied Rose's dusters up in knots, she had a mania for knots, she even tied strands of her own hair in knots, the way she'd tied strands of her life in knots. She heard whispers about *homes* and *hospitals* and in response to the whispers she poked her tongue out at Harriet and the doctor. But she went all the same, behind them. Meekly in fact. After all they were taking her on an excursion with a suitcase. And that night, as she lay in a bed beside ten other beds, she forgot her primrose wall, Horace faded to ghostlike substance, his cumbersome frame prancing lightly away into the shadows and she stared after him and raised an arm from the bedcovers to wave him goodbye. She closed her eyes for a moment feeling a tingling in her fingers, the need to tie a knot, a tingling in her fingertips which groped for the satin bow at the neck of her nightdress. She watched Elsie glide towards her, appearing from the self-same shadows where Horace had disappeared. Elsie, pretty, without a moustache, gliding and floating in front of her eyes. Elsie had a smile on her face and was beckoning to Lillian with a curved finger on her outstretched arm. Lillian tinkered with the satin bow at her neck. Elsie's smile was youthful and wide and her face the colour of light. Her face was open and forgiving. Elsie was her sister, her true and only Companion. She had known her from birth. Elsie had been her confidante, the life-long receptacle into which she'd poured the liquid of her mind. She'd gone away somewhere. Yet here she was again beckoning Lillian, inciting her to follow. Lillian tightened the fingers of both her hands on the satin bow, it was a sudden urgent movement, a paroxysm. She pulled the two ends of the satin ribbon taut and began, slowly, purposefully, to re-enact with the satin bow what she had many times practised with her strands of wool and the strands of her hair. Taut the two ends, she crossed them, crossing one of her wrists slowly, purposefully, as she did so, over the other. Elsie was smiling, nodding her head, pulling at Lillian's mind over which she, Lillian, as usual, had very little control. Lillian murmured through half-closed lips, I love you Elsie, I've always loved you. I do need you, you know.

Beguiling Elsie.

I could rest again if I went with you. You'd look after me, wouldn't you? Please. Look after me Elsie. I don't know any of these people around me. I'm afraid of them. What to her bedside neighbours was like a soft low rumble, to Lillian herself was an articulate plea to depend again upon her younger sister. How pretty you are Elsie. The light on Elsie's face had turned into a shimmering halo. You look like Jesus, the one I met years ago on the train, do you remember? She caught her breath and held it tight, in silence, waiting for Elsie to answer. The tingling in her fingers was becoming unbearable, the need to tie a knot ever more urgent. Elsie didn't answer her, she just continued to smile and stretched her forefinger in a slow and purposeful beckoning gesture. Lillian's fingers quivered, tensing the satin ribbon. Meticulously, she folded its one end under the other, her hands very close to her neck now. Did she know what she was doing? She pulled the crossed ends of satin slowly, purposefully. She pulled until the small satin knot touched the sagging skin of her old neck. The halo around Elsie's head shone with a brilliant light, it glittered enticing Lillian. Elsie was calm. Lillian was calm, Although she had a threshold to cross, the threshold which separated her from her sister. I'm going to come to you Elsie, she murmured, Just wait a minute. A minute of Lillian's customary dithering. Don't go. I'm coming. Wait for me. Those were the last words Lillian uttered, Wait for me, as she pulled the satin knot tight, tighter into the folds of her short, thick neck, into her dowager's hump, she kept pulling even though she felt herself choking and felt her breath escaping her, she gulped in suffocated spurts not much louder than a man's snores and she pulled and pulled with a vengeance at the satin. The only way to get herself across this threshold of pain, to find the relief of her sister's arms was to keep on pulling. Her eyes bulged out of their sockets and her body let out a final shudder, an excruciating adieu to life, her arms jumped outwards, splayed stiffly on each side of her body across white sheets. It was over. Lillian had gone to be with Elsie, to perpetuate her dependence in eternity.

They didn't tell Horace about Lillian's end. It might have killed him on the spot. Instead, Mavis' Adolescent, who had long ago turned her back on Britain in favour of Spanish climes, in a lusty burst of protectiveness, took him away to her foreign land. She spurned the pleas from the medical people, from those who administered him his soups and vitaminized liquids. Something had got into Mavis' Adolescent and she took it upon herself with uncharacteristic authority to wrench Horace away from all that was familiar with him. She became obsessed by the need to protect him from the end that had been Lillian's. She ripped him thoughtlessly from Harriet's tender care and whisked him away to the heat and the dust and the vibrant voices of the Spanish hinterland. Poor Horace. Spain was not his place on earth. It was not his Land of

Opportunity, just as Australia had not been a Land of Opportunity either for Lillian or for Elsie. He was cast amongst speakers of a foreign language, expected to make himself at home amongst a medley of words which meant nothing to him, he was destined to die *a foreigner* amongst people who understood nothing about him or his love of England or his love of whisky. Horace was not a wine drinker. It was a tragic way for him to spend the last weeks of his life. It was a greater shock to his system than the news of Lillian's suicide would have been.

After a lifetime of dedication, all soul and mind, to England, a lifetime of dedication to the British Way of Life, they had taken Horace away and buried him beneath Spanish soil.

§§§

Before You Go

If you enjoyed reading *Sisterly Love,* could you leave a review on the amazon.com site for the book, on *Goodreads* or on the website of the retailer where you bought it. This will help potential readers be able to decide if this is a story they will enjoy reading. Your input is indispensable ... thank you in advance for your valuable insight.

If you would like to contact me directly, please visit my website https://dianahutton.wixsite.com/spanishwattle and use the contact form there or post on my Facebook page with HPEditions at https://www.facebook.com/Diana-Hutton-Author-368640653536883/

About the Author

Diana Hutton lives in Madrid, Spain and has spent most of her career as a professional translator but has devoted the last few years to writing full-time. Her latest novel, "Sisterly Love" delves into the intricacies of the sister relationship in old age, treating the subject with remarkable humour and sensitivity. She is also in the process of working on a new novel.

Diana has written two other novels, "A Grave above Ground" and "Don't Call Me Lebohang" which can be purchased on Amazon. "A Grave above Ground" is also available as an audiobook at most retail audiobook outlets.

Although born in Southampton, in the United Kingdom at the end of the Second World War, Diana spent the first ten years of her life in London, then moved with her family to Sydney, Australia. She was educated there and dabbled in acting and contemporary ballet in Sydney on leaving school, then worked at the Australian Broadcasting Commission. As a young woman, she returned to London, but shortly afterwards moved to live in Paris where she met her Spanish husband-to-be whilst working in the Australian Permanent Delegation to UNESCO. She married in Madrid and has two grown-up children. She has lived there on and off since 1970 and has found life in Spain to be a deeply enriching experience.

Other books by Diana Hutton

"A Grave above Ground" see excerpt in the following pages. Available everywhere.

"Don't Call Me Lebohang" available from Amazon.

A Grave above Ground

Diana Hutton

This is a beggar's tale. It is the story of how easily life can change. An unwanted pregnancy brings a happy young university student with a bright future face to face with harsh reality, much worsened by the soulless poverty crushing Romania at the time of Ceausescu's cruel dictatorship. Family rejection is followed by a sordid kidnapping of the baby she had come to love and adore, a frantic search for the infant in the hellish confines of the many government orphanages, flight from persecution as a refugee, oppression as an illegal immigrant and even rape, abuse and eventual psychological collapse, all leading her to a life of squalor, discrimination and begging on the streets of Madrid.

While she inspires hatred in some people who look on her as refugee trash, others whose lives she touches see some good in her, offer love, care, a taste of normal life and even find inspiration in her humble self-possession.

But is hers a fate that can be escaped from or is there no possible recovery from the total eclipse of a heart?

Also available everywhere as an AudioBook

A GRAVE ABOVE GROUND

A BEGGAR'S TALE

DIANA HUTTON

Music by Jaime Cano

Published by HPEditions©

www.ingramcontent.com/pod-product-compliance
Lightning Source LLC
Chambersburg PA
CBHW031411290426
44110CB00011B/333